NOT TO READ

Alejandro Zambra is a Chilean writer, poet, and critic. His first novel *Bonsai* was awarded Chile's Literary Critics' Award for Best Novel. He is also the author of *The Private Lives of Trees* and *Ways of Going Home*, which won the Altazor Award and the National Council Prize for Books, both for the best Chilean novel. *My Documents*, published by Fitzcarraldo Editions in 2015, was shortlisted for the 2015 Frank O'Connor International Short Story Prize. His latest novel is *Multiple Choice*. His writing has appeared in the *New Yorker*, the *Paris Review*, *Tin House*, *Harper's*, *Granta* and *McSweeney's*, among other places. He was a 2015–16 Cullman Center fellow at the New York Public Library. He lives in Mexico City.

Megan McDowell has translated many contemporary authors from Latin America and Spain, including Alejandro Zambra, Samanta Schweblin, Mariana Enriquez, Lina Meruane, Diego Zuñiga, and Carlos Fonseca. Her translations have been published in the *New Yorker*, *Tin House*, *Paris Review*, *Harper's*, *McSweeney's*, *Words Without Borders*, and *Vice*, among others. Her translation of Alejandro Zambra's *Ways of Going Home* won the 2013 English PEN award for writing in translation, and her translation of Samanta Schweblin's novel *Fever Dream* was shortlisted for the Man Booker International prize in 2017. She lives in Santiago, Chile.

'There is no writer like Alejandro Zambra, no one as bold, as subtle, as funny.'
— Daniel Alarcón, author of *At Night We Walk In Circles*

'When I read Zambra I feel like someone's shooting fireworks inside my head. His prose is as compact as a grain of gunpowder, but its allusions and ramifications branch out and illuminate even the most remote corners of our minds..'
— Valeria Luiselli, author of *The Story of My Teeth*

'Falling in love with Zambra's literature is a fascinating road to travel. Imaginative and original, he is a master of short forms; I adore his devastating audacity.'
— Enrique Vila-Matas, author of *The Illogic of Kassel*

Praise for *My Documents*

'This dynamite collection of stories has it all –Chile and Belgium, exile and homecomings, Pinochet and Simon and Garfunkel – but what I love most about the tales is their strangeness, their intelligence, and their splendid honesty.'
— Junot Díaz, *New Yorker*

'*My Documents* represents a new form. When I think about Alejandro Zambra, I feel happy for the future of fiction.'
— Adam Thirlwell, author of *Lurid and Cute*

'If you are going to read Alejandro Zambra, which you should, don't just read *My Documents*, read everything he's done.'
— Chris Power, *Guardian*

'His books are like a phone call in the middle of the night from an old friend, and afterward, I missed the charming and funny voice on the other end, with its strange and beautiful stories.'
— Nicole Krauss, author of *Forest Dark*

Fitzcarraldo Editions

NOT TO READ

ALEJANDRO ZAMBRA

Translated and edited by
MEGAN McDOWELL

CONTENTS

I

III

Foreword

When I was 20 years old, I worked at a bookstore. One of my co-workers was Ukrainian, but oddly enough she recommended an Argentine book to me: *Hopscotch*, by Julio Cortázar. I read that book and loved it. Looking back, I think it moved something in me that eventually led me to learn Spanish and start translating. But a more immediate consequence of my obsession with that book was that I read many others – Cortázar name-drops a lot, and I picked up those names and read them. I read Céline because of him, and René Crevel, Raymond Queneau, Carson McCullers, I found books on Mondrian and Vieira da Silva. I wanted to better understand the things Cortázar's characters thought about, so I tried to redad the books they mentioned. I thought of the literary references in *Hopscotch* as recommendations from Cortázar himself, and some of those books came to be fundamental in my reading life.

There's another recommendation that has been very important for me. In 2007, after starting a Masters in translation, I visited Chile with the goal of finding a project to work on. I asked many people – booksellers, editors, writers – to tell me who the interesting younger writers in Chile were. I heard a lot of names, but everyone coincided on one: Alejandro Zambra. I came home with a lot of books, but yes, Zambra was the one I wanted to work with; that was the start of a literary relationship and friendship that is one of my most treasured.

Not to Read is 'a gem' of a book because it consists largely of recommendations from one of my favourite authors. There are many books mentioned here that I hadn't heard of before and that I've picked up while working on *Not to Read*; it has also made me go back to authors I haven't thought about in a long time, like Juan Carlos Onetti or Macedonio Fernández. It's true that some of the writers mentioned here have not been translated into

English[1], or have appeared only rarely. But you don't have to be familiar with the books discussed here in order to enjoy reading – Zambra's voice is that of a trusted friend telling you about a book he's excited about, and why. The fact that this friend is also one of the most interesting authors working today makes this peek into his reading life all the more fascinating.

The literary panorama portrayed here is a Latin America that is not the one English-language readers are used to. Boom writers are conspicuous in their absence, for the most part, and when they do appear it is often as a counterpoint – Vargas Llosa, for example, is the embodiment of a kind of smug 'professional writer' Zambra distrusts. Alejandro would rather talk about Nicanor Parra than Pablo Neruda, Mario Levrero than Gabriel Garcia Márquez. Bolaño is here, but it's his poems that get the longest look, not the stories and novels he's most famous for. Julio Ramón Ribeyro, perhaps the writer who comes with Alejandro's most effusive recommendation, is also referred to as a 'second-class citizen of the boom' who didn't fulfil European readers' expectations of Latin American writers – no magic, no local colour, no bombast.

And if many of the writers mentioned herein can be thought of as 'second-string' (which is not to say second rate), there is also a decided focus on 'secondary' forms. Many essays focus on diaries, letters, and hybrid novel/journals. One comes away with the decided impression that Zambra doesn't have much use for traditional conceptions of genre, which anyone who has read *Multiple Choice* already knows. In fact, one can read *No Leer* as a sort of inverse of Zambra's fiction. We can see Alejandro's early criticism as a kind of laboratory for his novels; we learn what he was reading and the questions he was thinking

1 Disclaimer: In quoting the works discussed here, I have used existing English translations when I could get my hands on them. If there is no English translation or if Google books was not forthcoming, I've translated from the Spanish.

about, his concerns as he was writing *Bonsai* and *The Private Lives of Trees* and *Ways of Going Home*. For example, Zambra's first mention of a bonsai was in a short piece on Adolfo Couve in 2003. Zambra's readers will recognize scenes and phrases here that appear later in his fiction, but most important and compelling is the way of thinking about literary practice that Zambra enacts here – the book is a kind of 'How to Read' that comes before the 'How to Write'.

The original version of *Not to Read* was *No Leer*, published in Chile by UDP press in 2010. Zambra wrote book reviews for the Chilean press from 2003-2008, and the original idea of *No Leer* was to collect those pieces, which, written as they were for the newspaper format, tended to be short and pointed. Since that first publication, revised and expanded editions have been published in Argentina, Mexico, and Spain, with a second Spanish version to be published later this year. That's to say, this book has had a long life and many incarnations, of which this English version is only the most recent. It includes additions and subtractions to the nucleus of the original book, and the essays concentrated in the later part of the book tend to be more recent, written after Alejandro stopped contributing criticism to the Chilean press. By then he has consolidated both a certain renown and a voice, and developed a way of thinking about literature.

Not to Read, then, is a kind of literary autobiography, and as such, the first person abounds. But just as frequently as Zambra writes 'I', he writes 'we'. The first person plural is where he feels most comfortable, and maybe that's appropriate for a writer who has come to be the standard bearer of his generation in Chile: that of the 'children of dictatorship', that of 'secondary characters'. 'I belong and I want to belong,' says Alejandro Zambra, and it's the honest declaration of a mature writer who has spent many solitary hours reading, who has read and loved many solitary writers. But for Alejandro literature is not a solitary practice;

as he says more than once, we write to multiply ourselves, and this book is moved by an individual's search for a voice and by a collective spirit.

Megan McDowell, February 2018

I

OBLIGATORY READINGS

I still remember the day when the teacher turned to the chalkboard and wrote the words *test*, *next*, *Friday*, *Madame*, *Bovary*, *Gustave*, *Flaubert*, *French*. With each word the silence grew, and by the end the only sound was the sad squeaking of the chalk. By that point we had already read long novels, almost as long as *Madame Bovary*, but this time the deadline was impossible: barely a week to get through a four-hundred-page novel. We were starting to get used to those surprises, though: we had just entered the National Institute, we were twelve or thirteen years old, and we knew that from then on, all the books would be long.

That's how they taught us to read: by beating it into us. I feel sure that those teachers didn't want to inspire enthusiasm for books, but rather to deter us from them, to put us off books forever. They didn't waste their spit extolling the joys of reading, perhaps because they had lost that joy or had never really felt it. Supposedly they were good teachers, but back then being good meant little more than knowing the textbook.

As in Nicanor Parra's poem, 'our teachers drove us nuts / with their pointless questions'. But we soon learned their tricks, or developed our own. On all the tests, for example, there was a section of character identification, and it included nothing but secondary characters: the more secondary the character, the more likely we would be asked about them. We resigned ourselves to memorizing the names, though with the pleasure of guaranteed points.

There was a certain beauty in the act, because back then that's exactly what we were: secondary characters, hundreds of children who crisscrossed the city lugging denim backpacks. The neighbours would feel their weight and always make the same joke: 'What are you carrying in there, rocks?' Downtown Santiago received us with tear gas bombs, but we weren't carrying rocks, we were carrying bricks by Baldor or Villee or Flaubert.

Madame Bovary was one of the few novels we had at my house, so I started reading that very same night, following the emergency method my father had taught me: read the first two pages and right away skip to the final two, and only then, only once you know how the novel begins and ends, do you continue reading in order. 'Even if you don't finish, at least you know who the killer is,' said my father, who apparently only ever read books about murders.

The truth is, I didn't get much further in my reading. I liked to read, but Flaubert's prose simply made me doze off. Luckily, the day before the test, I found a copy of the movie at a video store in Maipú. My mother tried to keep me from watching it, saying it wasn't appropriate for a kid my age. I agreed, or rather I hoped it was true. I thought *Madame Bovary* sounded like porn; everything French sounded like porn to me. In that regard the movie was disappointing, but I watched it twice and covered sheets of legal paper with notes on both sides. I failed the test, though, and for a long time afterward I associated *Madame Bovary* with that red F, and with the name of the film's director, which the teacher wrote with exclamation marks beside my bad grade: Vincente Minnelli!!

I never again trusted movie versions, and ever since then I have thought that the cinema lies and literature doesn't (I have no way of demonstrating this, of course). I read Flaubert's novel much later, and I tend to reread it every year, more or less when the first flu hits. There's no mystery in changing tastes; these things happen in the life of any reader. But it's a miracle that we survived those teachers, who did everything they could to show us that reading is the most boring thing in the world.

May 2009

BRING BACK CORTÁZAR

Sometimes I think the only thing we did in school was read Julio Cortázar. I remember taking tests on 'The Night Face Up' in each of my last three years of school, and countless were the times we read 'Axolotl' and 'The Continuity of Parks', two short stories that the teachers considered ideal for filling out an hour and a half of class. This is not a complaint, since we were happy reading Cortázar: we recited the characteristics of the fantasy genre with automatic joy, and we repeated in chorus that for Cortázar the short story wins by knockout and the novel by points, and that there was a male reader and a female reader and all of that.

The tastes of my generation were shaped by Cortázar's stories, and not even the Xeroxed tests could divest his literature of that air of permanent contemporaneity. I remember how at sixteen I convinced my dad to give me the six thousand pesos that *Hopscotch* cost, explaining that the book was 'several books, but two in particular', so that buying it was like buying two novels for three thousand pesos each, or even four books for fifteen hundred pesos each. I also remember the employee at the Atenea bookshop who, when I was looking for *Around the Day in Eighty Worlds*, explained to me patiently, over and over, that the book was called *Around the World in Eighty Days*, and that the author was Julio Verne and not Julio Cortázar.

Later, at university, Cortázar was the only writer who was undisputed. Dozens of wannabe Oliveiras and Magas milled about on the lawns at the University of Chile's College of Philosophy, while some professors endeavoured to adopt Morelli's speculative distance in their classes. Almost all seductions began with a pitiful rendition of with Chapter 7 of *Hopscotch* ('I touch your lips, with a finger I touch the edge of your mouth...') which at that time was considered a stupendous text, and there were so many people speaking Gliglish (amalating the noeme, as they say) that it was hard to get a word in in Spanish.

I never liked the stories in *Cronopios and Famas* or *A Certain Lucas*: the fleeting, playful prose was lacking, I thought, in real humour. But on the other hand I don't think anyone could deny the greatness of stories like 'House Taken Over', 'We Love Glenda So Much', 'The Pursuer', and another twenty or thirty of Cortázar's stories. *Hopscotch*, meanwhile, is still an astonishing book, although it's true that sometimes we're astonished that it has astonished us, because it can often sound old-fashioned and overwrought. But still today, the novel has some truly beautiful passages.

In a recent essay, the Argentine writer Fabián Casas recalls his first reading of *Hopscotch* ('it was all cryptic, promising, wonderful') and his later disappointment ('the book started to seem naive, snobbish, and unbearable'). That is my generation's experience: sooner rather than later we end up killing the father, even though he was a liberating and quite permissive dad. And it turns out that now we miss him, as Casas says at the end of his essay, in a happy, sentimental turn: 'I want him to come back. I want us to have writers like him again: forthright, committed, beautiful, forever young, cultured, generous, loud-mouthed.'

I agree: bring back Cortázar. It's a mysterious mechanism, the one that makes an admired writer become, suddenly, a dispensable legend. But literary fashions are almost never based on real readings or re-readings. Maybe now, when everyone drags his memory through the mud, we regret having denied him three times. Maybe we're only just now ready to read Cortázar, to truly read him.

February 2009

IN PRAISE OF THE PHOTOCOPY

Essays by Roland Barthes marked with fluorescent highlighters; poems by Carlos de Rokha or Enrique Lihn stapled together; ring-bound or precariously fastened novels by Witold Gombrowicz or Clarice Lispector: it's good to remember that we learned to read with these photocopies, which we waited for impatiently, smoking, on the other side of the window. As citizens of a country where books are ridiculously expensive to buy and libraries are poorly equipped or non-existent, we got used to reading photocopies, and we even came to find it charming. In exchange for a just few pesos, some giant, tireless machines could bestow on us the literature we so desired. We read those warm bundles of paper and then stored them on shelves as if they were real books. Because that's what they were to us: rare, beloved books. Important books.

I remember a classmate who photocopied *War and Peace* at a rate of thirty pages per week, and a friend who bought reams of light blue paper because, according to her, the printing came out better. The greatest bibliographic gem I have is a haphazard copy of *La Nueva Novela* [The New Novel], the inimitable book-object by Juan Luis Martínez, with its transparent insets, the little Chilean flag insert, or the page with Chinese characters intermingled in the text and hooks stuck to the paper. Several of us collaborated on making it, regressing back to our days in carpentry class at school. The resulting table was pretty wobbly, but I'll never forget what a good time we had those weeks of scissors, fasteners, and photocopies.

We felt the first campaigns against photocopying books as a kind of attack on us: they wanted to take away the only means we had to read what we really wanted to read. They said the photocopy was killing the book, but we knew that literature survived in those stained pages, just as it survives now on screens – because books are still scandalously expensive in Chile.

The discussion around digital books, incidentally, is at times overly elaborate: the defenders of conventional books appeal to romantic images of reading (to which I fully subscribe), and the electronic propagandist will insist on the comfort of carrying your library in your pocket, or the miracle of endlessly interlinking texts. But it's not so much about habits as it is about costs. Can we expect a student to spend twenty thousand pesos on a book? Isn't it quite reasonable for them to just download it from the internet?

Today, many readers have first-rate virtual libraries, with no need to use a credit card or buy the latest gadget. It's hard to be against this miracle. Editors, booksellers, distributors and authors unite occasionally to combat practices that ruin business, but books have become luxury items and absolutely nothing indicates this will change. Especially in countries like Chile, where books are, and have been for too many years now, the domain of collectors.

I myself have become a collector over time, because I wouldn't dare to live without my books. But in my case it's something more like atavism, an anachronistic and slightly absurd inclination to sleep wrapped up in a library. I remember a friend who would always offer me a storage room for my books, because he couldn't understand how I could forego so much of my living space to hang those shelves that were, according to him, dangerous: 'The next earthquake will hit and they'll fall on top of you and you'll die, all thanks to your encyclopaedias,' he'd say, even though I've never owned encyclopaedias.

Nor have I been able to throw away the old ring-bound photocopies, even when I later got hold of the books in original editions. Now that photocopies are on the wane, I can't help but feel a bit nostalgic, and I can't bring myself to throw them out; every once in a while I still page through those fake books that once provoked a genuine and lasting wonder.

July 2009

LIBRARIES

I first saw the library of my friend Álvaro five years ago and it was disappointing, because it seemed to be filled with bad books. Back then he and I talked almost exclusively about books, and our conversations had the charm of the tentative, the incomplete. We didn't need to go into much detail in order to understand each other: he would say that a book was good or that it was boring, and I felt sure his statement held an entire declaration of principles; we didn't feel the need to elaborate on our opinions, we simply enjoyed the complicity.

That afternoon at his house, I felt uncomfortable. I'd expected to find his shelves filled with books that I loved too, or maybe with unknown names of surprising new authors, and instead I met only with familiar writers who interested me very little. In any case I didn't really inspect the library because that has always seemed like bad manners to me. It's true, the fact that books are in living rooms authorizes us to look at them, but even so, I think the first time it's better to glance out of the corner of the eye, prudently, without abusing any trust. I had brought Álvaro my second novel, which had just come out, as a gift, and I spent the whole visit tortured by the possibility that it would end up in bad company. But it stayed right there on the coffee table, as is fitting when it comes to new acquisitions.

Two weeks later Álvaro invited me over again, and this time he showed me a very small room in his back yard, the study he shut himself into to read and write. I estimated there were some seventy or eighty books on the shelves, which of course were the ones that mattered most to my friend. I felt proud to see my few novels and even my old book of poetry taking up all of the letter 'Z'.

29

Later I discovered that there were books in other parts of the house, and that of all these places, the worst, literarily speaking, was the living room.

The books in the living room are supposed to represent you, I told him later, and his answer was marvellously vague: hhhmmmm. But later I realized he had thought long and hard about the matter. He was annoyed by the custom of putting books in the living room, but he didn't have any more space available, and after trying out various solutions he had arrived at this one, which among other advantages was good for loans, because he had no problem lending out those books. The others, the ones in his little study or his bedroom, he didn't want to share with anyone.

My friend still uses that system, which over time has gotten a fair bit more complex: as the tastes or moods of its owner change, a title can pass from the study to the bedroom, then from the bedroom to the living room, and finally from there to the street, because every once in a while he gets rid of a load of books. What seems strangest to me is that he differentiates even among the works of one author, so that someone's novels could be in the study, their poems in the bedroom and their essays in the living room. I should clarify that this division is not by literary genre, as demonstrated by the fact that, with good reason, there are many novels by César Aira in the study, and others distributed throughout the house.

This being the case, when I go visit Álvaro I'm always invaded by a sense of fatalism, and I worry I've lost ground, that my days in the study are numbered. When I find I'm still alone in the letter 'Z', a great happiness washes over me. But it doesn't last long, because then comes the fear that it's all a sham, and the truth is that I can perfectly well imagine my friend hurriedly moving

my books from one shelf to another every time I ring
the doorbell.

May 2012

FOUR PEOPLE

How lonely is it to be a writer?

I am asked this by a friendly stranger, out of pure curiosity, after a reading. I answer hesitantly; I'm not sure of the answer. I think about the cliché of the writer locked in for long hours, struggling with his convictions and desires. I remember that fragment, so dramatic and in a way comical, in which Kafka confesses the desire to shut himself away in a cellar with only a lamp and his writing materials: 'Food would be brought and always put down far away from my room, outside the cellar's outermost door. The walk to my food, in my dressing gown, through the vaulted cellars, would be my only exercise.'

When we write, we absent ourselves from the world, and sometimes entire days pass when we only go out to buy cigarettes or walk the dog (although in those cases it's the dog who walks us). But I'm not so sure that writing is a solitary profession. At least for me, it has always had a collective aspect. From my early days I got used to sharing what I wrote, and I sincerely believe there is no better writing workshop than getting together with friends over a manuscript and a few beers. Friends who are willing to listen, make suggestions, disagree, cross things out; friends whose opinions sometimes unexpectedly and decisively change what we write.

We constructed our first books thanks to those drawn-out sessions. They were entertaining and also disturbing, because it wasn't easy to accept that the poem written in transported solitude was starting to become a collective, somewhat foreign work. Nor was it pleasant to see others gloss right over a phrase or verse that we thought was important. There was a time when we got together almost daily to read, and I even remember a night when we gathered with the aim of translating some poems by Joan Brossa, even though none of us knew Catalan. How hard can it be? we said, armed with a hundred-page dictionary, back when there was no internet or Google shortcuts. The result was, naturally, disastrous and fun.

But I was talking about interlocutors, the ones who, according to Natalia Ginzburg, tend to be three or four people we trust in blindly and whose opinions matter most to us. In her case those four people were two girlfriends, a critic, and in particular her oldest son, with whom she had a strange routine. After listening to his mother's stories, the son hurled insults and abuse at her. When she heard those insults, oddly, the author knew that the text was good.

Natalia Ginzburg's opinion coincides with Ezra Pound's famous poem: 'I join these words for four people, / Some others may overhear them, / O world, I am sorry for you, / You do not know these four people.' In my case the interlocutors are six or seven or maybe even more people. Now that I think about it, when I presented my new novel in public, I wanted to write a piece to thank the people who had read the manuscript, but the list was so long that I just gave a general greeting instead.

The literary world has a bad reputation, and there are people who believe that writers are always fighting and elbowing their way past each other. There is some of that. A lot, maybe. But it's also a supportive world, a world where people give and take. I'm always impressed by how profoundly collective the work of a theatre or film director is, and sometimes I'm relieved to think that our job consists only of filling up pages in solitude. But I also never forget those generous readers whose opinions are ultimately, silently, affixed to the pages of a book.

September 2011

ERASING THE READER

'Discordant, wants to obscure everything.' That's what someone wrote in my copy of *Toda la Luz del Mediodía* [All the Light of Noon], the novel by Mauricio Wacquez that, clearly, was not a favourite of the book's previous owner. In impatient handwriting, that anonymous reader tempered his boredom by noting down in the margins adjectives that I of course don't agree with, especially because they often coincide with – in my opinion – the novel's best passages: 'stilted', 'snooty', 'pedantic', 'corny'.

Many years ago now, when Wacquez was still alive, I found this, his first novel, published in 1964, in a remainder bin. After reading and rereading it I lent it to my friend Natalia, and she liked it so much that she never gave it back to me. I even carried out a kind of raid: I went over to her house and we spent a long time talking, going through her books. 'I'm sure I have it, I didn't lose it,' Natalia told me as we downed a litre of coffee and talked, perhaps, of Wacquez's recent death. By that time, he was her favourite writer.

Days ago, in a bookshop on Manuel Montt, I came across the novel again, not as cheap this time, but in better condition than the copy Natalia kidnapped. I should have erased those pencilled-in notations right away, but I didn't; on the contrary, I reread *All the Light of Noon* with the anonymous reader keeping me company the whole time. It's strange to read that way, tripping over unfair opinions that get stuck in your memory anyway – as proven, in fact, by this article, which was going to be about Wacquez and not that buzzing voice that won't let me read Wacquez.

I've spent the afternoon imagining that noisy reader,

deciding on his features, his interests. I don't know why I think he's a man. Maybe because of his somewhat rough handwriting, which mixes print and cursive letters seemingly at random. In spite of how bad he found the novel, he read it from beginning to end: maybe he liked the idea of continuing to hand out infractions, or maybe, most likely, he had to read it for a test. 'Nothing longer and more tedious than reading the novel of a philosophy student,' he writes on page 48, though it doesn't have much to do with the text. Maybe he was a literature student who detested philosophy students. Or, more likely, a writer who had lost the novel competition that Wacquez won with this book.

'Truncated scenes that only insinuate communication,' finger-points the anonymous reader further on, and for once he is right: that *is* the book's style; the novel is made of fragments, of silences. Surely such comments were written decades ago, when this story was even more incorrect than it is now; the anonymous reader, however, doesn't seem scandalized by the voracious triangle of Max, Paulina, and Marcelo: Paulina loves Max, but Max loves Marcelo, Paulina's eighteen-year-old son; Marcelo, in his own way, reciprocates: he loves Max, or, more likely, he loves his mother through Max. *All the Light of Noon* is, as Fernando Blanco has said, one of the most transgressive novels of Chilean literature. And one of the best, perhaps.

The first time I read it I was impressed by the narrator's precision, his extreme freedom, his clean and sharp language. Wish to obscure everything? No: wish to illuminate – with sun or artificial light – the darkest zones. Fearless (and without fear of fear, Wacquez would say), the tale confronts bitter memories: 'As I advance through the past, I weigh every gram of reality. I measure exactly the intensity of each smile. Until when? What is the measure that applies to horror?' After a strange idyll in a house in Quintero, Marcelo starts to distance himself from Max, who now seeks out Paulina and proposes an outlandish marriage that she – recklessly and absurdly – accepts: 'I experience Paulina's happiness so intensely that sometimes I imagine it's my own,' writes Max, on the eve of his wedding. Now he *is* afraid, and writing, recording that fear, is more a destiny than a consolation.

'Sex burns up in suffering like sugar in insulin. A physical process, a fist converted into a kiss,' writes Wacquez, and miraculously, the anonymous reader passes, is silent. I've said that his handwriting is rough, that it unpredictably mixes print and cursive. But I've just looked at the book again and the truth is the hand-writing looks a lot like mine. A lot. I copy onto a piece of paper the phrase: 'Discordant, wants to obscure every-thing.' The copy is almost identical; I could imitate that handwriting to perfection. I know it wasn't me, it's not possible, but the similarity has left me stunned. I call my friend Natalia then, and disguise my unease badly. She tells me that yes, she has the book at hand, she always did; she doesn't remember the afternoon of the raid. 'Could you go get it?' I ask.

'Sure, wait a second,' she says, laughing at my ur-gency. In ten seconds she is back and she reads me the beginning: 'Again I see you drink from a glass that your hand squeezes jealously; I see your posture, always reclining, and I am easy because I know it will last all afternoon. Then I'll have to go with you to catch the bus that will take you to your house. And I do not want that; I want to keep you with me.'

'The book is fine, neither you nor I underlined anything,' says Natalia, and I breathe a long, inexplicable sigh.

'Can I have it?' she asks.

'It's all yours,' I tell her, 'now you can underline it.' After we laugh, I find an eraser and erase the intruder. This story ends with the scene of a reader who erases, in the book, the contagious traces of another reader. It is, I think, a happy ending.

March 2006

OTHER PEOPLE'S MAIL

It is hard to read other people's letters without thinking about one's own, those you've sent and those you've received. Only some of mine, very few, have survived my moves. My generation was the last one to write and receive letters. I say that without nostalgia. It's much better to spend the afternoon waiting for an email than to count the weeks while you wait for a letter.

What do we look for in the letters of others? Secrets, revelations, details? 'If my printing's crooked, it's only because I drank too much apple cider tonight,' writes Sylvia Plath to her mother. 'I tell you I am sad. I tell you I am alone. I tell you I am dead. I need a coffin and a ridiculous speech,' Violeta Parra says in a heart-rending letter to Gilbert Favre.

Sometimes the revelations don't come. The correspondence between Mishima and Kawabata, for example, is very strange. For long passages we are witness to nothing but an unflagging exchange of courtesies. Mishima sends a salmon, and Kawabata responds with chestnut candies and mysterious words of encouragement: 'Whatever your mother says, your writing is magnificent.' Mishima confesses to his teacher that he found Disneyland to be the most entertaining place on the planet, and we amused readers spend some time imagining the hyperkinetic Yukio poised at the peak of a rollercoaster.

In recent days I've read and re-read the letters that Julio Ramón Ribeyro sent his brother Juan Antonio. Alfredo Bryce Echenique has described this correspondence as 'testimony of one of the most intense and beautiful known examples of brotherly love,' which could lead us to think that the book compiles deep reflections on family ties; but Bryce is alluding, rather, to the absolute complicity that exists between the brothers. These are not necessarily emotional letters; they're cordial and affectionate, but at times quite practical, as Ribeyro asks Juan Antonio – from Madrid, Paris, or Berlin, among other places – for all kinds of favours. Nor are these 'literary' letters, not by a long shot, though Ribeyro confides details of the books he is writing or trying to write, and every once in a while he improvises funny reflections on contemporary and classic authors ('the great thing about Proust is that, aside from being a fag, nothing extraordinary happened to him in his entire life'). Particularly beautiful are the warm and meticulous letters in which he relays his first impressions about the cities he is seeing: we get the feeling that Ribeyro travels only so he can tell his brother what the world is like.

We recognize here, certainly, the hand of a great writer. This is without a doubt the author of *La tentación del fracaso* [The Temptation of Failure], *Prosas apátridas* [Stateless Prose] and 'Solo para fumadores' [For Smokers Only], an extraordinary story that Ribeyro wrote just for us. This is how a letter from 1958 begins: 'What would become of me if the cigarette had never been invented? It's three in the afternoon and I've already smoked thirty. The thing is that I've been writing letters and for me, writing is an act that complements the pleasure of smoking.' In a later message, Ribeyro signs off with an indication of the enormous congruence of the two acts: 'I have only one cigarette left, so I am concluding this letter.'

I'm sure Ribeyro knew this phrase of Paul Léautaud's: 'What I most like is literature that is written like a letter.' Léautaud was pointing to a style, the style of necessity.

When we read other people's letters, we are looking for a zone of necessity that is often absent in fiction. No clamouring narrators, no startling characters: every once in a while it's good to pause happily for a while on the steps that lead up to literature.

April 2009

MANUEL PUIG BRUSHES HIS TEETH

'I super-read it and studied it and it super opened my eyes, my blindfold fell off. There are three or four tricks that Mankiewicz uses to lighten and season dialog, and I super-adopted them,' Manuel Puig wrote in 1959 after reading *All About Eve*, the 'script of scripts,' as he says in a full-on fit of happiness.

The first volume of *Querida Familia* [Dear Family], which collects the 'European letters' that Manuel Puig sent home between 1956 and 1962, is a decisive close-up of his formative years as a writer, even though throughout the 172 letters it compiles, there is little to no talk of literature. The reader comes in through the window on a family scene that invariably repeats: the mother, deeply moved, reading aloud the news that Manuel (Coco) sends from Rome, Paris, London, or Stockholm.

Now this is a strange book, rather distant from the conventions of epistolary literature; by searching and researching it is possible to find a few stylistic secrets (the three or four of Puig's own tricks), but the character that predominates is, of course, the son, Manuel, Coco, an anxious and affectionate youth, genuinely interested in maintaining ties with his family, especially with his cinephile mother.

At times Coco turns into something like his mother's European correspondent: he tells her about seeing Marlene Dietrich, in the flesh ('in person she's a monster, to top it off she's skinny and scrawny, her face is deathly yellow and she wasn't wearing make-up'), or Sophia Loren ('even though she has zits on her face, she seemed beyond belief'). Simultaneously, Puig builds a sharp, invigorating portrait of the Europe of the time: almost everything amazes him and almost everything disappoints him, predisposed as he is to wonder and doubt. 'The Sistine Chapel as a whole gave me a monstrous impression of chaos; later, when you look at the detail, it's a wonder, but in general it really shocked me. If the Pope shared my opinion, he would break it up into pieces,' says Coco, who never stops being the son, the grown child out seeing the world: 'I brush my teeth after breakfast, in the afternoon and at night.' The good son, in any case, knows how to enjoy the distance; he misses his family, but not his country: 'Buenos Aires doesn't attract me in the slightest, with its evil and twisted people, always ready to fly off the handle.' Naturally, what Puig tells his parents is less interesting that what he doesn't tell them: positioned as we are to spy on young Coco, we conjecture, as well, about his European emancipation, the homosexual escapades that, as Suzanne Jill-Levine points out in *Manuel Puig and the Spider Woman*, he disguised in his letters as virginal 'camaraderie'.

Funny asides abound ('I dreamed Lauren Bacall was telling me about her husband's death!'), as do brushstrokes of film criticism in naïf mode: 'I couldn't resist the temptation to see *Summertime* with Katherine Hepburn. Lovely, but it disagreed with me: nothing but goodbyes.' But literature, as some heroine of Puig's would say, is conspicuous in its absence: after reading Henry James's *The Lesson of the Master*, he merely comments to his parents that it's a 'nice story'. The most attractive aspect of this book lies precisely in that absence of literary reflection: how is it possible that this provincial boy, who fills the page with exclamation points and visits museums at a trot, comes to be one of the greatest Argentine writers of the twentieth century? The reading of *Dear Family* leaves the response open: the myth of the 'involuntary' writer remains standing, as only toward the end of the volume, when Puig is thirty years old, do we glimpse the path that will lead to the writing of *Betrayed by Rita Hayworth*. On the other hand, from the very first pages we can see Puig's fidelity to his obsessions, his autonomy, his resistance to thinking and feeling according to the many traps set out before him.

'In Manuel Puig's writing there are careful, skilfully constructed images but no ideas, no central vision that organizes and gives significance to the fictional world, no personal style,' Mario Vargas Llosa wrote some years ago. Perhaps overcome by Puig's growing importance in the academic realm, Vargas Llosa painted him as an author of 'light literature', an 'undemanding, pleasing literature that has no other purpose than to entertain.' It's difficult not to remember, after reading this, Puig's ranking of the boom writers where he compares 'la' Vargas Llosa with Esther Williams, who was 'so disciplined and serious' (and 'la' García Márquez with Liz Taylor, who was 'beautiful but had short legs'). But beyond any settling of scores, the Peruvian writer's judgement represents the opinion of many writers and readers who still haven't found the key to Puig's novels.

And that confusion is healthy, of course. To hold that *The Kiss of the Spider Woman* or *Eternal Curse on the Reader of These Pages* are light novels seems, at the very least, a hasty assertion, especially because they are works that have not aged, or have aged well: most of Puig's narrations are still extravagant and innovative books, irreducible to any more or less canonical definition of the novel. Puig is the author, as Alberto Giordano has said, of a literature outside of literature, of an oeuvre that is simultaneously legible and inscrutable, one that calls the nature of the literary into question. Consequently, *Dear Family* is, certainly, one of the most eccentric epistolary collections that we know of, although this time the eccentricity points to 'normality', to that apparent absence of 'thought' that Vargas Llosa faults Puig's novels for. In this collection there are no altarpieces of high culture: Puig is just Puig, a middle class Argentine tourist, a voracious cinephile, a responsible son who brushes his teeth three times a day, a clever and super-awake kid who wants to absorb everything. He doesn't pose, or rather he does – a lot – but in the role of aficionado; he has fun, as Gil de Biedma says in a poem, 'alternating between nudity and disguise', and he demonstrates, along the way, that a good way to become a writer is to not want to be a writer.

April 2006

A BURNING LOVE

The publication of *Niña errante* [Wandering Girl], the collection of Gabriela Mistral's letters to Doris Dana, has provoked many reactions, some of them truly funny. Take, for example, the response from the poet Jaime Quezada, who said that the letters showed a 'friendship with a capital F', as if it were impossible to call things by their names. It's an understandable gesture though: it's a delicate thing to air the private life of a woman who jealously guarded herself against rumours, and not out of shame but rather the eminently reasonable wish to live in peace.

Other distinguished Mistralians think that the revelations in this book do not alter the reading of Gabriela Mistral's literary work, since the important material is in her poems, in the texts that she authorized and wanted to publish. This claim is correct, but also ill-timed: the knowledge that the author was a lesbian is worth as much (or as little) when one reads her poems as the belief that she fit the nun-like image the conservative Mistralians have always promoted. If we are going to put on structuralist airs, then let us do without the biography entirely.

The book's editing has also been criticized, in particular for certain regrettable gaps that make its reading more difficult. It seems it may have been possible to better contextualize some of the letters, but Pedro Pablo Zegers' work is, in other aspects, vital. I do think it was unnecessary, though, to use so much euphemism in the prologue. The fact that Mistral spoke of herself using the masculine is evidence, according to Zegers, of 'a paternal and protective streak'. There's no reason, however, not to think that she simply felt more comfortable speaking as a man.

Also in the prologue, Zegers describes how the two women established a bond of teacher and pupil that 'little by little' gave way to a 'complex' relationship. But the letters tell, rather, of a burning love: a fascinated Doris Dana approaches the famous poet thirty years her senior, and in a matter of months they are already planning to live together for the rest of their lives. Soon Mistral is sending Doris checks, and then she opens an account for the two of them, pays Doris's debts, and plans to leave everything to her when she dies. She also advises Doris to continue writing stories, although in a way they both know that she is not going to become a great writer, but rather a great writer's secretary, nurse, and life partner.

Most of Doris Dana's letters were lost, but they must have been rare and short, judging by Gabriela Mistral's persistent complaints: 'I am like those crazy people who write letters to themselves and then answer them,' she says at one point, and the image reappears regularly, because her beloved runs away or holes up in a silence that hurts, torments: 'I have never asked you for long letters that would steal your time, which belongs to your friends; I have asked you for fast and frequent lines.' She always sounds cross, wounded by the lack of contact: 'Even the manager of an American bank, Doris Dana, takes the time to write his friends when he knows they need his words. Not you.'

That's why the title is so spot-on: what the reader shares with the writer is that constant flight, that absence she feels, senses, and exaggerates: 'Love is very delicate. It can break out of nowhere, or it wears out, grows old, ugly, becomes a cold habit. Care for it, my love, watch over it.'

Just whom could a book like this offend? The same

47

people who are scandalized by homosexuality and the morning-after pill. Only people who are very conservative and very stupid.

September 2009

A DREAM COME TRUE

To reread Onetti is to read him for the first time. Or at least that's what I think now, as I read his stories again, return to his novels: there are entire sentences I remember, atmospheres, plots, characters and scenes, but as long as the reading lasts my memories lose their precision, while the newness of the words always wins out, the contingency of reading here and now.

I guess that's always what happens when we re-read the work of a writer we admire: we are able to articulate our admiration, give reasons for our preferences, sketch out articles or columns, but when we return to the texts themselves all our certainties break apart, and we build new memories – ones that also seem definitive, for a while.

I say all this in order to return to the question – to me inevitable – about the first time I read Onetti. It was in the mid-nineties, during my serious period of voracious reading. Back then we read in a hurry, trusting in speed, as if we wanted to recover time that we had never had. I remember how Onetti's work resisted that speed; it asked for a long look, and it didn't fit into the boxes that our teachers taught us with categorical gestures.

The first thing I read were his stories, and the one I liked the best is still the one I like best now: 'A Dream Come True'. That permanence is strange, maybe contradictory: I remembered some phrases from the story ('I understood, now without a doubt, that she was crazy, and I felt more at ease'), I remembered the characters, and Blanes' joke about *Hamlet* and the staging of 'intimate' theatre. But now I unheard those memories; I felt it was the first time I was reading a story I already knew.

The narrator of 'A Dream Come True' is

compassionate and reasonable: he knows more or he thinks he knows more than the woman and than Blanes, and that's why he doesn't react to the joke about *Hamlet*, doesn't clarify it; he knows it wouldn't make sense to clear things up. He hasn't read Hamlet, and as a form of twisted revenge he proposes to himself to never read it, to never understand the joke. Back then, when I encountered this story for the first time, I thought of Hamlet, of the play within the play, the scene of the prince proposing to the actors that they put on *The Murder of Gonzago*, and also about Borges, the similarity of 'A Dream Come True' with some of Borges's poems and stories.

As you can see, I used to be much more intelligent than I am now, since after re-reading the story I haven't come to any 'literary' conclusions. I've only thought about the Madwoman's dream, about the desire to control the staging of one's own death, the gesture – clearheaded or capricious, we don't know – of dying onstage, as great artists do, but with no more audience than the empty seats, the secondary actors, and that witness who sooner or later will agree to tell the story.

Reading Onetti brings a certain intimacy, an enormous complicity, that is very difficult to describe. I used to like 'A Dream Come True', but now, for different reasons, I like it more. Maybe in that story I used to see literature, and now I see only a gesture: the gesture of reading, of trying to read life. It's a poor conclusion, although I think it's necessary to say it: Onetti wasn't writing to make literature, but rather to get close to – and bring us closer to – the questions no one can answer.

August 2009

THE SILENCE OF THE VACUUM ON SUNDAY AFTERNOON

I've been reading Elias Canetti's notes according to the only method he judged possible: paging through it endlessly, getting lost in the multitudinous tyranny of the phrases, waiting for an interruption; 'It would be awful, absurd, to read it all at once,' Canetti said in reference to *The Secret Heart of the Clock*: 'Some have tried and are annoyed when they can't manage it. They should not manage it. The author makes no effort to achieve concentration in order to facilitate things for the reader. On the contrary, he wanted to force the reader to stop. Perhaps that is a harsh way of saying it, but that's how it is.'

To read in order to stop reading? Yes. This is the kind of text that calls for the jumpy reader so desired by Macedonio or Machado de Assis, among so many other enemies of the straight line. But Canetti's laughter tends to be inverse, elegiac: 'He is eaten away by thoughts he'd forgotten sixty years ago,' he says and right away we close the book and open forbidden drawers of memory, or maybe we go on reading, getting our breath back, little by little, with difficulty: 'A man remembers things the way things would have liked to be: more terrible, better, wider.'

I received Canetti's collected notes one week before the publication of *Veneno de escorpión Azul* [Venom of the Blue Scorpion], the death diary of Gonzalo Millán, a poet who could well have written some of Canetti's phrases. I read the two books simultaneously, jumping to Canetti and reading straight through the stretch that goes from 20 May 2006 through twelve days before Millán's death, on 14 October of the same year.

Last year, I say to myself out loud, as though solving an absurd math problem. It is unsettling to read a diary written less than a year ago. It's strange to know that exactly twelve months ago, on 22 July 2006, Millán woke up at eight in the morning, and, after eating his daily marijuana cookie, wrote: 'I realize what's happening, but I don't believe it, it's not happening to me. I deny three times while my cough destroys me.'

I was saying I've been reading Canetti's notes and *Venom of the Blue Scorpion*, surely searching or hoping for a zone of confusion. I write, now, from that confusion, from that wish for solitary phrases, in prose or in verse. (Canetti: 'A single phrase is pure. The next one already takes something away from it.')

I read, for example, that Millán says goodbye to his pens, and I go to Canetti and look in the index for the word *pen*, and I find phrases that describe much better than any review what is happening in *Venom of the Blue Scorpion*, what is happening – or happened – in Gonzalo Millán's life. I transcribe a few of these single phrases: 'At the edge of the abyss, he grasps hold of pens.' 'The last pen has been devoured.' And especially this one: 'The pen, his crutch.' And this one: 'They threw him out of the world with all of the pens.'

I think about Millán in exile, losing the language of the tribe and discovering or recovering a stutter, a foreignness: learning to speak in a language of his own. I think of this image of Canetti's: 'I feel at home when, pen in hand, I write German words and everything around me is English.'

I don't know if Millán liked Canetti. I think he did: at least, there is a poem in *Vida* [Life] that includes these lines of Canetti's as an epigraph: 'The days are distinct, but the night has only one name.' Millán cites, on the other hand, two phrases by George Oppen that Canetti could very well have written: 'It is possible to use words provided one treat them as enemies.' 'When the man writing is frightened by a word, he may have started.'

In sum. 'They've got you marked like the tree they're going to cut down,' says Millán towards the end of *Venom of the Blue Scorpion*, a book that for now strikes me as almost impossible to describe. It is, to be sure, a detailed goodbye to love and travelling, to childhood and to poetry, to friends and beloved daily objects – because Millán also says goodbye to the metal sugar bowl, the eyelash curler, the vibration of an electric shaver, the silence of the vacuum on Sunday afternoon.

'I'm the one who has changed his voice / The stranger who does not like to hear himself,' he says.

'I am a particular cell extinguishing itself,' he says.

'The tears say goodbye forever to the eyes,' he says.

'I shed tears in dust,' he says.

'I agonize among my plush trophies,' he says.

'I leave a gap: a necessary lacuna / an initial and final indentation as an offering,' he says.

And he doesn't say but could have, with Canetti: 'The most imprecise word of all: I.'

July 2007

THE CARETAKER OF A GIANT
WHOREHOUSE

Alejandro Rossi preferred books that 'with no regret, we can open to whatever page we feel like,' and that predilection acts, when we recall it, as a friendly instruction. There are definitely many of us who consult his *Manual del distraído* [Manual for the Distracted] as if those loose notes actually did constitute a manual, as if we really wanted to perfect the art of opening books to a random page. We blindly seek 'just the right advice, the perfect diagnosis, the crucial word, the big idea expressed in four decisive pages,' and we are never truly disappointed, as Rossi himself consoles us: 'It never happens like that, but it doesn't matter, because the hope for the miracle is strengthened in failure.'

'It's the easiest thing in the world to read a text wrong,' says Rossi, but it's difficult to read *Manual for the Distracted* wrong, since the author closes the door to intruders with enthusiasm and delicacy. Those who are anxiously in search of important conclusions ('as if we were victims of a tedious ritual that forced us to write pages and more pages before reaching the five or six essential sentences'), or those who believe the first paragraph is enough to guess what comes next, will not go beyond the first lines or reach the final ones of *Manual for the Distracted*.

It's good to speak of Alejandro Rossi in the present tense, and thus to forget that he died last week, at seventy-seven years old, due to his habit of 'chewing cigarettes like they had vitamins,' as Juan Villoro has said. It's entirely a privilege to write about *Manual for the Distracted* imagining that it's a new book, not one that was first published thirty-one years ago. In spite of the funereal reason, it's a pleasure to remember the man who defined his interests and his methods like this: 'I'm devoted to quick, dazzling intuitions, the kind whose exposition fits in a few well-polished sentences. There are no recipes for inducing them, except to remain still, motionless, without moving a finger. This runs the risk, if it's night-time, of also inviting mosquitos.'

An enemy of grandiloquence and the telephone, alarmed by 'the enormous number of words that fit on a page', and convinced that 'the truth taken to its ultimate conclusions doesn't always favour social well-being,' Alejandro Rossi was an observer of the minimal. Though this observation is fairly misleading, since he didn't shy away from the macro here and now, either. He certainly didn't place any trust in dogma, manifestos, or declarations of principle, although his own, over time, has become fairly celebrated: 'I've always tried not to get too close to truth, or at least not to large truths, and have decidedly preferred peripheral lands, blind alleyways, ideas with no future.'

Rossi at times changed his position within his writings; the first person came easily to him, but he wanted to avoid falling into anecdotalism: 'I am sick of this kind of story. It is not my aspiration to demonstrate that I possess my own gallery of monsters.' He didn't want to limit himself to biography, although *Manual for the Distracted* is also, of course, a brilliant autobiography written by a lover of secondary characters.

'It's sometimes a relief to be able to express oneself through another,' says Rossi in his magnificent manual: 'They made the effort, we merely discover commonalities and passively agree.' That is what happens upon reading *Manual for the Distracted*: we discover commonalities, we agree, we would like to quote the entire book. I'll content myself with one final fragment, my favourite: 'How often I find myself thinking about the countless people who are making love at this precise instant, behind those windows. It's a realization that never ceases to amaze me and that makes me feel, as I walk through the streets, as if I were the caretaker of a giant whorehouse.'

June 2009

TOY CATALOGUE

The Toy Catalogue, by the Italian writer Sandra Petrignani, is a beautiful and satisfying book. The exercise is so simple that it even seems naive: the author precisely describes the toys of her childhood, once coveted and now rather lost to memory: scooters, water pistols, teddy bears, dolls, kaleidoscopes, spinning tops, buckets, toy soldiers, among so many others. Autobiographical scenes inevitably emerge, but that is not exactly the author's purpose; she rather steers clear of confession. While from time to time she comes out with some whimsical and funny phrase, she more often employs a curiously impersonal tone. Thus she advises, at one point: 'One doesn't learn to yo-yo – you get it straightaway or never at all.'

I've spent over an hour trying to say this another way, but fine, what can we do: this book is a gem. I love this description, for example, of the moment when a soap bubble bursts on the skin: 'Your mouth caught the bitter taste of soap, your eyes pure enchantment and your mind a disturbing realization of insubstantiality.' Or when the author recalls the hours spent jumping rope and she writes this unexpected sentence: 'If you've never had long hair you can't imagine what a lovely feeling it is to feel it fly up and then slap back down on your shoulders.'

In another entry, Sandra Petrignani remembers that, more than playing with marbles, the delight lay in treasuring them ('holding lots of them between your hands and listening to the music they made cracking against each other'), and then she talks about perfection and stability and then concludes: 'If God exists, he is round like a marble.' I completely agree. I do not agree, on the other hand, when she laments the fact that model cars no longer have passengers painted on their windows, which provokes, in her opinion, an 'alarming strangeness' that comes from their 'unreal emptiness'. I think those silly cartoons that imitate drivers and passengers are much more unreal. I remember, in this regard, an essay where Martín Kohan complains about Hot Wheels ('my son is fascinated by them, and I can't get on board,' he says), arguing that the cars represent non-existent models, unlike traditional miniatures, which are tranquilizing copies of real cars. Kohan thinks of Walter Benjamin's obsession with miniatures, and of the possibility – so important for a child's way of thinking – of conceiving a world to scale, because those toys 'don't just imitate the world, they promote the illusion that they *are* a world, that they are *the* world.'

Between those empty but realistic miniatures and the Hot Wheels of today are the toy cars of my generation, which were not only cars but also robots. Though in some cases not even the argument of that supposed saving – that of buying, for the same price, a car and a robot – would let us get our hands on an Optimus Prime or one of his cheaper followers. Speaking of scale models, much more important than Transformers, for me, was the section 'Chile in Miniature' at the now disappeared Mundo Mágico: I remember the fascination I felt on seeing at my feet, within reach of my hands, the miniature version of the immense Votive Temple of Maipú. And it wasn't one visit, but many. Over and over I asked my parents to take me there, and my parents, with the same consistency with which they refused me whatever toys were in style, indulged me with that innocent form of tourism: to contemplate the model of a city that in reality, back in the mid-eighties, was falling to pieces, but that in fantasy was pleasant and manageable, compact, definitive.

The Toy Catalogue is one of those books that we could all write. I mean: only Sandra Petrignani could do it, but the exercise is contagious, and as we read we already know that sooner rather than later we will end up imitating not only her process but also her gaze; that we will talk about our own toys, about our own memories, now without sentimentalism or moralizing, perhaps even without nostalgia. Or maybe moved by a new nostalgia: a less abstract, more truthful one.

February 2012

PEEING WHILE IT RAINS

'Peeing while it's raining, now that's being part of the world,' said Hebe Uhart a few days ago, in a lecture on Simone Weil, and those of us in the room laughed as one often laughs when reading Uhart's stories, because that kind of joke abounds in them. Sometimes she tells them with utter ease, other times with a bit of timidity or innocence, like one discovering, all of a sudden, an unexpected tone. Reading Hebe Uhart we laugh a lot, although we are never sure if what we've read is just a joke, because in her words there is also, above all, precision and wisdom. That joke about the rain, for example, is true. At some point we've likely had that feeling: at some point, we were peeing and it was raining outside, and we felt at one with the world.

Hebe Uhart's books are full of these small revelations, which are born of a religious attention to detail while her ear goes deep into the ups and downs of language. Some months ago, in her previous visit to Chile, her intention was fundamentally to look for and discover our language. Hebe tells of how she walked freely through Santiago, eager to get lost, as though trying to let the city enter her unawares. She also walked a lot in this most recent visit, which coincided with the student demonstrations. She made her way among the protesters, trying to understand for herself what is happening in Chile, happy to get lost in the crowd.

Hebe Uhart's non-fiction chronicles seem like stories and her stories work like chronicles, or like loose and very lively observations. Her prose moves generously away from habitual models. Generously and naturally, with the discretion of one who is not trying to impress, because in her work we do not perceive, either, those juggling acts writers often perform in order to set themselves apart from the tradition.

'My Basque grandmother's house was a great centre of learning for me,' says the narrator of 'Señorita', in my opinion one of Hebe Uhart's best stories, and she explains it this way: 'They celebrated if someone fell to the ground, farted, or made a mistake speaking.' At nine years old the girl finds out that girls practice to be young misses (señoritas), and señoritas practice to be ladies. And she tries, in her own way, to understand those mysterious categories. Later she meets a couple that has separated, and when she thinks for the first time about that exotic custom of separating, she concludes: 'I'm not going to get married, because if I marry, I'll have to separate, and that's sad. But I'm going to have a lot of boyfriends, when I'm nineteen, twenty-nine, thirty-nine, and maybe a little longer.'

I very much like that fairly strange girl, who in adolescence decides not to ever go to a party again, but who always sends the birthday boy or girl a telegram that says 'Happy birthday'. She also refuses to look for words she doesn't know in the dictionary, because 'it says "see" and then "see" again,' and she doesn't want to lose, as she calls it, 'the impetus of reading'. Later she finds this quote by Paul Claudel: 'Youth was not made for pleasure, but for heroism.' And although she doesn't have too many opportunities to display her heroism, the phrase becomes a kind of intense emotion that stays with her always.

Now it's Hebe Uhart who puts together phrases, but ones less sententious than Claudel's, because she does not want to impart lessons, though we do learn a lot from her. But I don't know if we learn about literature. I think that she is not so interested in literature, but that life is very important to her. That's why after we read her we don't have the impression of having closed a book: after reading Hebe Uhart, the stories and words echo the way they do when we come home after spending long hours conversing with a stranger, and discovering a new and valuable complicity.

August 2011

THE SOLITUDE OF JOSEFINA VICENS

The Mexican writer Josefina Vicens preferred the slippery simplicity of natural phrases, even if she had to spend years searching for them. In one of the few interviews she granted, she tells of the time Juan Rulfo asked her why she was taking so long to publish another novel. The joke made sense, since in the end Vicens' oeuvre turned out to be even smaller than Rulfo's: her two novels were recently published together in a volume that could fit in a shirt pocket.

Her most well-known work is *El libro vacío* [The Empty Book], from 1958, which took eight years to write and which depicts the process of a man fighting against the blank page: 'What you see here, this notebook full of words and smudges, is nothing but the null result of a desperate tyranny that comes from an unknown place,' notes the narrator, and he tops it off with this bitter phrase of forced and useless self-pity: 'All this, and everything I will write, is only to say nothing. The result with be, in the end, many full pages and an empty book.'

It may sound like a dilettante's nightmare, but Vicens had no interest in the adventures of writing workshops. Quite the contrary, what the character feels is the lucid desire to construct a work that deserves to exist, in spite of the rampant prolixity. We know the author's own habits were similar to those of her character. Although *An Empty Book* received the highest praise on its publication, it was only in 1982, twenty-odd years later, that she published her second book, *Los años falsos* [The False Years]. She died in 1988, as she was sketching out a third work.

'We've all come to see me,' says Luis Alfonso at the beginning of *The False Years*, and there is pain in that phrase. Pain and irony, really: he is nineteen years old, but his father's death has turned him into an old man, or into a poor, pathetic guy who imitates, faithfully and with cowardice, someone else's life. Thanks to the deceased man's friends, Luis Alfonso inherits his father's job as advisor to a politician who soon enough becomes an undersecretary, and who will reach the heights so often reached by those who obey their bosses and harangue their underlings.

Luis Alfonso has the same name as his father, and everyone says that the physical resemblance is astonishing. What they don't know is that the son even practices his father's gestures before the mirror – repugnance and admiration intermingle to the point that he no longer wants to live for himself. He wants to occupy a secure place or disappear, to be the one in the cemetery so the dead man can return and spend his days drinking, playing dominos, and sleeping with Elena, the lover who, now given over entirely to imitation, Luis Alfonso also inherits.

The novel shows a political class willing to do anything to get rich, and the character's drama is precisely that: he has been prepared for opportunism and greed, and the desire to go against the grain gets him nowhere, since he doesn't have the strength to be anything more than the caricature his father was. 'We've all come to see me,' he thinks then, in the cemetery, where he has gone with his mother and sisters to commemorate the fourth anniversary of that death he feels as his own: 'I could talk to you about what it's like to be there below, with you, in your seeming death, and about what it's like to be up here, with you, in my seeming life.'

It's possible to read *The False Years* and *The Empty Book* as intimate stories, resistant to larger dimensions, but that emphasis would be unfair, since in Josefina Vicens' beautiful books, privacy is a condemnation, the last and obligatory refuge within a shattered space. The characters would like to integrate into the world, but the only way they have to do it is by recognizing their radical solitude, their definitive, subterranean madness.

August 2009

THIS IS LIKE A STORY BY ALEJANDRA COSTAMAGNA

In one of his brilliant literary essays, the poet W. H. Auden gives some guidelines about what he considers the ideal training for a writer. I don't have the text to hand, but I think I remember that he advises writers to learn several languages, and that they study – among other subjects – mythology, meteorology, cooking, and also – last but not least – that they keep a vegetable patch and a pet. I don't know how much Alejandra Costamagna knows about mythology or meteorology, nor do I know if she is a good cook, because although I have had her over for lunch many times, she has never returned those invitations. I am sure, on the other hand, that Alejandra has cats, because a conversation with her is only sometimes about literature, but almost always involves her cats. So, to say it with just a slight drumroll, I know a lot about Alejandra Costamagna's cats, although sadly I have never met them, because – I think it bears repeating – she has never invited me to her house.

I don't know if Alejandra has ever had a vegetable patch, or at least a garden. Now that I think about it, it's not hard to imagine one of her characters watering or carefully pruning plants. I feel like I've read a story by Alejandra – a non-existent story that I still feel like I have read – a story about a character who gets up at four in the morning and instead of drinking a glass of water or smoking a cigarette, gets up, goes out to the yard, starts to water the garden, and as the water falls and soaks her slippers, starts to feel something like happiness. I've never read that story of Alejandra's because Alejandra hasn't written it, but I think she should. I think it would be a beautiful story, one that only she could write. Because there are certain situations, some atmospheres and above all a restraint and rhythm that are recognizable in Alejandra Costamagna's writing. I have thought about that more than once over recent days, in relation to certain moments, as a result of certain everyday sensations. I've thought: 'This seems like a story by Alejandra Costamagna.' Because there is a world we intuit and through which we sometimes move, but which is hers alone. It's a world that, if it sounded good, we could call Costamagnian, but the truth is it doesn't sound very good.

That world, as I say, looks very much like our own, and nevertheless it maintains a side that is irreducible, at times even proudly secret. I think about endings, above all. What the stories in *Animales domésticos* [Household Pets] tell is not exactly what they seem to tell, and it takes us a little while to realize that. At first we let the story carry us along and we think we recognize it, and for a while we even feel at home and walk securely around those territories we think are familiar, but suddenly we discover a shade, a discreet lilt, a mark we couldn't foresee. Then we understand that we had not understood, we realize that the story is another, that we are and aren't there. We recognize ourselves in those lives because we're like that too, those are our problems as well, but at the same time we know that only they, only those characters would act like that. Because Alejandra Costamagna's characters possess an air of truth that provokes that famous and pleasurable confusion, the genuine miracle of literature: it's what happens when life seems to be on the side of the book, when suddenly the characters are so real that for a long and valuable second we ourselves become, with the book in our hands, less real.

Household Pets is a book about sons and daughters

without children, about people who talk to themselves or to the cat, about sick people who don't believe, 'not in doctors or in miracles or in exceptions,' and about solitary beings who, as one story says, don't believe 'in Patanjali or in Christ or the middle road or survivors or successors or, especially, in parents.' But mainly, *Household Pets* is a book about the limits of the everyday; about the presences that we have so on top of us that we are unable to see or feel them.

One aspect I admire about Alejandra's work is that kind of friendly sobriety that beats within her writing. It's her tone, her hallmark: she never shows off her authority, although in fact she almost always knows very well what she is talking about. She knows her people, she knows her garden, her cats, but she doesn't spend time on gesticulation or rest on maxims. And she respects her readers enormously. I think it's necessary to emphasize that. Alejandra respects readers and in that sense distinguishes herself from that crowd of writers who publish novels already underlined, with words in bold or italics, since they are afraid that readers won't understand and so they accentuate and show off and yell.

That fear, the fear of ending up talking to yourself, is understandable – it's a whisper that's impossible to separate from the profession. But a person who writes must be willing to talk to herself, because a writer is one who tries to say something that hasn't been said, something that is probably difficult or even impossible to say. Alejandra Costamagna writes from that awareness; her writing is a search for the unsayable, and this book is the unmistakable testimony of her discoveries.

NATIONAL HOLIDAYS

The façades of Barranco harmonize with a strange elegance: risky colours abound, but the assemblage doesn't look tawdry. I walk like a tourist and I describe Lima's skies with the same adjectives as always: grey, ashy, overcast. There is sun, but it's as if something were preventing it from fulfilling its function.

I buy a newspaper at random – they have so many here. A rise in fuel cannot be ruled out, the IMF recommends Peru lower its inflation, Eva Ayllón is working on a new show. There are also dozens of items which seem cryptic to me and that I read closely, as though solving great mysteries: 'Doc' will be questioned in the Cuatro Suyos case, the Colombian Vargas can wear blue, the *misilera* is doomed.

One story catches my eye. It's about a woman in Trujillo who painted the façade of her house with the colours of the Chilean flag. The reason for this gesture, according to her, was that for 15 years she had a relationship with a Chilean man. She meant it as an homage and not an insult, but the neighbours complained at what they considered a provocation – especially now, on the eve of Chile's national holidays – and the hullaballoo was such that the mayor had to go and ask her to cover the single star with blue paint. The story isn't over yet, because the neighbours are now asking the woman to cover the blue with red: to turn the Chilean flag into a Peruvian flag.

There is a strange aggravating circumstance: the place has a liquor shop that the enamoured woman has baptized *botillería*, like in Chile, and not *licorería*, like in Peru. The photo shows the woman smiling and waving a little Peruvian flag in a sign of remorse. Behind her is a small house, now without the star, but with the Chilean colours in perfect proportion. That façade would be unimaginable in Barranco, I think, in a kind of uncertain joke. I close the newspaper, look around me for Peruvian flags, and I find 15, maybe 16.

Later I remember, out of pure dilettantism, Cesare Pavese's phrase: 'We need a village, even if only for the pleasure of leaving it.' At night I see some friends who give me books that I've read but don't have: *Dichos de Luder* [Luder's Sayings] by the great Julio Ramón Ribeyro, and the first edition of *El libro de Dios y de los húngaros* [The Book of God and the Hungarians] by Antonio Cisneros, who has just published a new book of poems, *Un crucero a las islas Galápagas* [A Cruise to the Galapagos Islands].

I buy Cisneros's new book, page through it and put it away for later, like a precious gem. Meanwhile I recall seeing the poet in 2001 as he read, standing on balcony of La Moneda, reading these lines from one of his greatest hits: 'To forget you and not look at you / I watch the flies winging through the air / Great Style / Great Speed / Great Height.' Cisneros was completely drunk, and it was awesome to see his anti-solemn performance: it's the closest I've come to seeing the Rolling Stones.

From which it derives that, I don't really know why, I didn't go see the Rolling Stones when they came to Chile. And now I remember that there is a book called *Los Rolling Stones en Peru* [The Rolling Stones in Peru] and I resolve to read it some day. The conclusions of my trip to Peru are, as always, fairly strange: I like Lima a lot, I like the sound of the word *huachafo*, and I find it excellent that someone, in a gesture of love, could paint their house with another country's colours. Even if the façade ends up kind of ugly, of course.

August 2008

THE PUNTA ARENAS CEMETERY

I wanted to go to the cemetery in Punta Arenas and recall Enrique Lihn's poem, the one he wrote after going, with a tourist's serene anxiety, to tour that space so heavy with disconcerting symbols. The poem speaks of 'a peace that struggles to be shattered', and that is the impression that remains after looking at the cypress trees ('the double line of obsequious cypresses,' says Lihn), the inspired mausoleums, the headstones in foreign languages, the miraculously fresh flowers. I look towards the sea while the poet Galo Ghigliotto plays with some blocks of ice, and our guide, the writer Óscar Barrientos, takes the opportunity to visit his grandfather's grave.

One way or another all Magellanic writers talk about their region. *El viento es un país que se fue* [The Wind is a Country That Departed], the novel that Barrientos has just published with Das Kapital press, is set, like almost all the writer's fiction, in Puerto Peregrino [Pilgrim's Port]. But that fictional place sounds realistic in this corner of the world that seems to have been baptized by obsessive and melancholic novelists. I like Barrientos's books a lot, but now that I've been to Punta Arenas I like them more, because I'm starting to understand that his literature is less literary than I'd thought. The things that happen in Pilgrim's Port could happen in Punta Arenas; I can't even bring myself to rule out the supernatural episodes.

How to flee from the wind, from history, myth, the sea? Magellanic writers don't want to flee that inscrutable landscape – Barrientos turns to fantastic literature not to escape but to remain, to understand a reality that doesn't fit on a postcard. I try to say some of this to him, but Barrientos is very famous in this town, and while we walk he greets an average of 0.9 people per minute. Then he tries to convince me that we should have what everyone has for breakfast in Punta Arenas: five sausages in a roll (*choripanes*) and a glass of banana milk. I dramatically refuse, and he pretends to be offended.

That night, we have a reading at the Pablo Neruda Neighbourhood Association, which, in one of life's great ironies, is on a street named after the poet's worst enemy, Pablo de Rokha. The Cultural Council has a long-running writing workshop for the locals, and our reading is the least of the event: the important part is the conversation at the end with those men and women who write to learn about themselves, to learn how to live after the death of a mother or a child.

I think how the vanity that abounds at literary events has to give way, sometimes, to these unforeseen and authentic moments. I talk about that with the poet Christian Formoso, who has come to hear the reading with his son Dante. Last year, Formoso published 'El cementerio más hermoso de Chile' ['The most beautiful cemetery in Chile'], a long poem that delves into that commonplace of the area: people in Punta Arenas are proud of their cemetery, the same way that Chile celebrates the supposed beauty of the flag or the national anthem. It's a beautiful and harrowing book, which at times calls to mind Neruda, de Rokha, Zurita, *The Spoon River Anthology* by Edgar Lee Masters, *Los naufragios* [The Shipwrecks] by Alvar Núñez Cabeza de Vaca. Formoso searches in the regional memory, he collects and assembles the voices of a community broken by the official discourses. The result is an inexhaustible book.

Back in Santiago, I think of the value of remaining in one's city and searching for a place in the world. I think of that peace Lihn spoke of, the peace that struggles to be shattered. And like that, little by little, the chronicle begins.

July 2009

THE CITY WILL FOLLOW YOU

'The city will follow you,' says Constantine Cavafy's most famous poem, and it is hard not to agree, especially if we have spent our whole lives walking along and looking at the same streets. I like Santiago, and sometimes I think I couldn't live anywhere else. But like most of its inhabitants, I'll admit that it is not a beautiful city, or at least not one whose beauty is obvious. That's why it's hard for us to show people around: we can't figure out where to take the friends who decide to spend a few days in Santiago.

When a visitor says they like the city, Santiagoans immediately ask, a little surprised and even a bit alarmed, why. A few days ago a foreign friend – Dutch; that is, a traveller *par excellence* – gave me this funny and logical reply: 'I like Santiago because it's close to Valparaíso.' And sure, Chile *is* full of beautiful places. It's a little absurd to spend two or three holiday days in a city that isn't even especially entertaining, although on this point everything is relative: I, at least, have never gotten bored in Santiago. I think there are plenty of places where good times are to be had, but sometimes I think I'd have a good time anywhere.

Santiago is many cities at once. And sometimes it seems sad that it's been carefully designed so that people's paths never cross. When I think about Santiago, I think especially about its downtown, where everything mixes together, where everyone – whether they want to or not – comes into contact. When I was eleven years old and started to travel to school every day (I lived on the city's outskirts, an hour and a half from downtown) I fell in love with that landscape, dirty, interesting, crowded, dangerous, impersonal, chaotic. A place where everything was happening, where no one belonged. I started class at two in the afternoon, but I left my house very early so I could wander through those new streets, whose names I only knew because they appeared in the local version of Monopoly.

I can perfectly imagine Roberto Merino on those same walks ten, fifteen years before me: walking eagerly but also distracted, sincerely inhabiting the city, free of previously held theories, blissfully lost.

I think there would be consensus in pointing to Merino – a reporter by intuition and necessity; by vocation, an inconstant and excellent poet – as the best 'Santiagologist' of our literature. Recently collected in the volume *Todo Santiago* [All of Santiago], Merino's articles about the city total around 150, and the vast majority of them are short, maybe 600 or 700 words. That is plenty of room for the author to unfurl his inimitable and perhaps untranslatable style: syntax *à la* Borges, somewhat 'English,' otherwise very Chilean, colloquial – though not at all quaint – plus some bookish asides that are never pedantic, and frequent, unexpected rhythmic shadings.

If Merino's columns have awakened growing interest in readers (though he continues to be, at 50 years old, a semi-cult writer), it has been precisely for his style, the elegance of a prose that has little or nothing to do with average journalism. One of his feats is the perfect manipulation of emphasis and a persuasive sobriety that allows him to sneak in the most capricious observations: at one point he says that Parcheesi boards are stupid, for example, or that McDonald's French fry boxes can seem mysterious. Speaking of fast food, there is one column in which Merino confesses that he has a habit of stopping in front of the restaurant Dominó to observe the way people eat hot dogs: 'Some do it cheerfully, taking giant bites; others sadly, with the absent gaze of too little sleep.' It must be said that Chile's original and delicious hot dogs – which we call *completos* – are among our greatest inventions, perhaps the only thing that foreigners end up remembering of Santiago. And nevertheless, in that article, Merino confesses he has never tried one. To have lived one's entire life near downtown Santiago (as Merino has) without ever trying a *completo* from Dominó, unless you are a vegetarian (and Merino is not), is almost utterly unbelievable. You don't have to believe him; the image is a good illustration of his slightly distanced, absent position.

All of Santiago is, to a large extent, an involuntary book, composed of texts written against the clock, minutes before a deadline. Almost twenty years ago, when an editor gave him the job of writing a column about the city, Merino followed a certain pattern of bibliographic reports and inquiries, but the lenses grew blurry little by little until his writing became more personal, with the city cut back to the modest range of action of a subject, one who moves with curiosity and calm through a setting that he knows by heart, but in which he always finds more nuances. In these columns there is a great deal of observation and concrete description, and little conjecture or fixation on idiosyncrasy or national identity. And although in a couple of columns he outlines a convincing and very well-named 'route of boredom', Merino never condemns the city, not by any means: if he had to choose between hate and love, doubtless love would win.

The city that emerges in Merino's articles is discernible but also private, very personal, and even – as are all things when we look at them up close – a little hermetical: the author tends to allude to sounds, smells, moods, the way the light falls in certain spaces. All the while, he takes on the subjects that are inevitable when talking about Santiago: pollution, the constant demolition of valuable buildings, the paranoia about crime that affixes metal bars and alarms everywhere, the endless honking horns and traffic jams at rush hour, the rising numbers of beggars, sellers, and artists on the street.

It's the city that we know, the city that would follow us if we wanted to flee from it (from ourselves), with its permanent architectural eclecticism, with the dirty river, almost always a mere trickle, cutting the landscape in half, with the stray dogs napping at all hours on the corners, with the most beautiful sky imaginable those few days of autumn or winter after it rains, when we rediscover the mountains. And with fairly strange people, like Merino himself, for example, looking at us from the other side of the window pane as we sadly chew our magnificent hot dogs.

June 2013

NOT TO READ

How to Talk About Books You Haven't Read is the title of an essay by Pierre Bayard that these days is being read, or at least sold, all over the world. I can't say much about this book because, unfortunately, I haven't read it. But the subject strikes me, just now, as familiar.

In recent years I've experienced countless times the happiness of not reading certain books, ones that, if I had gone on working as a literary critic, I would have had to read. Once, for example, I had to comment on a shoddy novel by Jorge Edwards inspired by the figure of Joaquín Edwards Bello, so that a few months ago, when I heard that the new target of Edwards' novelistic fumbling was the poet Enrique Lihn, I breathed a long sigh of relief at not reading *La casa de Dostoievski* [Dostoyevsky's House]. People less lucky than I read the novel and thought that it was detrimental to Lihn's memory, for which Edwards – praised almost unanimously for his previous work – was this time attacked unjustly, since as far as I know his book wasn't a biography, but a novel.

The attacks on Edwards were so furious that I even felt like coming to his defence, but then I would have had to read the three hundred plus pages of the book. I'm sure several of Edwards' detractors didn't even read *Dostoyevsky's House*, but there's no reason to blame them, since the father of this tradition of non-readers is precisely Edwards himself. Some years ago he presented *Epifanía de una sombra* [Epiphany of a Shadow], the posthumous work by Mauricio Wacquez, by saying that he had only made it halfway through, but that it was without a doubt a splendid novel, considering that Mauricio wrote very well. Edwards also presented *The Savage Detectives* with the confession, before an astonished

Roberto Bolaño, that he still hadn't finished reading the novel. And at the last Madrid Book Fair, Bolaño was once again his victim: in the frame of an homage, Edwards said that he had tried many times to read *2666*, and that he had even bought several copies, to the point that he planned to organize a raffle for all those unread books.

Maybe that afternoon Edwards was responding to the impropriety I myself had committed at the same table minutes before, when asked a question about Bolaño's reception in Chile. I couldn't resist remembering the polemic between Óscar Bustamante and Agustín Squella, which for me was a key chapter in the history of Chilean non-reading. Squella's argument was excellent, but much better, in terms of its stylistic challenge, had been Bustamante's rebuttal, in which he admitted that he hadn't read *2666* but confirmed that without a doubt it was not a great novel.

Lately the writer Marcelo Lillo has joined in this tendency, affirming that he is not interested in Chilean literature and at the same time declaring that, with his book of short stories, he is attempting to revitalize Chilean literature. It's strange to want to revitalize a panorama that one isn't familiar with, although this kind of cockiness is, in a way, healthy. I *have* read Marcelo Lillo's very proper book, thanks to Rafael Gumucio, who gave it to me with the assurance that Lillo was a great short story writer. 'I haven't read it and I don't plan to read it,' Gumucio told me, 'but it's very good. I don't need to read it to know it's very good, better than Cheever, better than Carver, better than everyone.'

Incidentally, the recent Nobel Prize to Jean-Marie Le Clézio has caught us unprepared. I've only read *The African*, which is a brilliant book, but it would be inappropriate to make a pronouncement as to whether the prize is deserved or not based on such a precarious foundation. 'Who the hell is he? I don't even know his name,' wrote a disconsolate Alberto Fuguet on his blog. Much more diligent than her colleagues, apparently, is Carla Guelfenbein, who said she had read Le Clézio on a recommendation from another Nobel winner, J. M. Coetzee, whom she met at a writer's conference in Iceland.

Some years ago I wrote a pretty unfavourable review about Carla Guelfenbein's first book, and in light of the current commentary about *El Resto es Silencio* [The Rest is Silence], her most recent effort, I was wrong back then, or maybe the proximity to Coetzee has improved Guelfenbein's prose. It's too late to find out, I have to say, since no one is going to deprive me of the pleasure it gives me not to read certain books, and the truth is I wouldn't read another novel by Carla Guelfenbein even if Coetzee himself recommended it to me.

October 2008

GENIUS KIDS

I have never read and hope not to read *Stories and Poems for Extremely Intelligent Children of All Ages*, an anthology-essay that professor Harold Bloom published a couple of years ago. Since then I have endeavoured, with model perseverance, not to read it, to ignore it completely. But now, a friend of mine – one unaware of the proud relationship of not reading that I have with this dreadful book – has told me that it is an 'important' work (he didn't say 'good' or 'interesting'; he said 'important'), and that he had enjoyed Bloom's toys 'like a child would' (that's what my friend said). And it's only now that I have realized the true reason for my phobia: it's that I can't imagine myself, as a child, reading a book called *Stories and Poems for Extremely Intelligent Children of All Ages*. I'm trying, but I just can't do it.

If instead of Transformers or toy highways of dubious provenance I had received, for Christmas, a book with that title or one like it, I would probably have faked deep gratitude. After all, a parent who gives his child a gift like that does so inspired by an intuition that is boastful, but legitimate. Extremely intelligent children, I tell myself with certain indulgence, don't read the books that adults make them read: they don't want to be extremely intelligent, since wanting to be intelligent is extremely unintelligent. Intelligent children dominate to perfection the art of playing dumb, and thus they reach adulthood absolutely unscathed, perfectly free of the harsh punishments that intelligence tends to bring.

Many Chilean children from the eighties owe our literary initiation to the Ercilla Library, a numerous collection of books without pictures, prologues, or footnotes that came as free gifts with the magazine

Ercilla; it included several of the titles that appear among Harold Bloom's favourites. We are, for better or worse, the *Ercilla* generation: we read *The Metamorphosis* or *The Portrait of Dorian Gray* or Poe's stories basically because all we had to do was reach out a hand to get those books, and because they captivated us and didn't bore us, since within them throbbed lives less safe but more fun than 'horrendous authentic life', as Enrique Vila-Matas tends to say, citing (I think) Italo Svevo.

The *Ercilla* generation grew up in a world not at all apt for literature, a world where it was healthier to play dumb than to be a wise guy. We were not, in any case, extremely intelligent, but I like to think that over the years we grew sensible enough to distrust the tireless rankings and sermons of professor Harold Bloom.

June 2005

SUMMERING IN HUNGARY

Maybe Sandor Márai's novels take summer holidays too. Maybe the same book that looked so splendid last summer beside the tennis rackets and buckets is now returning to the usual beach, a few grains of sand still impregnated in the unread or half-read pages. I don't know. I haven't read Sándor Márai. Nor do I go to the beach in summer. Maybe I haven't read Márai precisely because I don't go to the beach in summer.

In *La vida descalzo* [The Barefoot Life], his surprising essay about the beach, Alan Pauls insists on the dissonance between the act of reading and the habit of summering, in spite of the supposed existence of an entire genre, the beach read – which, incidentally, has very little of the genre about it. After all it's pretty difficult to demarcate a set of books as being sun-proof: maybe novels about romance or adventure or detectives who are anything but savage.

Publishers invoke the idea of catching up: the holidayer aspires to rehabilitate herself as a reader; that is, to read what she had to put off during the rest of the year. And why? With respect to what would she have to catch up? This concept is strange, since it presumes a slavish fidelity to fashion. I tend to think that the people who read in the summer are the same ones who read in winter, autumn, and spring: people rather more opposed to propaganda, who pass up novelties with pleasure.

'You should read Márai, it's good literature,' a friend tells me, holding back, barely, an ambiguous laugh. She asks for recommendations and I advise, seriously and in jest, that she take with her on holiday *Celestial Harmonies*, the great work by the great Péter Esterházy (since we were already talking Hungarians), or that she read *The*

Beach or *The Beautiful Summer*, the wintery 'summer-time' books by Cesare Pavese, or *Alto Volta*, by the poet Yanko González, or any book by Mario Levrero, the photophobic Uruguayan author who wanted to write a luminous novel.

It's really strange to recommend books for summer (or winter, or waiting rooms). The summers of those of us who don't go to the beach are, in any case, much more compatible with reading: at least there are no friends denouncing anyone who would rather stay back and read, or – worse – write. Beach readers, on the other hand, seek the elusive shade where they can doze off a while with the badge of Jonathan Littell on their chests. Not to mention the parents who evade their children thanks to the five hundred pending pages. And more than one teenager tolerating what will be – he swears – the last summer he spends with his parents. He only goes down to the beach at night, now with neither book nor family, happy.

And that's sort of what happens at the Proustian end of *The Barefoot Life*, when Pauls relates his moment of initiation when, because of a fever, he trades in sand for books: after he was forbidden from going to the beach, the boy feels a natural discontent ('he thinks of all the games he won't play, all the waves he won't dive into, all the ice cream cones he won't eat, all the times he won't pee in the water'), but then he discovers the happy freedom of being left alone, in bed with his book, all afternoon. It's a very beautiful image. The image of summer, perhaps.

January 2008

OUT LOUD

Sometimes I think a literary work is only good if it passes the test of being read aloud, subjected to someone else's patience or one's own ticklish ear. That's why I like audio books, which recover the old custom of listening to words, of receiving their rhythm as well, the delayed music of the narration.

In his book *A History of Reading* Alberto Manguel reminds us that silent reading only became the norm in the tenth century – before that, it was understood that reading meant reading aloud, so that in antiquity, libraries were noisy places. It was believed that reading involved the eyes and the ears, so that the image of the isolated reader was unthinkable, and even communicated a mysterious selfishness.

For us, on the other hand, there is beauty in the image of the solitary reader. I remember a classmate who used to go to the National Library in the afternoons not to read, but to watch other people reading. He, in fact, didn't like to read, and he only used books as masks so he could watch without being seen. From time to time he drew the readers' poses in his sketchbook, usually the female readers, because he thought that a beautiful woman looked even more beautiful when she was reading.

I'm sure that he would enjoy the images in *On Reading*, André Kertész's book of photographs: readers appear in cities or peripheries, in parks, bars, or domestic interiors, but always immersed, absent, solitary, with just a few exceptions, like the famous photograph of three boys sharing the same book. To me, what is even more beautiful is the sudden moment when someone spells something out or repeats a passage in a quiet voice, as though discovering the sounds that sleep on the page, as though wanting to memorize, once and for all, their favourite verses or scenes.

Poetry tends to resist the page, and that's why for a poet, sound checks are necessary and important. Those of us who came of age with those terrible and eternal poetry readings learned it the hard way: the poem must break the circuit of solitude, even if it does nothing other than talk about that solitude. Now that I think about it, the first audio book I listened to was Pablo Neruda reciting his poems, and it's difficult to read him now without remembering that odious nasal accompaniment. But listening to Enrique Lihn reading the poem 'La pieza oscura' ['The Dark Room'], or Nicanor Parra reciting 'Soliloquio del Individuo ['The Individual's Soliloquy'] (with that direct phrasing that is just slightly different from the original line breaks) is a way to access unexpected subtleties.

It's unusual, on the other hand, for fiction writers to read passages of their novels out loud, and sometimes I think it would be good to instate this custom, at the risk of being bored to death. In that regard, I remember a traumatic experience: at the end of 2003, the fiction writer Juan Manuel de Prada came to present his award-winning novel *La vida invisible* [Invisible Life], and out of pure bad luck I was tasked with introducing him to the students at Diego Portales University. In my consummate naïveté I suggested he read us an excerpt from his book, since in Chile his work was not widely known. The man began to read unhurriedly, convinced he was about to captivate the auditorium, and even pausing from time to time to gulp down two litres of mineral water. We spent an hour and a half in the hall, desperately waiting for the moment when the next full stop would be the final one.

What failed that time was not the reader; what failed was the text, the story, the music. The ear doesn't lie, and to be sure of that all you have to do is press play. You'll either get bored or keep listening all night long.

July 2009

AN EMPTY BOOK

'I write just in case,' was José Santos González Vera's reply when he was asked the classic question about why he wrote. I like that answer – I think his phrase manages to communicate lightly the serious illness that comes over some fiction writers and poets when they confront the proverbial blank page. Far from having a way with words, writers tend to be very insecure people who harbour fundamental doubts about their profession. I'm not referring to writer's block or problems merely technical in nature, but rather to essential apprehensions that rear up frequently for writers. It is likely that, at the end of the day, many authors subscribe to what the Mexican writer Josefina Vicens said in a passage that's always healthy to recall: 'All of this and everything I will write is only to say nothing. The result will be, in the end, many full pages and an empty book.'

Blank pages or full pages that make up an empty book: there is melodrama in these images, but I prefer that melodrama, that perpetual domestic ordeal, since on the opposite pavement prowl writers so self-satisfied they're incapable of any reflection. It's staggering, the conviction of some novelists as they argue the transcendence of their work. They will claim, blasé as hell, that they represent a group or a generation, even an entire country or continent. They don't write just in case so much as just because: they don't do it for the love of it, and that's why they complain so much about negative reviews or lack of readers or the lack of government subsidies.

It's often forgotten that publishing a book is a very strange occurrence. Writing a book is already pretty strange, but publishing implies that what one does could interest someone else, and that's supposing a lot. Many fiction writers take on – without an ounce of guilt – the logic of the 'cool-hunter': they research the panorama, review the list of new releases, and quickly churn out the books that people supposedly want to read. But the books people want to read are not always the books one wants to write. And the best books are those that we didn't know we wanted to read. 'I don't have a way with words, not at all,' says Andrés Anwandter in a brief essay that he wrote, somewhat duty-bound, for an anthology. In that text, Anwandter slips in an idea that is, for me, essential: poets trip over tongues, language comes to them the way it does to a stutterer, as a problem. I once heard Armando Uribe cite Thomas Mann alluding to this: 'A writer is one who writes with difficulty.'

Unpleasant, in any case, that image of the suffering artist. Sometimes, on days when I'm down, I think it would be better to spend my time on some happier activity – writing detective novels, for example. The problem is that I've never liked detective novels much. I've read two or ten very good ones, but it seems so exhausting to go around the world looking for the culprit and taking up witnesses' time that was doubtless very valuable. The murderer, in the end, is always the author, who in the final pages confesses what he's known since the beginning. Writing detective novels is an undeniable exercise in skill, and that is what the genre's biggest followers tend to extol: a strategic excellence in distributing the clues, and the ability to build, using the same elements as always, a story that surprises.

I think of detective novels because they represent a clean example of writing. Literature without last names, on the other hand, always struggles against indeterminacy. Writing a detective novel must be, in this sense, similar to writing a sonnet: the difficulty is technical above all. The job well done prevails, and it matters little whether the author had something to say or not. To think that one has something to say is, of course, an act of extreme vanity. That's why, many times, the page stays blank and the book empty.

January 2009

FESTIVAL OF THE LONG NOVEL

Some years ago, I organized the first-ever Festival of the Long Novel. It never actually happened, but I still think it's a good idea. I still have the emails I sent out to dozens of writers and professors inviting them to share their experiences as readers of long books, although I never knew the exact minimum number of pages, and I got a little lost in a series of brilliant conversations about which novels genuinely counted as long. Some time later I published a very short novel, and there were those who thought I was a champion of brevity. Not at all. I prefer long novels, the ones we reserve for the first flu of the year, the ones that oblige us to invent the first flu of the year so that we can stay home reading them.

At some point in my adolescence I started faking illnesses that would let me progress at my leisure through important readings. My parents might have had suspicions, because always they made me go to the doctor, but I didn't even need to fool the guy; he invariably found me sick and blessed me with antibiotics and two or three days of absolute rest. Maybe as a kind of punishment, during my second year of university I spent a month suffering from an atrocious – and very real – bronchopneumonia that I struggled to make the most of by reading, little by little and a bit unenthusiastically, James Joyce's *Ulysses*.

Unemployment also favours readers. I remember the days, in the winter of 1999, when I got up early and went to drop off artful resumes. I did it with very little hope, but relieved at the imminence of a day spent reading. I walked home around eleven in the morning along Vicuña Mackenna, and sometimes I quickened my steps thinking of the moment when I'd flop onto the bed and pick up my novel again. I've never read as much as I did then, with only brief pauses to prepare the habitual pasta that I ate slowly, back in bed, always with the book open, progressing through the novel as though through a slow and urgent promise. That's why there are tomato sauce stains on my copy of *The Magic Mountain*. I didn't have a fever, but with a reader's solidarity, and probably a touch of hypochondria, I took my temperature every five pages. I even mistrusted the thermometer, since I wanted to fall as ill as the characters in the book.

Shortly afterward, a friend helped me get a job as a night-time phone operator at a travel insurance company, and those nights beside the telephone were also very conducive to reading. The boss let us sleep or do whatever we wanted as long as we were there when the phone rang, but hours would pass without anything happening. Now that I think about it, I've never again had a job so compatible with reading freely, untouched by the duties of writing a review or preparing a class.

Years later, for example, my reading of *2666* was a true marathon: I cancelled the classes I had to teach and also closed my life, so to speak, since I had to read fast to comply with the journalistic tyranny that demanded we get out ahead of the competition. I liked reading that way, the novel fascinated me, and I wasn't even unhappy with the review I wrote. But I prefer the re-reading of *2666* that I started a few days ago, with no precise reason or greater obligation.

I don't exactly know why the project of the Festival of the Long Novel didn't prosper. I guess it was my negligence when it comes to organizing that kind of exhausting event. Or maybe it was then that I started to read *The Manuscript Found in Saragossa* and reality was suspended, which is what always happens when we hide out in the lasting intensity of a magnificent long novel.

October 2009

RIGHT TO LEFT, UP AND DOWN

In Adolfo Couve's prologue to his book *Cuarteto de la infancia* [Childhood Quartet] he defends literary realism, basing his arguments, naturally, on Balzac and Flaubert, but also mentioning Fitzgerald and Truman Capote, and even poets like Ezra Pound and T. S. Eliot. What Couve valued in those authors was an idea of style, a commitment to form that went beyond literary genre. Some of Couve's novels, in fact, certainly approach poetry at times, as tends to happen with good novels, which are always closer to poetry than bad poems are.

However, Edwardo Molina held that 'Novels are the poetry of fools,' and this is surely what many poets think: that novels lack true intensity. Pound himself defended the writing of short texts by saying that the unwritten part would be 'the narrated part', that is, the boring part of the story. Gonzalo Millán, meanwhile, justified his affinity for *Madame Bovary* by saying that Flaubert was, really, a poet.

For their part, some prose writers reduce poetry to the narcissistic spectacle that Witold Gombrowicz denounced in 'Against Poets'. In *Book of my Mother*, Albert Cohen says that poets' feelings 'are short-lived, and that is why they start a new line' and some time ago, along the same lines, the writer Marcelo Mellado – who recently proclaimed himself public enemy number one for Chilean poets – accused them of 'writing downwards' and not left to right. The poets responded humourlessly, maybe confirming Mellado's caricatures of them in his brilliant novel *Informe Tapia* [The Tapia Report]. The charge of writing downwards is funny but also accurate, since many poets forget that writing a verse is a bit more complex than adding words to a shopping list.

It's not the same, certainly, to write from side to side as downwards. But there *are* great novels written downwards – *Spoon River* by Edgar Lee Masters, or books by the Catalan writer José María Fonollosa – and brilliant poems written side to side. Roberto Bolaño thought the best poetry of the twentieth century had been written in the form of a novel, and while that is a fairly doubtful claim, I think it is healthy, on this point, to mix apples and oranges.

In a 1968 conference, Borges lamented that the word 'poet' had ever been split into two, and he said that he hoped – a rhetorical hope, perhaps – that the poet would again be the person who, long ago, sang and told stories. This assertion is valuable: to mix genres is not innovation, but rather a return to a lost spirit. That's what we celebrate when we praise the lyricism or, more exactly, the epic breath, for example, of *2666*.

We are too full of labels: people talk about prose poems, poetic prose, 'proems', novels in verse, narrative poems, even the poet-novel and – I mention this for the sake of abundance, thinking of Marosa di Giorgio's *Rosa mistica* [Mystic Rose] – the erotic novel written in the form of a prose poem. Every time a work calls the division of labour into question, the critics react as if the mixing of genres were a new and endlessly disconcerting phenomenon.

This gesture is not so serious, except on occasions when labels fill up the whole debate and we lose sight of the fact that these forms mean something. To put it a different way: we don't wonder if *Spoon River Anthology* is a novel or a book of poetry in order fit it in with our reading habits. On the contrary: what matters is understanding that Edgar Lee Masters *needed* that ambiguity in order to say what he wanted to say.

March 2009

PAULO COELHO AND HIS PREDECESSORS

Sometimes Neruda could get dangerously close to cheesiness. His most well-known poems don't look out of place on scrolls at craft fairs, or on the typical post-cards with images of the waves at twilight. It's true that the best of his oeuvre has proven irreducible to these formats, but we also know that Neruda was capable of beauts like this: 'Take bread away from me, if you wish / Take air away, but / do not take from me your laughter.' Or these lines, maybe a little unnecessarily honest: 'There are taller than you, taller. / There are purer than you, purer. / There are lovelier than you, lovelier. / But you are the queen.'

And yet, 'Muere Lentamente' ['Slow Death'], the poem that the internet has been attributing to him for a while now, is not worthy of Neruda. Its widespread acceptance proves that many people still understand poetry to be the mere expression of emotions. In reality written by the Brazilian Martha Madeiros, the text endorses the primitive idea of poetry 'with a message'. The message, in fact, is clear: one must 'accept help', life must be enjoyed before it's too late; we must travel, listen to music, and read (read Martha Madeiros?); otherwise, guess what: we'll die slowly. And they say that a slow death is a whole lot worse than a quick one.

A similar story occurs with 'La Marioneta' ['The Puppet'], the letter supposedly written by Gabriel García Márquez in 1997 and that is often presented as a 'poem', perhaps because it includes a call to value one's neighbour, as 'today could be the last time you see those you love'. More interesting is the case of the famous poem 'Instantes' ['Instants'], in which a pseudo-Borges affirms that in another life he will make sure to be dumber, more relaxed, and – oddly – less hygienic (first time I've heard that hygiene could be harmful). The text was published in 1989 in the prestigious Mexican magazine *Vuelta* and presented – with no suspicions as to its legitimacy – as 'a reconciliation of the distinct human side of this great figure of the literature of the ages'.

Many writers and academics took the bait, but the usual party poopers patiently investigated the misunderstanding and established its true authorship. The subject had already incensed Borges' widow María Kodama, exasperated with having to clarify over and over that he had never written anything that bad (though maybe she would have been a little more excited if she'd been earning the royalties). The poem's admirers could not resign themselves to the truth and went on arguing that if Borges were alive again he would doubtless agree to write poems that bad in exchange for contemplating more sunsets, climbing more mountains, eating delicious ice cream cones, and never, ever showering. 'Because in case you don't know, life is made of that, only of instants; do not lose the now,' the false Borges advises us, and García Márquez agrees: 'Tomorrow's not guaranteed to anyone, young or old.' Neruda couldn't be left behind, and in the end his advice is the most elaborate of the series: 'Let us avoid death in gentle quotas, remembering / always that living demands a much greater effort /than the simple act of breathing.'

Self-help wins out, what can we do. 'With Paulo Coelho young and in good health, all the countries of the world have a reserve of cheap spirituality at their disposal for a long time to come,' says Iván Almeida in his funny study titled *Jorge Luis Borges, author of the poem 'Instants'*. But it would seem that not only are people desirous of bad literature; there are also those who would attempt to alter literary history in order to understand it as the distinct intonation of a few sultry sighs. Coelho and his precursors: none other than Borges, Neruda, and García Márquez. Demonstrating that these are false texts is useful, but it isn't enough: 'Even if the poem "Instants" isn't by Borges, we have to admit that it is a beautiful and profound poem,' says one stirred blogger, and his opinion is that of the majority. Conclusion: we're surrounded.

January 2009

CONFESSIONS OF A WOODEN CAT

In writing her book *Solar-Lunar Astrology: Affinities for Love*, María de los Ángeles Laso says that she had help from a Wooden Tigress, a Water Dog, a Fire Dragon, a Water Buffalo, and a Fire Snake. With this singular staff of collaborators, the author – a Metal Tigress known to the masses as the ex-panellist of a show on public television – put together this manual of psycho-astrology that is destined to promote self-knowledge among its readers.

There is little one could object to in a book such as this one: nearly five hundred pages written with more enthusiasm than eloquence and not without its grammatical errors, which it would be wise not to attribute to the Tigress, but rather to the editors. I am entirely ignorant of their astrological identities, but it's not hard to presume they are at the very least Dogs or Rats, or perhaps even a bunch of Pigs.

The reader can only hope that there are not factual errors as well. 'Be careful about reading health books. You may die of a misprint,' counselled Mark Twain. Proportionally speaking, a slight slip-up in dates could lead, for example, to a Snake reading this book and going through life believing himself a Monkey. The consequences of this imbalance could be fatal (or not). There aren't many reasons, it's true, to distrust in María de los Ángeles's knowledge, since – as the jacket of this book confirms – she has studied Art, Philosophy, Yoga, Psychoastrology, Ecoagriculture, I-Ching, Tarot, Dream Symbolism and Astroarcheology.

In my humble condition as a Wooden Cat, I must confess that it is particularly difficult for me to review the book of a Tigress: I have an inclination to admire and respect her, but I secretly think that she looks down on me. I try to position myself in her heart, but as I know that there are many privations and sacrifices to which I must submit in order to achieve this goal, I think that I will not be able to bear this relationship for very long. Sooner or later, I will return to my comfortable and bourgeois nature.

I am, moreover, manipulative, insecure, sybaritic, indolent, apathetic and indecisive. She, though it pains me to admit it, is lucid, respectful and practical; I am a dreamer and independent (like Arthur Miller or Pedro Almodóvar), and she is an energetic but warm Virgo Tiger, like Agatha Christie, Nicanor Parra, or Julio Cortázar.

IN TANNIN COUNTRY

In writing *Uncorked 2004*, Patricio Tapia tried a total 844 wines – nothing to sneeze at. The result of this magnificent feat of tasting, after some inevitable pruning, is a series of over four hundred short texts in which the author displays to full effect his remarkable ability to create unexpected and disturbing metaphors. For example, in 'Don Melchor 2000', one of the best texts of the series: 'The fruit is like a spear that pierces the entire palate to the end, leaving behind a sweet, warm sensation.' Further on we encounter this funny, lysergic variation on the same image: 'Just look at the strength of the tannins as they attack the palate like a band of Indians firing their arrows.'

With a fine sense of irony, Tapia speaks, for example, of a wine that is 'so commercial it's touching', going on to describe it in this assertive manner: 'It's like a popular song you hear on the radio, hum all week and then forget.' Honourable mention goes to this beautiful hyperbole: 'The maturity of the fruit dazzles me until I'm almost exhausted.' The author often launches into lavish recommendations, as when he affirms that a certain Cabernet 'has serious potential as an excellent companion for some pork chops on the grill'.

I very much like the defiant tone that Tapia adopts on occasion. 'The notes of yeast join with the mature fruits, generating a note that's very difficult to describe. Try it yourselves,' says the author, who dominates to perfection the art of addressing his readers, as can be seen in this passage that, incidentally, sounds like a veiled autobiographical confession: 'Let's return to the mouth feel. Sense how the wine surrounds the tongue like an affectionate hug from a clumsy, plump woman who has just

gone swimming in the cold Pacific Ocean. You will enjoy this wine. I assure you.'

2004

THE POETRY OF KAROL WOJTILA

'This is a canonical book within the history of contemporary world literature, indispensable for the
interpretation of modern culture,' proclaims the cover
of *Pensamientos de Luz* [Thoughts of Light], a selection
of poems by the eighty-something Polish author Karol
Wojtila, of whose literary work we previously knew almost nothing in this little corner of the world.

This enthusiastic blurb is seconded in the volume's
prologue by Doctor Bogdan Piotrowsky, who proudly observes that 'it's not every age that can boast an
anthology so interesting and surprising.' As it seems
the recommendation is hardly impartial, it is only natural for the good poetry reader to react with distrust,
especially if he notices that Piotrowski dedicates his introduction ('with devotion, admiration, and thanks') to
Wojtila himself, seriously and unnecessarily compromising his own credibility.

In any case, the reading of *Pensamientos de Luz* (recently published by Editorial Norma), constitutes a full
display of the Wojtilian poetic proposition, which immediately catches one's attention for its extreme expressive
concision. Strictly speaking, many of the texts collected
here are really aphorisms: 'It is only given to man to die
one time; and then, Judgement!' declares Wojtila, in a
poem that is somewhat alarmist, but certainly striking.
I would also mention that the author has certain distinctive habits, such as his way of writing certain words with
capital letters, for no apparent reason (the pronouns He,
You, and His, mostly), in alluding to a series of characters who, nevertheless, are never specified: 'Although
I look with admiration upon the Son, I do not know
how to become Him.' As can be seen, the poet wants to

become Him, that is, 'the Son', but it is never clear what the benefits of such a conversion would be.

The best moments of the book, in any case, are those in which Wojtila leaves aside the tribulations of identity and confronts, bravely, the always difficult task of writing love poems: 'I am inscribed in You by means of hope; outside of You I cannot exist.' The sombre and somewhat mystical tone with which Wojtila refers to the erotic experience, in truth, feels less strange. The same can be said of this unusual invitation to imbibe alcohol, which seems to have been written by a teetotaller: 'Now, I pour the cup of wine to the brim in Your celestial celebration – a prayerful servant, grateful for your strange enthrallment of my youth.'

Although Wojtila makes honest efforts to write decorously, it must be said that *Pensamientos de Luz* shows a poet who is still not fully developed. His texts in general are hermetical, somewhat tiresome, and overly solemn, although it is true that it's perhaps that very solemnity – so abandoned by contemporary poetry – that bestows a weird attractiveness on this Polish author's proposal. Points given here, taken away there; the reading of this book is an interesting experience, as it demonstrates the enormous diversity of lyrical poetry today.

May 2004

RELEVANCE OF HAMLET
IN THE MODERN AGE

It must be said happily, gratefully: our job is ideal. Even if every once in a while an editor calls and asks us to be more current, we know very well how to get around that demand; we are capable, even, of dedicating our Sunday column to talking about *Hamlet*. What's more, if the editor insists, all we have to do is add one or two lines at the end of the column. We can say, for example, that on rereading some passages from that marvellous work we discovered Shakespeare's deep relevance to the modern age. There's no need to specify which passages are so very current, since we all know that the culture sections don't have much room for argumentation.

And what does it matter, when we also know that no one reads us? All the columnists of all the culture sections of all the newspapers in the world know that. Out of pure neuroticism we take care of our prose, savour every adjective, lose valuable time deciding between a colon or semi-colon, and it pains our souls when we find that some error slipped through or that we spelled the word *idiosyncrasy* wrong.

We know that very likely, absolutely no one reads our columns. At first it hurts, but now it makes us happy. Because how exhausting it would be to think, on the contrary, that what one does is important, that many people are going to read what we say in the newspaper. That we have a responsibility.

Speaking of responsibilities, we have one to take care of the culture pages. We have to love them. It's true that in the end someone will use our thoughts to pack up glasses or wrap fish. But we have to care for these spaces, because they are rare and we perform real juggling acts in order to coexist with the advertisements in a dignified way. We are the ones tasked with giving the matter a little sparkle. Luckily, our role is decorative: no one asks us, for example, to condemn the self-importance of Minister Rodrigo Hinzpeter, the brutal intransigence of Mayor Labbé, the unrealistic conservatism of appointed senator Von Baer. No one asks us to talk about president Piñera, and it's a relief, because if we did we would have to say who knows how many unpleasant things. Fortunately we don't have to speak out publicly about the uncomfortable truth that we live in one of the most unequal countries in the world. It's good to know that no one forces us to tell the story of a country that, with a great deal of rage and a little melancholy, is realizing that the only remaining option is to take a stand.

It's true that at times we are filled with a certain unease. Within fifty or a hundred years, there will be people studying this dark time of Chile's history, and it could make one a little nervous to think that on reading through the newspaper someone will find our names and our opinions on the contemporary relevance of *Hamlet*. Maybe they will think that we were complicit, that we were cowards. We feel guilty imagining that scene, maybe because one time, when we were still very young and innocent, we were the ones who spent afternoons at the library reading newspapers from the eighties. And we feel a deep and lasting sadness.

Sorry, there's no need to get so serious, so pessimistic. Why think so much about the past, or the present? Why think so much? Why think? I'm happy, I think it's magnificent to have the chance to talk about Shakespeare, about *Hamlet*, or about prominent poets or fiction writers, about truly good novels. What an immense relief not to have to review that devastating and badly written novel that Chile has been for so many years.

March 2012

AGAINST POETS

At twenty years old they already have some important experiences behind them: they've published poems in journals and anthologies, taken part in workshops, written articles for school yearbooks, and maybe they have granted one or two premature interviews. They already have their first books ready, and they're about to come out from emerging publishing houses. They are very bad books, but for now that doesn't matter. They write long and sententious poems that abuse the gerund, the exclamation mark, and ellipses. They read Vicente Huidobro, Delmira Agustini, and Oliverio Girondo, but above all they read each other, in interminable sessions that are only friendly at times.

By twenty-five they have disavowed those first poems, which they consider distant sins of youth. They hope that soon they will find maturity as poets, which is much more important to them than finding maturity as people. The second book goes above and beyond their goal: it's not good, but it is inarguably better than the first. They talk about how they are still looking for a voice of their own, and meanwhile they plan anthologies that include their whole peer group; no one wants to write the prologue, though, because no one wants to run the risk of becoming a literary critic.

By thirty, they've suffered several discouragements. They have been included in national and Latin American anthologies, but they've been left out of some other publications and that's been very hard for them to accept. At times they write only to demonstrate how arbitrary those exclusions have been. They have published, by this point, three books of poetry. They have founded two publishing houses and four literary

110

magazines. Their biographical notes proclaim that they have participated in over thirteen – fourteen, that is – poetry conferences and that their books have been partially translated to Italian. Really, it's only one poem that's been translated, but it doesn't matter: they've been translated, and that's enough.

Only at thirty-five do they start to feel uncomfortable when they're introduced as young poets. Now they give writing workshops in which they advise their students to avoid gerunds, to be careful with adjectives, to declare war on ellipses and exclamation points. They inculcate the utmost creative freedom in their pupils, but they forbid a pretty long list of words: void, anguish, desolation, desperation, dusk, twilight, soul, spirit, heart, vagina. They talk to them about molopoeia, phanopoeia, and logopoeia, but they get a little tangled up in the explanation. They fall in love with sixteen-year-old poets and compare them with Alejandra Pizarnik, but they've never seen a photo of Alejandra Pizarnik.

When they're forty years old no one thinks to introduce them as young poets; their faces and bellies have changed, perhaps irreversibly. Poets suffer more during the so-called mid-life crisis than common people do. They didn't decide to become poets just so they could be forty years old. From now on it'll all be downhill. They've become inoffensive. It's much easier to ask them for prologues than to fight against them, better to invite them to readings and applaud them without enthusiasm, respectfully. They are, in other words, true failures.

For the failure to be complete they must receive, from time to time, misleading signals. At fifty, at sixty, at seventy years old the poets will win two or three minor prizes; timid undergrads and perhaps one or another attractive doctoral student will analyse their books, which will maybe be translated to French, German, Greek, or at least Argentine. What's more, there will always be some emerging publishing house interested in rescuing them from oblivion.

It's pitiful to see them next to the phone, waiting for the news of a prize, a government pension, an homage, a little trip to the south, whatever. They look like frightened children, teenagers now too old to commit suicide. Sometimes a compassionate reporter will ask them what good poetry is in this dehumanized and consumerist world. They sigh and reply the same as they always have: that only poetry will save the world, that amid all the confusion we must seek out true words and hold on tightly to them. They say it without faith, routinely, but they are entirely right.

October 2008

AN INCOMPLETE PORTRAIT, FULL
OF SPOILERS, OF BOLAÑO AS A
FOOTBALL FAN

I don't really like 'Buba', Roberto Bolaño's story about football. There are many Bolaño stories I like, and it would be hard for me to choose just one, but there's no doubt when it comes to choosing the one I like the least. When I read 'Buba' the first time, I thought it was clear that Bolaño was not a football fan, and that impression stayed with me until yesterday afternoon, when I reread it and discovered there was nothing in the story that would allow the inference that Bolaño was uninterested in football. The problem was, rather, that we his readers are *too* interested in the sport.

'I always thought it was more interesting to score an own goal than a goal,' Bolaño said, and the argument is baseless but funny: 'Unless one's name is Pelé, a goal is eminently vulgar and impolite to the opposing goalie, whom you don't know and who has done nothing to you, while an own goal is a gesture of independence.' We respond right away: more than a gesture of independence, a premeditated own goal would be an act of betrayal. We respond seriously, and it's that seriousness that Bolaño is laughing at. But we don't laugh with him, since we think that football is the most serious thing in the world. I am writing, in fact, in a state of utter nervousness because of the imminent and decisive match against Peru this afternoon. These are not the best conditions for writing a column or rereading a story, but what can I do, this is my job.

'Buba' is a melancholy and funny story that focuses on the Chilean Acevedo, the Spaniard Herrera, and the African Buba, three players who for various reasons are left out of Barcelona's starting line-up, and who change their luck thanks to a ritual of Buba's. Suddenly they start scoring strange goals, or goals that seem very strange to Acevedo, and from one day to the next they become the most important figures of a team that wins the Spanish League and then the Champions League and also the next Spanish league and the one after that, though now without Buba, who is transferred to Juventus and then dies in a car accident.

It's never directly stated in the story that the club in question is FC Barcelona, nor is a specific time period mentioned, but more than one Barça fan believes he's seen, in this story, an allusion to his team back in the eighties. 'Only Buba's miraculous black magic could have saved my childhood,' one blogger says with emotion, remembering the miseries his club went through in those days: 'So many years of humiliation and defeat. And Buba never showed up.'

We, on the other hand, focus our attention on the narrator Acevedo, a Chilean left-winger who at a young age goes to La Plata to play for Gimnasia y Esgrima, and then has a difficult period of adjustment in Barcelona after he is injured, when his only pastimes are whisky and whores. The first pages of the story are very good, deeply Bolañan, especially in the quick rhythm of the brushstrokes and the author's enormous skill in the art of imitating voices.

As in many of Bolaño's stories, the enigma is not resolved: we don't know if the players' success was owed to magic, or even if Buba died because of some curse related to the practice of rituals. But the story isn't disappointing because of its denouement or its turn to magic. The problem with 'Buba' is a problem with reality: we find it ultimately unrealistic that a Chilean could ever have such a track record, especially if we know he has gone, as Acevedo has, to several consecutive World Cups.

It's painful to accept, but the truth is that if Acevedo were Argentine or Uruguayan, the story would seem irreproachable to us. Bolaño knew this and laughs affectionately at us as he bestows on us great, imaginary triumphs. We have one consolation, minor but perhaps useful in facing the game this afternoon: we wouldn't believe the story, either, if Acevedo were Peruvian.

March 2009

IN THE SERVICE OF GHOSTS

Enrique Lihn once defined childhood as a time that was 'in the service of ghosts,' a kind of 'prehistory of the adult,' through which the memory wanders erratically, at will, inventing or avoiding memories. The subject of *La pieza oscura* [The Dark Room], one of his essential books, is the urgent persistence of certain childhood images, and one especially: that of children abandoned in a forest-garden or garden-greenhouse, that is, a protected and artificial environment, an imaginary space that the adult has no choice but to assume as real.

Published in 1963, *The Dark Room* is Enrique Lihn's first great move towards a critical poetry, distanced from both idealization and disbelief; a poetry that refuses confessionalism but that also distrusts simple abstraction. The book's central image – that of the poem that gives the book its title – is, in this sense, apt and disquieting: the poet isolates a scene with precision (two boys and two girls playing in a dark room), and he is able to affix certain details (the parents who turn on the light and ruin the game; the children who feign innocence, taking refuge in their usual routines as if nothing had happened), but instead of archiving it along with other images of the time, he delves into the bitter depths of the past.

Over the memory of that scene drifts, then, a tragic air, 'an indistinct, bloodied drizzle', associated with the guilty challenge of certain warnings of the adults, and linked as well to the disturbing appearance, in close-up, of eroticism: 'And I bit at length my cousin Isabel's neck.' The suspicion prevails that the boundary between game and truth is diffuse. Laughter and happiness become, suddenly, oppressive: 'We stopped turning with a strange sense of shame / ever unable to formulate any reproach / other than of having tried for such easy success.'

Childhood is, then, a time in the service of ghosts, a place to put images that, seen from the present, form a kind of foundation. A difficult foundation, of course, unsteady: the dark room is the place where photographs are developed, where images appear, for the first time fixed on paper, that simultaneously authorize and destroy identity.

May 2005

NIGHT IN THE PLAZA

'I wrote *Lumpérica* at a moment when I simultaneously felt a great aversion and attraction to literature,' Diamela Eltit has said about her first novel, published in 1983 and republished a few months ago. A similar thing happens upon reading it, as the novel both dazzles and repels the reader, or at least that's what I felt when I read it for the first time, ten years ago.

Lumpérica did not reach my hands as a subversive text, but rather as a work already consecrated by the academy. It seemed to me, however, that the novel escaped theoretical reductionism. I remember having thought then, very concretely, about the censor, the dark functionary tasked with approving the manuscript's publication. I smugly imagined some guy nodding off at phrases that I found beautiful and for him were incomprehensible. What words did the censor underline? What novel did he read? What did his face look like?

Now, in the re-reading, I've thought more about the author, the woman who wrote knowing that the censor would read her work. It's said that when we write we imagine an ideal reader, someone capable of fully understanding what we are doing. But then I had to also imagine that enemy who turned the pages in search of forbidden allusions, with a criteria that was maybe unimaginative, or perhaps sophisticated, who knows.

The evocation of an empty plaza gives way to an elusive story that is at the same time unerring, documentary. The plaza is any plaza in Santiago in the middle of the seventies. There is no story or precise plot: Diamela Eltit investigates the possibilities of the scene, describes and conjectures about the experience of spending the night on a bench, looking at the street signs with a convalescent's greed, with innocence, with rage and surprise.

'Suddenly the lights come on, just when the darkness is nearly absolute,' says the narrator, who has first asked, in various ways, what those lights are for, what hand turns on the public lighting system. The working street lights compose a sort of stage set; that's why the protagonist acts or wants to act, but at the same time must protect herself, since the stage should be empty; the lights exist to demonstrate that no one challenges the curfew, that no one occupies the place now abandoned by vendors, panhandlers, children and lovers.

The protagonist of *Lumpérica* struggles to get her senses back, to recover her body, her thought, her own language. She metamorphoses to find herself and hide herself. That's why she shaves her head, becomes an animal, changes her name, babbles in a foreign language. That's why she gives herself over to the crowd, or at least she imagines that surrender. The body awakens or tries to wake from the anaesthesia, to recognize itself: 'I myself had a wound, but today I have, I am weighed down by, my own scar. I no longer remember how or how much it hurt me, but from the scar I know it hurt.'

Still today the novel accepts and rejects us, shakes us; it conserves its original power and its beauty. Those of us who were born during the first years of the dictatorship lived only during the day of the long night *Lumpérica* relates. I think that few books portray our parents' generation with such force. Few books allow us, as *Lumpérica* does, to really delve into the meaning of inheritance.

May 2009

THE DEFEATED NOVEL

'Though it may not seem like it, though it tries not to seem like it, this is a work of fiction,' says Rodrigo Rey Rosa at the start of *El material humano* [Human Matter]. But pretty soon we forget that warning, and we go along with the author without asking too many questions. We don't know what he is looking for, but neither does he with any certainty: he merely crosses the city to study an archive that has just been discovered; it holds eighty million documents in which the history of Guatemala pulses.

The likelihood of finding something 'novelable' in the archive is very high, but the narrator can't find the novel, or rather he finds it, but decides to lose it. He observes and analyses the materials, but he refuses to normalize them literarily: he doesn't want to, and perhaps doesn't believe it's necessary to build fiction on the foundation of those documents that speak for themselves, and speak loudly.

The image of the writer defeated by the material is decisive. We see him with his notebooks, copying down details that have slept for decades in the archive: people who have files opened on them for terrorism, for sedition, sabotage, for insubordination, mistreating the national flag, shining shoes without a license, for damaging trees in the public way, for family abandonment, practicing occult arts, for publishing obscenities.

The narrator does not develop heroic images or round off emotions. He proceeds with patience and melancholy, as from the start he knows he will not solve any enigmas, that none of the stories will provoke the illusion of meaning. Some discoveries and certain conversations, however, leave him vulnerable: suddenly he

120

finds clues that would allow him to write, not the story of Guatemalan police, but rather the story of his mother, his own story. But the narration does not turn toward that possible family novel. He doesn't write that one either, for now.

This is one of Rey Rosa's best books. His familiar prose style, so sober and measured, now coexists with the dusty style of police files. It would be absurd to waste paper arguing over whether *Human Matter* is or is not a novel, as the author breaks conventions with ease: he chooses the boundary because only from there can he tell the story he wants to tell.

Some years ago, after a prolonged absence, Rey Rosa returned to his country. That is, in a way, the subject of *Human Matter*: the possibility of roots. In one passage of the book, someone asks the narrator if he feels threatened living in Guatemala. 'To say yes would be an exaggeration, but to deny it would be to fall short of the truth,' he replies.

The search in the archives coincides with wide-ranging readings, including Voltaire's *Memoirs*, the novel *Fouché* by Stefan Zweig, or the mesmerizing *Borges* by Bioy Casares; they all mix with his project and alter it. Perhaps because of this, the protagonist constantly feels himself to be a kind of impostor: he suspects himself, he thinks that it should be an ex-combatant who takes on the task or mission that he, almost without wanting to, has begun. Readings, trips, playing with his daughter, the uncertainty of love, the confusion of the literary scene: that's what his life really consists of. He is a dilettante, and nevertheless, what he is investigating matters to him a great deal.

Sometimes, to write is to discover what we already knew. The narrator of this novel knows that there is no hope for Guatemala, and that it would be better to go far away and recall the lost country. But writing is also a way of staying. And he stays. He doesn't know why, he doesn't know for how long, but he stays.

April 2009

THE SILENCE OF TELLING

As I was reading *Lost City Radio* I was constantly reminded of 'Murke's Collected Silences', a story by Heinrich Böll that, like Daniel Alarcón's novel, is set in a radio station. It's no surprise that a novel set in a radio station would remind me of a story set in a radio station. Nor is it strange for me to remember that story by Heinrich Böll, which I think of fairly often because it's probably one of the two or three best stories I've ever read. But of course, there is more to the similarity than the mere coincidence of settings.

'Murke's Collected Silences' is the story of Peter Murke, employee of a German radio station who, while everyone else is arguing over the essence of art or the meaning of existence, spends his free time collecting silences. It sounds strange and clumsily metaphorical, but it's literal: the technician who edits the recordings cuts out pieces of the tape that contain the overly long silences the announcers leave between one word and another. Instead of throwing out those pieces he presents them to Murke, who little by little assembles a tape of faltering breath. The image is decisive and beautiful: it is 1945, Germany is vacillating between pain and the uncertain conviction that life goes on; some people bellow their empty opinions shamelessly and without memory, but luckily there are others who, like Murke, would rather collect silences.

I don't know if Daniel Alarcón has read this story by Heinrich Böll, but I'm sure he would like it, that he *will* like it, since the strength or integrity of *Lost City Radio* comes from a similar ethic. For Alarcón, telling a story well does not mean making it understandable, but rather respecting the empty zones it is made of. Alarcón prefers the silence of telling: he avoids literary noise through the simple method of writing no more than the necessary words. Thus, the novel makes visible the silence of those who were and are no longer. And the silence of the answers that don't come. The radio is the place of the voice and of silence. We hear more than the announcers and more than the listeners. We hear, as well, what is not heard, what is not aired, what the listeners don't know or what they know and prefer to keep silent. What the announcers choose not to say, or only half-say. The silence of the silenced. The silence of the victims and the victimizers.

In more than one interview, Alarcón has recalled an observation of Borges' about the bad habit of exaggerating the differences between countries. If we exaggerate differences, the country of *Lost City Radio* is Peru. But Alarcón has chosen not to call the country in his novel Peru. Maybe because the country in his novel is and isn't Peru, the same way it is and isn't Chile. I say this thinking that for a Chilean, it's impossible to read the novel without remembering our own disappeared. After reading *Lost City Radio* I reread *Cartas de petición* [Letters of request], the book by Leonidas Morales that collects messages that, in a kind of last resort, the relatives of disappeared prisoners sent to the authorities, which replied only by archiving the letters or delegating them or with disappointing and rhetorical answers. It is always urgent to go back over these letters in which relatives appeal to governors as if they really trusted them, as if they didn't know that the people they were writing to were the very ones guilty of the disappearances of their siblings or parents or children. Sometimes they even make clear their adherence to the regime and ask for forgiveness for the behaviour of the disappeared. *My son had crazy ideas that we do not share. But help us find him. Tell us where he is.*

What good is a novel, then, when faced with the howl of reality, the inarguable authority of documentation? Why even write novels? The cliché says that sometimes truth is stranger than fiction. Perhaps it's right there, in that kitchen-table phrase, that the meaning of fiction-writing lies. Maybe we write to confirm that defeat of fiction. To demonstrate that fiction is not enough, it won't suffice. That it is only good for interrupting life during the time the reading lasts.

Fiction only triumphs when it fails, when it lets us see the traces of reality. Alarcón is conscious of that essential imbalance, that loss, and that awareness impresses on the story a constant elegiac inflection. As such, the characters and spaces refuse the black and white. The existence of the programme *Lost City Radio* is, in itself, problematic: its goal is to bring lost people together with their relatives, but the goal is also to get an audience. Norma's secret legitimacy comes from her condition as victim, the fact that she is contemplating pain from the same side of the street. Her miraculous voice is a balm that from the start shields and welcomes listeners. It's the same voice that gives news, the same voice that, as the narrator says, reads good news with indifference and bad news as if it held uncertain hope. When they listen to Norma's programme people cede to the illusion that it is possible to repair ruptures. But war is not spoken of. That's the rule: stick to a personal idea of history, or rather reduce the story to its minimum: someone who was with me is no longer here. And I want to see him again. The causes and the events are disguised in the pact of mutual trust, and if someone betrays it there's an easy solution: anyone gets lippy and they are, simply, taken off air. An untimely and perhaps happy music destroys the communication.

A new and deficient language, the neo-language of figures and acronyms, threatens to invade the space of intimacy. But it doesn't quite manage it: if there is a triumph in this novel it is that of these private stories, which by dint of their honesty preserve the memory of a better or less bad time. Telling any one of these stories is to tell them all. But one must know how to tell them. And Daniel Alarcón does: he chooses Norma as a protagonist, but he could have chosen Zahir, a secondary character who in the long run prevails as both victor and vanquished, or Adela, perhaps the true abandoned woman. The precision, the sense of detail, the skill in creating unexpected images with the same materials as always, are consistently in the service of the story; with the same virtues, other writers practice an exhibitionism that's entirely absent in this sober and beautiful novel that progresses with the disconcerting speed of memories.

Many are the scenes, the images that *Lost City Radio* leaves on the retina: green trucks that take children away forever, new maps that erase an imprecise past, a war that no one knows for sure when it began; a portrait artist whose work women treasure with quiet desperation; a lover's betrayal that becomes the acrid denouement of a story that was already bitter enough; a man who writes his surveillance reports imitating the style of the only detective novel he knows; the violence circulating through a cloud of tear gas; a battle that no one tells of and an old man who utters these perhaps definitive words: 'Talking doesn't help. I've learned that. It's why I never ask.'

And a puzzle, of course. After enduring a revelation

that readers already intuited, Norma and Victor take on the outlandish exercise of putting together a puzzle. It's the auratic image of the old town square: 'The puzzle,' says the narrator, 'suddenly absolved them of the need to speak, and they fell quickly into the rhythm of it: examining a piece, its colours and textures, scanning the box to see where it might fit. Her city as it had once been, the city where she'd fallen in love with Rey.'

Now Norma knows that her long wait has been less legitimate than others. She still is not prepared to accept it. She still doesn't know if it is possible to accept the end of one story and the beginning of another. And again, the silence that invades everything.

I end with this paragraph that demonstrates to what point silence wins the game: 'Norma had one hand over the boy, enough to feel him breathe; in the other, she held the list, which had been touched by a dozen people in the past week, had been creased, folded, nearly destroyed, saved, and stolen. It felt good to have it, but not like a victory so much as a reprieve. Ten years had passed, ten years that comprised a vast, inviolable silence, and then these three days, of which, she suspected, she would remember only noise: the chattering dissonance of many voices, sounds at once indistinct and pressing, calling her urgently in different directions. Wounding her, certainly, but no worse than the silence had.'

October 2007

A CORRUPTED LANGUAGE

How can one trust in language if over and over it has demonstrated its inability to communicate horror, solitude, death? How to write in a language corrupted by history? The novels of J. M. Coetzee continuously put forth the need to confront these questions, which he intuited – as he relates in *Youth*, the second volume of his memoir – in his reading of twentieth-century poetry.

London, 1962: Coetzee is a dreamy youth who has left Cape Town in pursuit of poetry. He finds work with some ease, but it turns out to be much more difficult to fulfil his vocation as a writer. During those days he reads Rilke, Vallejo, Neruda, but especially Ezra Pound and T. S. Eliot, in whom he not only sees literary models but true life examples, mirrors to look into: 'If Eliot chooses to seem dull, chooses to wear a suit and work in a bank and call himself J. Alfred Prufrock, it must be as a disguise, as part of the necessary cunning of the artist in the modern age.' So thinks the protagonist of *Youth*, who wears a suit and works at IBM, though his mask does not fit comfortably. He did not choose to seem boring, he really *is* boring, on the verge of desperation, lost in a city that is forcibly showing him his place in the world.

It's then that Coetzee takes the step from poetry to prose. For him this is, without a doubt, a regression, as he sees prose as merely a 'second-best choice', a compromise solution thanks to which he will no longer have to take responsibility, for example, for these imposing precepts from Eliot himself: 'Poetry is not a turning loose of emotion, but an escape from emotion; it is not the expression of personality, but an escape from personality.' Sure that he has found something important, John copies these fragments into his diary, including Eliot's sad afterthought: 'only those who have personality and emotions know what it means to want to escape from these things.'

John is not a youth without personality, but rather an immigrant in search of convictions who encounters only suspicions. 'Prose, fortunately, does not demand emotion,' he tells himself as a way to confront the setback. 'Prose is like a flat, tranquil sheet of water on which one can tack about at one's leisure, making patterns on the surface.' Neither Pound nor Eliot do anything for him now. In search of a new model he turns to Henry James, understanding that one of James's merits is having transcended nationalities. This, for a colonist of Afrikaner origin wishing to reinvent himself, constituted a valuable opportunity: 'People in James do not have to pay the rent; they certainly do not have to hold down jobs; all they are required to do is to have super subtle conversations whose effect is to bring about tiny shifts of power, shifts so minute as to be invisible to all but a practised eye.'

Very soon Coetzee finds out that it is truly difficult to manage super subtle conversations among interesting people. He understands, then, that narrative action demands a precise stage: while poetry tends to do without spatial details, prose asks for a particular setting, and Coetzee's stage is South Africa, not London. John wants to be English, like Eliot, the poet who was not English but convinced half the world that he was. But is it possible to convince half the world that he is not South African? Is John a good actor, as good an actor as Eliot? At times he hates or believes he hates his place of origin: 'South Africa was a bad start, a handicap.' 'If a tidal wave were to sweep in from the Atlantic tomorrow and wash away the southern tip of the African continent, he will not shed a tear.' In London's inhospitable streets, on the other hand, artistic passion throbs: 'London may be stony, labyrinthine, and cold, but behind its forbidding walls men and women are at work writing books, painting paintings, composing music.' For now he doesn't want to accept it, but he knows that his story is not Eliot's: he knows that to be a writer he must become South African; he must become what he already is.

Poetry is an escape from emotion, but John, who believes he lacks emotion, doesn't know what to flee from. Prose, meanwhile, doesn't need emotion, but rather a particular stage – that is, South Africa, the country from which he has escaped, and not England, the country from which he doesn't want to flee. Coetzee is born when he accepts that South Africa is the stage he flees when he writes. That is the subject of *Boyhood* and *Youth*: the life of someone who, rather in spite of himself, realizes that there are no parallel worlds, that it is impossible to marginalize oneself from history. Emotion – the pain that, in its most varied forms, runs through every page Coetzee writes – requires a direction, and that is what he learned from Pound and Eliot. In his own way, of course: he wanted Eliot to teach him how to be an English poet without being English, but he ended up learning how to be a South African writer, a writer from nowhere. From the best poetry of the twentieth century, Coetzee forged the best literature of recent decades.

'This letter is not a baring of my heart. It is a baring of something, but not of my heart,' confesses the protagonist of *The Age of Iron*. The moral imperative that reigns in Coetzee's books is the need to name – without a whimper, bravely – that which must be named, even if doing so entails a brutal exercise in honesty. *The Age of Iron* also contains this valuable and urgent declaration of principle: 'These are terrible sights ... They are to be condemned. But I cannot denounce them in other people's words. I must find my own words, from myself. Otherwise it is not the truth ... To speak of this ... you would need the tongue of a God.'

In *Disgrace*, reality demonstrates to David Lurie that when it comes to describing South Africa, English is a dead language. 'Like a dinosaur expiring and settling in the mud, the language has stiffened,' he realizes. This is what sooner or later Coetzee's characters end up discovering: that there is no room for fiction in the world they live in, that all they can do is communicate, precisely, what they see. Coetzee's challenge is, in practice, the same as Eliot's: purify the language of the tribe. What changes is the emphasis: Coetzee proves that it is possible to write in a contaminated language. From that language in decline, the writer extracts that which can still be said, and he says it with the greatest clarity possible, crisply and completely. In one of the most beautiful and astute passages of *Elizabeth Costello*, Coetzee expresses it like this: 'I merely write down the words and then test them, test their soundness, to make sure I have heard right.' That is, without a doubt, what a great writer does: put the language of his age to the test.

November 2005

CHIT CHAT FROM THE HEREAFTER

It's not a novel, or maybe it is, in the same way that it is and isn't a book of poems and even a collection of stories. Sticking close to home, Roberto Bolaño recommended story writers read the *Spoon River Anthology*, and it wasn't idle coquetry: the fragments of Edgar Lee Masters' masterwork are, in reality, stories that the author chose not to finish. Instead of appealing to fiction, he wrote in quick, free verses that conserved the illusion of a world half-made. Masters wrote a great, strange book, a book of monologues that recreate, so to speak, chit-chat from the hereafter.

Going on about genre is, in this case, mere academic atavism. More than a plan, there were intuitions: Edgar Lee Masters wondered what the dead of a Midwestern town would say if they could talk. He wanted to give voice to the dead, and then he killed the living so that they could speak too. He imagined the entire town dead, full of a bunch of ghosts still very attached to life: generous, stingy, jealous, vengeful. Masters invented two hundred and fifty testimonies, two hundred and fifty replies that led to new questions, to other books that we imagine as we read this one.

The genesis of *Spoon River Anthology* is legendary: in 1914, at forty-five years old, Edgar Lee Masters discovered Book VII of the *Palatine Anthology*. In the funeral epigrams of authors like Callimachus, Meleager, and Leonidas, the poet could see the unexpected possibility of a new, national art: he mixed the Greek form with the idiosyncrasies of an average US town, which he baptized with the name of a river from his childhood. And starting then he wrote, at home or in his law office, brief monologues that he published in instalments under a pseudonym, as was appropriate for a lawyer who wanted to remain respectable. And he went on publishing them later, now without a pseudonym and with a New York publisher, to be met with immediate success and scandal: this was a dirty poetry, immoral and realistic. Until the *Spoon River Anthology* appeared, Edgar Lee Masters had been a failed writer, the non-essential author of books that not even he liked, as Borges said with his usual venom. After receiving recognition, after the fame from *Spoon River* – one of the few poetry bestsellers in history – Masters went back to being a failed writer, that is, the originator of only one great book, condemned to perpetually repeat the joke. 'He has imitated Whitman, Browning, Byron, Lowell, Edgar Lee Masters. All in vain: he is, by autonomasia, the author of *Spoon River Anthology*,' sentenced Borges, again, and it is a consensus judgement: the only one of his many posterior works that had any resonance was, fatally, the *New Spoon River Anthology*, a second part that in any case no one considered better than the first.

It's not hard to imagine Edgar Lee Masters as the involuntary author of a masterpiece, something like that character of César Aira's who writes a great poem without realizing it. It's a simplification, of course: Masters was, in reality, an epic poet who was more comfortable with a light, conversational verse; a heroic poet in a world without poets, without music. He zealously imitated Homer, but he had no Achilles or Ulysses to hand. Rather, on the contrary, he had people as inglorious as Frank Drummer, a man who wanted to memorize the *Encyclopaedia Britannica*, or Yee Bow, the child of immigrants who had a very bad time of it in Spoon River, as the people there forced him to disown Confucius and attend catechism. Edgar Lee Masters directed a rebellious choir, a chorus that didn't want to respond in unison: each character demanded a voice of their own, a specific perspective, biased and obstinate, so that, as in Shakespeare's tragedies, we never really know to what extent the author was speaking through his characters. The critical editions, of course, offer many clues, especially about the abundant autobiographical references and the private jokes scattered throughout the book; but in its reading, individual viewpoints prevail, the true chaos of life, and the author disappears in that crowd of sporadic disguises.

The poems of *Spoon River* are urgent messages, last-minute clarifications almost always directed to no one, to the town, to the world, to memory, and at times to specific people, as late-arriving love notes or settlings of scores. They are not really epitaphs, per se. Often, even, the poems function as anti-poems; that is, as versions that give the lie to the official story. Such is the case of Cassius Hueffer, a man kept from resting in peace by the rhetorical gap left by his epitaph: 'While I lived I could not cope with slanderous tongues / Now that I am dead I must submit to an epitaph / Graven by a fool!'

One key character in the *Spoon River Anthology* is, precisely, Richard Bone, the carver of gravestones, who is not the fool Hueffer speaks of: the real fool is the one who dictates the epitaph, not the man who earns a living pounding away at the stones. The headstone engraver is paid to write a truth that he himself distrusts. Edgar Lee Masters, on the contrary, wrote to shine light into a dark and slippery zone. The beautiful poem that he puts into the mouth of Mrs Sibley is example enough: 'The secret of the stars – gravitation. The secret of the earth – layers of rock. The secret of the soil – to receive seed. The secret of the seed – the germ. The secret of man – the sower. The secret of woman – the soil. My secret: Under a mound that you shall never find.'

January 2007

PLAYING DEAD

'In order to confront life without any pretension, or emphasis, or illusion, it would be necessary, every morning before starting the day, to read a couple of pages by Paul Léautaud.' This devastating comment of Julio Ramón Ribeyro's is evidence that he read *Journal Littéraire* by Paul Léautaud. Léautaud is one of the most radical diary writers in the history of literature, or, to put it without fanfare, a lonely and stubborn man who spent his life laying bare the least visible recesses of the private self.

Léautaud's work is slightly familiar to Chilean readers thanks to *Léautaud y el otro* [Léautaud and the Other], a crucial essay published by the poet Armando Uribe in 1966. Through numerous digressions, Uribe reveals his feelings of bewilderment and enthusiasm on discovering Léautaud, who was then – as now – considered a French writer of the second or third rank, perhaps because he shared the first half of the twentieth century with a long list of luminaries, or maybe because of his intransigence regarding the conventions of literary life. *Léautaud and the Other* is a veiled autobiography of Uribe himself, as he recreates with precision the arduous yet revitalizing experience of confronting the sharp and forceful prose of a man who threw himself, without anesthetic, into the savage revelation of his foibles.

Léautaud was not driven by a literary aim; in fact, he considered poetry and the novel to constitute 'the lower rungs of literature'. Doubtless, it must have been difficult for Uribe to take up poetry again after considering a paragraph like this one: 'Verse is a decidedly childish thing. These people who write following a measure, set cadences, with every line ending in a similar sound, a purr like a child reciting – these people are deeply ridiculous.' The novel also struck him as uninteresting work, bothersome and even disconcerting: 'How can a fifty-year-old man still write novels? How can one read them, even, at that age?' He judged that novelists were 'people lacking in vivacity', and he detested, especially, works of a romantic nature, since in them 'we are never told anything about the small, wet mess that follows the embrace, of the dirtiness it produces and the pregnancy that comes as a result. Always rhetoric instead of the truth.'

Heir of Stendhalian egotism, reader of Chamfort, Diderot, Voltaire, Montaigne, and La Rochefoucauld, Léautaud sought in books a certain adherence to the self, an originality that came not from invention and much less from ingenuity, but rather from the genuine flaring of the subject in language: 'What gives merit to a book is not its qualities or its defects. Everything lies in this: no one other than its author could not have written it. Any book that could have been written by another is good only for throwing into the bin.' Enemy even of the dictionary (whose use he advised against, since it implied an alteration of voice, or the possibility of alteration), Léautaud acted, according to his own definition, 'like an invalid studying the phases of his disease in himself'.

As Roberto Calasso noted in *The Forty-Nine Steps*, for Paul Léautaud, writing was a way of burying experience, a very personal way of 'playing dead', of protecting himself from the hounding of life. 'What is written has been laid to rest,' says Calasso, thinking, especially, of *Le Petit Ami* and *In Memoriam*, two autobiographical books published in 1903 in which Léautaud recounts his relationship with his mother and his father, respectively. His father, Firmin Léautaud, was an incorrigible seducer for whom his son's existence was an inconvenience.

His mother, a very young aspiring actress, abandoned him three days after giving birth: 'I have never had luck with women. I had just been born and my mother had already abandoned me.' Nine years later the young Léautaud had the luck or the misfortune to get her back: of this experience – of the memory of his mother lavishing him with affection, enamouring him – there persisted an Oedipal inclination that a decade later gave way to an episode that nearly ended in incest.

In spite of how, as can be seen, his biography set the scene for tragedy, Léautaud knew how to avoid any plaintive inflections and focus on the truth, which does not require tricks but rather bravery and rawness. During much of his life he kept two diaries: the *Journal Littéraire* and the *Journal Particulier*, or a literary and a personal journal, so that his record encompassed two forms of life, or rather two lives that only sometimes coincided. Seix Barral published *Diario Personal*, a title that tends toward misrepresentation because it corresponds only to Léautaud's private journal entries from 1933, an especially tumultuous year for him. At that time he was a sixty-something addict of 'beautiful obscenities', an old libertine debating between two attentive and dangerous lovers. The spot-on Spanish translation by Rodrigo Rey Rosa brings us close to Léautaud's hard yet reflexive language, which at times proceeds with striking brutality: 'Transformation of the face during pleasure: Much less ugly,' he says, for example, of one conquest.

Love is only physical and patriotism complete stupidity, just like religion and science, thought Léautaud the misanthrope, detractor of 'fools who walk around without hats', of 'the rabble who go around and around in a velodrome for six days', and also of 'the other rabble who attend that intelligent spectacle'. One who, nevertheless, took in every cat and dog he found in his path, cared for them, spent a good part of his modest salary as an employee of the *Mercure de France* on buying them food, and even held funeral ceremonies for them in his yard. Léautaud was also an original and incisive theatre critic, who preferred to talk about the audience – and, why not, about himself – instead of commenting on the play, which he almost always found lamentable. His true passion, in any case, was to lock himself in and write, with no real reason.

As César Aira says well in *Las Tres Fechas* [Three Dates], 'Privacy was for him the fertile ground of attention, the only medium in which the subject can fulfil his function in relation to the world: experience it, record it, make it real.' To do so he chose a sparing, quick language, a prose of solitary phrases joined with the naturalness of thought, without patches or compromising solutions. 'Certain moments of my life I've lived twice: first, seeing them, and later, on writing them. Without a doubt I have lived them more deeply as I wrote them,' said Paul Léautaud, an old invalid, a contagious old invalid who loved and hated and raged and wrote.

September 2005

139

THE OLDEST TOURIST IN BARCELONA

'I live more off rancour than pasta.' This phrase of Céline's, cited in passing in one of the three novels that make up *Historia de una absolución familiar* [History of a Family Absolution], to a certain extent sums up the mood that prevails throughout the twelve-hundred-plus pages that Germán Marín has just published.

This is the novel of a person who would have preferred to write a different book; History, in bloody capital letters, has infected daily life to such an extent that the act of conceiving fictions seems like a luxury that the author cannot allow himself, or can only allow himself if he first accepts, as Marín does, that literature cannot straighten out the past. After becoming in the 80s – as he puts it – 'the oldest tourist in Barcelona', Marín spends a good part of his exile wrapped up in the reconstruction of his genealogical tree. In that search he must abandon his idealizations of family, sink into the bottomless pit of private life, and comply, as much as possible, with the standard of not sweetening his memories.

'The desire to accept failure terrifies me,' he writes in *Círculo vicioso* [Vicious Cycle], 'because if I stopped writing, in an act of will, I would be even more vulnerable, abandoned like a cork to the ebb of the days.' Writing, he says, is a way of eluding the sensible god of tedium, or rather a way of coexisting with failure, of not disguising it in the appearance of a few little achievements. With a bitter and at times agonizing humour, Marín proclaims that finishing a novel is not difficult: one only needs a pen, a table, a notebook, a chair, and a well-sharpened knife so the writer can put his free hand on the table and impale it there.

The author of these novels refuses to disappear, given

140

that there are no truly private experiences, or any historical events that, seen from the present, have not contaminated private life. Towards the end of *La ola muerta* [The dead wave], in Buenos Aires, the young protagonist begins to seriously consider the possibility of becoming a writer, a profession that he had until then considered rather comical, as he'd assumed that being a writer was to be a kind of Enrique Lafourcade. His previous professions had included military cadet, DJ, smuggler, literature student, and he had just barely avoided establishing himself as a pimp or a police informant. Marín spends time on these past lives without giving in to the impulse to assume they were landings on a single staircase, to order them in a sequence dignified by the present. It is in that way, in the disorder of real life, that Germán Marín becomes a kind of Germán Marín.

To stay close to the self, in this case, is to display partial images that don't come to encapsulate an identity or a belonging. Much to the contrary, what Marín shows over and over is a radical discomfort with the faces that appear in the mirror. 'I am a Philippine woman who doesn't speak Spanish,' he says. 'I'm a tourist who forgot to leave.' And he goes on: 'I am a person who dreams a lot, but who salvages little to nothing of the night;' 'I always seem to be dreaming what's left over of the night'; 'I am a shadow apt for conversing with other shadows, but perhaps clumsier when dealing with people who come from reality.'

Viscious Cycle reconstructs the origin of the family, *Las cien águilas* [The Hundred Eagles] recovers Cadet Marín's childhood and adolescence, and *The Dead Wave* is the tale of a youth dominated by sexual discoveries and existential wallops. But it is the diary intermingled in

141

the narration that makes this trilogy an essential work, one that breaks with the tradition of the family novel in Chile to the extent that it emphasizes an inner, fragmented alienation that no longer fits within the moulds of bourgeois transgressions. There arise, precisions, digressions, dreams, trips to the movies, tooth pain, acidic commentary on the news arriving from Chile, dinners that end badly, fits of happiness, summers in a city where only crazy people stick around, the dogs and the old people no one wanted to walk, voyeuristic arousals, fetishistic outbursts, sexual adventures refuted immediately after, bolero lyrics, family rituals, broadsides, mystifications, self-censure, and a long series of elegiac annotations, because while Marín survives there are others who do not. Equal in death are: Jean-Paul Sartre, Cortázar, Borges, Rulfo, and Enrique Lihn, Tucapel Jiménez, Sebastián Acevedo, Rodrigo Rojas Denegri and José Carrasco. It is in the diary where he records, especially, the anxiety of a fiction writer, invariably convinced that he has not said what he really wanted to say. Not to mention a decisive uncertainty about the future, faced with the supposed democracy that is approaching. I give just one example, from 8 October 1985: 'The Pinochet dictatorship will someday be a tragic memory, and there will be no lack of people who, looking nostalgically at the photo of a loved one, will ask why destiny treated us so cruelly. It will be worse for those who sigh for someone and say taking up arms was a useless death, as I fear will be heard in the future. Meanwhile, the politicians far away in the salons will be living it up to celebrate the resuscitated democracy, even at the cost of the annoyance that Allende existed.'

Marín holds a grudge. He writes a novel interrupted by the exigencies of the present, or rather a diary that tends to take on the form of a hand-me-down, family novel. It's worth making clear that *History of a Family Absolution* is a great novel, the masterwork of a writer who has managed to depict Chilean violence and melancholy with an ironclad integrity, with firm strokes that nevertheless convey, as well, the vacillations, the muted zones of experience.

April 2006

TWO URGENT NOTES ABOUT
PEDRO LEMEBEL

I. ON 31 JULY 2004

It seems like a miracle that the work of Pedro Lemebel has found a place in Chilean literature. Not only did Lemebel have to write about what he saw and lived through and do it in a new way; he also had to dodge the media circus that tried to make him into one of those characters the press recruits every so often so they can create the illusion of pluralism: one more weird guy who supposedly says what no one else dares to. There was also, conversely, the danger of writing for the academy, the temptation of constructing an 'intellectual' discourse and staying there, high and dry and bored, betraying the impulse of his writing.

Lemebel knew how to get beyond the expectations of the press and all the paralyzing theoretical frameworks. His work, studied in dozens of universities around the world, has demonstrated a consistency and relevance much greater than that attributed to him by those who used to belittle him at the top of their lungs, and who now, resigned to a different scale of the politically correct, go on belittling him *sotto voce*.

I have no doubt that Lemebel deserves the National Literature Prize, but I'm less sure that the prize deserves Lemebel. The media take advantage of this time of year to display writers fighting like they're wrestlers on *Titans in the Ring*, when the real news is that this prize is terribly conceived and doesn't seem to matter to anyone. I understand Diamela Eltit wouldn't let herself be submitted, and I can imagine and admire her reasons, especially after the shame – not Diamela's, but Chile's – four years ago, when the prize went to Isabel Allende.

That Diamela Eltit deserves the national prize is, I think, inarguable; likewise Germán Marín, who *was* submitted this year, and a few others who should win if the prize were yearly, as it should be.

But before anyone else, Lemebel should win, as he has achieved what very few manage: to build an audience, create readers, many of them young people who have little to no interest in obligatory readings. I think of the people who came out of the closet thanks to Lemebel, and I don't mean only – though they would be enough – those who dared to confront their sexual identity after reading him. Rather, I mean those who, homosexual or not, discovered or rediscovered the shine and the power of words thanks to him, the need for writing, its urgency. Because to write truly, looking head-on at those we love and those we hate, and above all trying, much as it costs or hurts us, to look into our own depths, is always a coming out of the closet.

To give Lemebel the prize would be to award that whole horde of readers who more or less by chance came across some texts that were provocative, strange, very Chilean, cantankerous, bitter, funny, sentimental, sharp, elegant, entirely legible and at the same time complex, readers who then kept reading Lemebel and maybe other writers too, and who also dared to raise their own voices. Pedro Lemebel reminds us that literature is not inoffensive, that it's not mere decoration, that it does something to society. To give him the prize would be to honour that. It would be, I think a collective prize.

II. ON 23 JANUARY 2015
'If you don't read Lemebel in this course, you won't read him in any other,' Soledad Bianchi told us one winter morning. We had just met her, and she was going over the

syllabus of Hispanoamerican Literature V. It shouldn't have included any Chilean authors because that's what the Chilean Literature classes were for, but she wanted us to read some non-fiction pieces from *La Esquina de mi Corazón* [The Corner of My Heart]. It's difficult to explain the bravery of that gesture today. It wasn't easy to question an academy that jealously guarded the pigeonholes of knowledge, where homophobia and classism were still entrenched, and Lemebel's voice provoked bewilderment, repudiation, and unease. I'm talking about the nineties, which seem so nebulous now but would be even more so if we hadn't read Lemebel.

For one or two weeks there were rumours of a scandal, and even a couple of classmates who wanted to collect signatures for a formal complaint: we only had one semester to go over fifty years of Hispanic-American literature, and dozens of poets and a few fiction writers would be left out of the syllabus, but Soledad had chosen to sneak in the Chilean Lemebel, who didn't even write 'literature' but rather non-fiction, a lesser and contemptuous genre.

In the end no one complained, but I remember those discussions. Who knows what our language was like back then, when we still felt the prestige of academic jargon, but I guess that soon the joints and the beers kicked in, and we ended up talking about life, our lives. I defended Lemebel, but not because I'd read him, but rather because I'd seen him, I'd met him once, and that was reason enough for me. But maybe I defended him more because I had fallen in love at first sight with Soledad Bianchi, and I was willing to accept anything she said as an automatic truth.

I'm recalling all of this to lead up to a more recent scene which took place in October 2013 in the same

146

setting, at the College of Philosophy of the University of Chile. I sat next to Soledad at the back of the auditorium to watch the raging and brilliant performance that some students from Lastarria had put together using Lemebel's 'Manifiesto'. Afterwards he went onstage, with his wounded voice stolen by the cancer but transformed through the subtle miracle of a microphone into a metallic, enveloping whisper. Maybe in the middle of a long round of applause, I remembered that old class, the discussions in the grass, the constant disparagement of those years. Now the name Pedro Lemebel is in the syllabus of Chilean literature where it belongs. His work is studied all over, he is talked about in the press, on the radio, on TV, because his books created an audience that didn't exist before. His books changed lives. To say that his work is important for Chilean literature would be stingy: his work is important for Chile.

'Not even your face stamped on the front page of the newspapers could revive the globetrotting street carnival of your inexhaustible party,' wrote Lemebel three years ago, after Andrés Pérez's death. It's difficult not to remember those words, which express so well, now, a collective emotion. It's difficult not to imagine the impossible story he would write about his own funeral. We would laugh at his comments, so pointed and astute, we would be grateful for his outlook, so acidic and generous at the same time, his inimitable gossip, his bravery, his bald-faced tenderness, his language battle-hardened in the street and not in the university. His work was forged in the night, in the streets, the *barrio*: in life and not in literature.

BETWEEN QUOTATION MARKS

Of the over one hundred films by Raúl Ruiz, I have seen, sadly, only six. I want to watch them all, of course. I want to see the ones that were lost, and the ones that were never shot. I want to see the lost ones twice. And the ones that were never shot three times.

'And that, my friends, is what our art consists of: beating around the bush, straight to the essential,' writes Ruiz, and he is very right. There is nothing original or ingenious that I could add to the bibliography about his work, but I do have a ton of examples. In the Chilean press it tends to go the other way: someone talks and talks and throws out theories like mad, without ever getting to the treasured examples. I, on the other hand, only have examples. After flying through the thousand pages of Ruiz's diary and underlining his interviews almost entirely, I have dozens of examples to demonstrate, convincingly... I don't know what.

I'm referring to *Ruiz: Entrevistas escogidas – filmografía comentada* [Selected Interviews – Filmography with Commentary], and *Diario: Notas, recuerdos, y secuencias de cosas vistas* [Diary: Notes, Memories, and Series of Things Seen]. Putting together a book using interviews and editing a journal – these are editorial operations of major surgery: we must thank the poet Bruno Cuneo for his meticulous and impeccable work on these books. They are quite different from each other, of course. Interviews presume the more or less deliberate construction of a public image, while journals are always marvellously ambiguous, rambling, multi-vocal, open to contradictions, to repetitions, inconsistencies. We read interviews waiting for our turn at the hairdresser, but when we read someone's journal we inevitably become jealous lovers rummaging through drawers.

Ruiz is an ideal interview subject, one who answers the good questions and the bad – and the well-intentioned questions, which aren't necessarily good, and the malicious questions, which are almost always bad – with unwavering generosity, without pedantry or demagoguery, almost as if he enjoyed it. Regarding the effects that a work of art should provoke, for example, Ruiz improvises this precise, perfect definition: 'Art should provide people with emotions they have never experienced before, ones they've never felt. It's not about making people cry, but rather that the tear should fall in a certain way, when one least expects it, and for reasons he doesn't understand.'

He talks a lot about Chile in his interviews, which we could attribute to a fixation on the part of the interviewers, except that he does it even more in his journal. 'Chile is not a country, it's a military encampment,' he throws out at one point, and then he adds: 'To be Chilean does not describe a personality, but rather a sexual perversion: the search for orgasms through peals of laughter.' There are hints of reconciliation, passages of out-and-out nostalgia, but what prevails is resentment, the monologue of exile.

'Why do I tend to write the word *chancho* (pig) with a capital letter?' Ruiz wonders, and two lines on he answers his own question: 'Could be that in my brain the word Chancho is linked to the word Chile?' On a more casual note, I very much like this to-do list: 'Eat crab. Cut my hair. Make the truffles. Encourage free time. Take advantage of the few moments of solitude by not doing anything. Call Chin Cheung. Don't be afraid of Chile (the most difficult).'

Raúl Ruiz's journal is a long and radical film projected

149

in an enormous empty cinema. As is usual in the great personal diaries – because this one is, if you'll allow me to raise my voice, a truly great one – discomfort and unease live alongside untamed enthusiasm and infinite curiosity. There are jokes, there are excesses, there is speechifying. There are real dreams and invented dreams. There is innocence and cruelty. There is absolute fealty to Fernando Pessoa. There is a simply beautiful story that Ruiz wrote after his mother's death. There are lists of books, of people, of projects. There is decadence. There are theories on cinema and theories on cinema theory. There is a hesitant preoccupation with Chino Ríos's tennis matches. And there are so many literary references that at times this seems more like the journal of a writer than a filmmaker. But it's a little dumb to put it that way, because Ruiz was also, in private, a writer: a poet given to the compulsive production of sonnets, a tremendous essayist, and an occasional novelist I haven't read.

I'm afraid I'm running out of room, and there's no way I can sneak in the other quotations I'd prepared. Well, I can fit one more, fairly taken out of context but still very apt: 'Every Chilean speaks only in quotation marks.'

December 2017

HOW TO BE SILENT IN GERMAN

Macedonio Fernández is my favourite writer every other year. I admire his humour, his strange elegance, but sometimes my relationship with him falters, because that's how we readers are: sometimes we ask a writer for what he never wanted to give us. Macedonio is brilliant, but we don't always desire that brilliance, because we are not always, as he wanted us to be, 'artist readers'.

That's what I think while rereading two of his books: *Papeles de Recienvenido* [Newcomer Papers] and *Continuación de la nada* [Continuation of Nothingness]. I quickly discover that this is a year I love Macedonio, so much so that it seems strange to me there could be times when I don't. In any case, I should clarify that I always – the years when I love him and the ones when I don't – laugh at his jokes. This one is very good: 'The calf named Ton died, the black calf died, the Moorish calf died,' says a boy, but when they ask him for a happier story, he corrects himself: 'The Moorish calf was resurrected, the black calf was resurrected, the calf named Ton is resurrected.'

'I invented the parentheses with only one arch', says Macedonio, the writer who, referring to his impending birthday, confesses that he's never turned so many years in just one day. I like it when he promises to stay out of the country until his return, or when he discovers that his absence 'has extended to places abroad where he has never been'. And this sensible reflection strikes me as important: 'Travel: one is exposed to speaking languages one doesn't know, so as not to be silent in German, which I do not know how to do either.'

There is also the Bobo of Buenos Aires, that character who when it rains lets us know that our umbrella is getting wet, or when we smoke warns us that the tobacco at the end of our cigarette is on fire. Or who questions a policeman indignantly: 'You only met me a minute ago, and already you take the liberty of arresting me.'

I would like to endlessly quote this man who feared 'confusing one stranger for another', who thought that 'the hairstyle is a way of thinking outside the head,' or who, in one of his marvellous toasts, paid homage thus to the artist Alejandro Sirio: 'He was shorter than me, less existent, less thick, he didn't understand music like I did, in metaphysics there was no reason to wait for him at any corner, and moreover he hadn't achieved what I had, what few seductive tenors have managed: that no woman goes to bed with him.' Special mention for this opinion on Rodin's famous sculpture: 'Thinkers are more cold-blooded; this one takes off his clothes so he can think.'

In the emotional obituary that Jorge Luis Borges wrote when his master died, this definitive and beautiful phrase appears: 'One of the joys of my life is having been Macedonio's friend, of having seen him live.' Borges had also said that for years, he had imitated Macedonio 'to the point of transcription, to passionate and devoted plagiarism', since he used to believe that everyone who came before were drafts, 'imperfect and early' versions of Macedonio. As many critics have noted, in the end Macedonio was a draft of Borges. And sometimes – every other year – we like drafts more than the clean version. That's not true: we always like Borges; Macedonio only every other year. But during the year that we like him, we like him a lot.

'Don't read so lightly, dear reader, or my writing won't reach you all the way there where you're reading,' says Macedonio in *Newcomer Papers*, and he ends with this phrase that strikes me as perfect for the end of this piece: 'For now I'm not writing anything: deal with it.'

January 2012

Two tireless friends spend the last night of 1970 translating Shakespeare. The friends are named Borges and
Bioy Casares. They are not exactly teacher and student,
but in a way old man Borges has invented Bioy. Or it's
more that Bioy, with consummate good manners, has
let himself be invented, provided that he can maintain
a few distinctive characteristics that favour him: next
to Borges he will always be young; next to Borges he
will always be long, because he writes novels, the novels Borges has agreed not to write so that Bioy can write
them.

That night of 31 December 1970, after dining on
turkey and mashed potatoes, the tireless friends lock
themselves in to translate Shakespeare. 'Borges and
I slept a while, versifying in Spanish the witches of
Macbeth,' writes Bioy in his diary, and the image reappears in varying forms: on 10 January he says that they
worked 'nodding off between one hendecasyllable and
another,' and on the 13th that they translated 'with droop-
ing heads', and on the 18th it's Borges who only agrees
to work 'out of resignation'. To encourage themselves a
little, they comment with inflexible contempt on other
translations – regarding Guillermo Whitelow's version:
'If the actors were to perform Macbeth with Whitelow's
text, they would die asphyxiated, suffocated. He must
have done it to make a few bucks.' They grow bored to
the beat of the syllables, they get distracted: much more
than Macbeth, they are interested in Shakespeare. It's as
if they were translating Macbeth to escape Macbeth, to
forget a plot of betrayal through the constant recalling of
a face that 'even in the bad paintings of the time, does not
look like anyone else': Shakespeare's face. The face of

a man who, after having been many, wanted to become someone, and couldn't.

The work is interrupted by a trip Borges takes; on his return the translation becomes arduous and unnecessary: 'Shakespeare is the pinnacle of the human spirit? Better not to translate him; better not to look at him too close; we'll end up feeling contempt for him. He has such difficulty saying the simplest things! Or was he so used to the grandiloquent style that he couldn't say anything simply?' To look from close up is dangerous, thinks Borges, and Bioy looks at him from close up and transcribes, in his diary, every one of Borges' sentences, with affection and a certain prudence or loyalty that keeps him from criticizing or mythologizing him ('in general, ideas that aren't his don't strike him as good; I say this without bitterness, as a simple statement.') Bioy needs Borges, Borges needs Bioy. The inventor needs his invention, the invented one needs his creator to keep dreaming him. That's why he transcribes every word the inventor says. That's why he invents his inventor, why he allows himself that luxury. And we know that Bioy likes luxury.

Translating Macbeth is not a luxury, and it isn't a need. It's a joke: 'Tomorrow, maybe, let's work... on something other than Macbeth,' says Borges. The project is left unfinished for years, forever. One night in 1985, in one of their last meetings, Bioy proposes to Borges that they finish the translation, and Borges says yes, that no matter how bad it turns out it will be better than Gide's *Hamlet*. Maybe by then Borges had already decided to leave that version of *Macbeth* half-finished. In 1980 he had published 'Shakespeare's Memory', his last story – 'the one we imagine (surprised at the perfection of that ending) as Borges' last story,' says Ricardo Piglia

155

in *Formas breves* [Brief Forms] – whose protagonist, Hermann Soergel, is also the author of an unfinished version of *Macbeth*.

When Soergel is offered Shakespeare's memory ('from the earliest, most infantile days until the beginning of April of 1616'), he immediately thinks about writing the definitive biography on Shakespeare, but then he understands, chagrined, that the memory 'is not a sum; it's a disorder of undefined possibilities'. Soergel possesses only the circumstances, the 'cheap material' that Shakespeare turned into poetry: 'Chance or destiny gave Shakespeare the trivial and terrible things that every man knows; he knew how to turn them into fable, into characters much more vivid than the grey man who dreamed them, into verses that will live on through generations, into verbal music. Why un-weave that web, why undermine the tower, why reduce the sound and the fury of *Macbeth* to the modest proportions of a documentary biography or a realist novel?'

And Bioy? What did Bioy do with Borges' memory? He didn't try for a biography or a novel. Nor did he write a diary of his friendship with Borges, not really. What I mean is: he wrote a diary of 20,000 pages, and very graciously separated out the 1,600 that referred to Borges; he wrote 1,600 pages about Borges, and destined the other 18,400 to *not* writing about Borges.

A diary should be indiscreet, thought Borges, and Bioy's complies with that rule marvellously well. But Bioy doesn't want to write the truth about Borges – he can't. No one can. Bioy officiates as memorious anecdotalist; he wants to capture the cheap material, the grey life, the 'trivial and terrible things' that every man knows. He chooses to give life to Borges, to turn him into an indispensable secondary character. He chooses to turn Borges, in the end, into someone.

December 2006

ON WAITING

Affected by a minor ailment, Giuseppe Corte checks into a hospital where the patients are distributed according to the seriousness of their disease: those who suffer slight maladies are on the seventh floor, and the illnesses are still trivial down on the sixth, but by the fifth and the fourth the matter gets nastier, and the third and second are only extreme stopgaps before the same ending as always: a doctor closing the blinds on the first floor in a sign of mourning, and right away reopening them to receive a new terminal patient.

The story is by Dino Buzzati and it isn't hard to guess how it will go: in Buzzati's stories there is always someone who waits or leaves someone waiting. Or maybe there's a great event – a storm, a battle, or, to speed things up a bit, the very end of the world – that takes its time in coming or occurs while the characters remain isolated inside some obsessive idea. In this story, Giuseppe settles in on the tranquil seventh floor to wait out the brief time of his recovery, but we already know that the illness will worsen; we already know that, due to reasons simultaneously absurd and logical, the character will irrevocably descend.

Few works provoke the utter complicity that arises when reading the stories collected in *Sixty Stories* and *The Colomber*, in the novels *Secrets of the Old Forest*, *A Love Affair*, *The great portrait*, *Barnaby of the Mountains*, and in two truly strange volumes that allow us to measure – and admire – the artistic bravura of this illustrator/writer: *Poem strip*, a graphic novel *avant la lettre* that would gobsmack Wong Kar-wai, and *The Bear's Famous Invasion of Sicily*, a story in verse and prose with beautiful and delirious drawing that would make Tim Burton pale (even more).

The Bear's Famous Invasion of Sicily is the story of Leoncio, the king of the bears, who goes to Sicily to save Tonio, his son who was captured by men and turned into an odd tightrope walker (they call him, mockingly, Goliath). The story is very funny and dark: the bears take control and govern wisely for years, but little by little their vices turn them human, as they develop a taste for alcohol, gambling, and especially luxury (in spite of the heat, they love to wear coats they don't need). This is a fable about power that moralizes very little: if it teaches anything, it is to distrust one's teachers. It's no accident that a fearsome punishment in the bear's Sicily is to memorize 'educational poetry' like 'The Ant and the Grasshopper'.

Sixty Stories, meanwhile, includes almost all of Buzzati's greatest tales, including the already mentioned 'Seven Floors', and a long list that, if I were thorough, I would mention here and that would take up all the room in this article. I have to mention at least: 'The Seven Messengers', 'The Child Tyrant', 'The Collapse of Baliverna', 'The Dog who Saw God', 'The Saucer Has Landed', and 'The Changed Brother', among so many others. *The Colomber*, on the other hand, is a more uneven collection, at times approaching non-fiction or exhausted on parodies that aren't always convincing. But with Buzzati, the theory of indulgence works: we laugh anyway, we lower our guard, and even accept ten or twenty 'middle' stories (that's what John Ashbery replied when he was asked how he ordered his poems in his books: like everyone, the good ones at the beginning and the end, and the rest in the middle). Consequently, the book starts out with some masterful pieces ('Creation', 'The Lesson of 1980'), and closes with 'Voyage to the Hells

159

of the Century' a kind of novella in which the reporter Buzzati – maybe anticipating the turn towards so-called 'narrative journalism' – relates his adventures in a city that looks like Milan but is actually Hell. 'It was calming that the signs in the store and the advertisements were written in Italian and referred to the same products that we used every day,' says the narrator at one point, with consummate elegance.

In Buzzati's world, men fall in love with their cars (one of the author's obsessions – his critique of modernity perhaps hides a genuine enthusiasm for ever-faster models), while young people go out into the street and beat up the old, and children spend their afternoons making fun of a little classmate named Adolf Hitler. Echoes of the wars appear frequently and reverberate even in the placid landscape of the night-time garden, when the amoebas, the mosses, larva, and spiders engage in silent pitched battles. Because silence, also, is tension, a microscopic threat: 'The house itself seemed to be waiting for something, as if the walls, the beams, the furniture – everything – were holding its breath.'

Buzzati's versatility extolls, certainly, an enormous attachment to his few and intense obsessions: the imminence of an attack, a surprising turn that was, perhaps, to be expected; the solitude of a man whose pain is, for the world, an anecdote barely worthy of more or less affectionate ironies. It doesn't hurt to remember, by the way, the passage in *The Tartar Steppe* when, with tepid good judgement, Giovanni Drogo intuits his fate: 'It is difficult to believe in a thing when one is alone and there is no one to speak to. It was at this period that Drogo realized how far apart men are whatever their affection for each other, that if you suffer the pain is yours and yours alone, no one else can take upon himself the least part of it; that if you suffer it does not mean that others feel pain, and that brings about loneliness in life.'

September 2008

FIRST AND LAST WORDS

'Kosztolányi's prose is quiet and sharp. Today our books are noisier and perhaps more blurred,' says Péter Esterházy, author of noisy and blurry novels that in another hundred years will seem, perhaps, silent and sharp.

Esterházy is alluding to the distance that separates us from the classic, or at least from certain ways of narrating that we accept and perhaps prefer as readers, but that we renounce at the moment of writing. Not long ago I started reading a novel that begins like this: 'On a February morning, in the year 1960, in the city of Milan, Antonio Dorigo, architect, forty-nine years old, telephoned Signora Ermelina.' Everything in order: time, month, year, place, profession, first and last name and age of the protagonist, an action, a secondary character. I would surely have abandoned the book if I hadn't known that Dino Buzzati had written it, and that it's very unlikely I will end up not liking a book by Buzzati.

I'm not talking about the desire for originality, exactly. It's not that. I once heard José Emilio Pacheco roar with laughter over a translator of *The Waste Land* who, in order not to repeat the most reasonable Spanish translation of the first line (*'Abril es el mes más cruel'*), had arrived at this fairly statistical phrase: *'De todos los meses del año, sin duda abril es el más cruel'*, or 'Of all the months of the year, April is without a doubt the cruellest.' Translation is a good example of what I want to say, since it supposes a concrete task with words. And words are little talked about. We waste, on the other hand, valuable time responding to long questionnaires about the new paths of Latin American literature, or about the possible death of the novel, or about the important advances of narrative

162

journalism.

In the opening pages of *La arquitectura del fantasma* [The Architecture of the Ghost], Argentine writer Héctor Libertella remembers that the only book in his house when he was little was an old dictionary, so that writing became for him a way of filling those shelves, covering those gaps with books, 'even if they were only ghost books and the emptiness would remain, in the flesh,' he adds, perhaps thinking about the noise Esterházy spoke of. Libertella's prose is silent and sharp, but also noisy and blurry: his books are necessarily strange, because they obey an internal necessity and seem to find, along the way, a kind of new genre that is completed on reaching the last word.

Will our books be even noisier and blurrier than Libertella's, Esterházy's? Maybe not. Maybe they'll start with the name of the main character and go on with the day and the month and the year and the place. And maybe they'll end with some phrase so new we haven't even invented it yet.

April 2008

TRAVELLING WITH BOOKS

I.

I always take books when I travel, even on short trips. When it's time to pack, I choose them fairly impulsively, but the decisions do follow a kind of logic. For example, I tend to bring two or three novels whose company I feel I need. It's absurd, it's romantic, but I can't help it: I just feel safer surrounded by those two or three novels that I've read many times and that I always have close by. I can forget my favourite medicine or the cloth for cleaning eyeglasses, but I never forget those novels. I think it would be dangerous to travel without them.

I also bring a book I've never read, some large tome that I'm wary of, but I also think that once I'm all in on page one hundred and something I won't be able put it down. I have the feeling I'll skip appointments and parties, that I'll only see a few plazas and a couple of monuments because of how absorbed I'll be by that book I didn't believe in and that has utterly captivated me. Needless to say, of course, this never happens, and I return home without having gotten beyond the first paragraph, because it has also become a sacred custom not to read it.

I often bring books by friends on trips, almost always single-spaced typescripts, in small print, that I read or devour on the plane to wherever I'm going, hunkered down in my second-class seat, pretty uncomfortable but wrapped in the wonder those books tend to arouse in me. Because although I write books, it always astonishes me that people write books. It's strange to imagine the people one loves laboriously gathering words together, absent from the world for such a long time.

It was, come to think of it, on a plane a few months ago

that I read a piece by my friend Rodrigo Olavarría in which he remembers an episode from the old magazine *Disneylandia* that could be applicable here: Huey Dewey and Louie invites a cousin – a turkey or a goose, according to Rodrigo – on an outing, and when they get to the countryside it turns out that the cousin's backpack holds nothing but books.

We shouldn't be like that turkey or goose Rodrigo Olavarría talks about. We shouldn't travel with books, because they take up the space where a second pair of shoes could go, and every trip has a moment when we hugely regret not having a second pair of shoes. We shouldn't travel with books, moreover, because we always end up accumulating more books when we're travelling. I suspect that's what the second bed is for. I used to find it confusing: I'd arrive at those small, dark hotels, and when I entered the room I thought that instead of those two narrow beds, I could have used a single, more spacious one. But then I understood that the second bed must be for storing all the new books that keep adding up.

I don't think there is any other country where books are as expensive as they are in Chile, and so every trip, whether we like it or not, at some point for Chileans becomes an anxious tour of bookshops. Julio Ramón Ribeyro summarises that kind of outing this way: 'I usually leave without buying anything, because right away, at the sight of the books, my desire to possess extends not only to several possible books but to all books in existence. And if I do happen to buy a book, I leave without any kind of contentment, because its acquisition signifies not one book more but many books less.'

My experience is different, but equally guilty. I start out focusing on titles that would be hard to find in Chile, or whose prices are double or triple in bookshops at home. The problem is that very few books escape those criteria. And so I end up buying a lot, and over it all hangs the annoying doubt of whether I'm actually going to read them. I almost always do, in any case, even if it takes me months or years.

There are also the books given as gifts, usually by their authors. Some writers give away their books as though they were business cards: along with their name and email we find ourselves, suddenly, with thirty-something poems or fifteen stories or a very long novel, and there arises a strange impression of abundance or excess: we've just met this person, and already we have a generous entry into their obsessions, their desires and fears.

Then there are those who give you their books hoping that you'll reciprocate with one of your own, which is certainly awkward, and there are also those who don't give you anything, but somehow manage to insinuate that they have a few copies left and could sell them to you at a reasonable price. But my favourites are those modest souls who refuse to give you their books, seemingly resolved that no one should ever read them. I have a fond memory of a Peruvian author whom I asked where I could find his books, and he told me not to even try, because they were terrible; instead he gave me publications by other poets he considered to be good.

II.
I'm in Mexico, at the end of a four-month stay. A trip with books, of course. When I was packing I made the same mistakes as always, but at the last minute, quite reasonably, I decided to lighten my luggage considerably. I even took out the big tome, and in the end I flew

only with those two or three books without which, as I said, it seems dangerous to set off on a trip.

During my first weeks in Mexico City I became again, as I was in adolescence, a prudent reader who only buys what he is able to read immediately. And I rediscovered, then, the charm of the half-empty shelf. In this sense, our first libraries are exemplary: we have barely ten books, but we know them almost by heart. Over time, though, we lose integrity: the shelves accumulate uncertain volumes, and too frequently we give in to the urge to collect, that marvellous and incurable illness that brings us to treasure first editions or bibliographic rarities or even books that catch our attention with their design, their typography, their size.

One terrible variation of this illness comes when we buy books knowing not only that we're not going to read them, but that we wouldn't know how to read them because they are written in languages that are mostly unknown to us. But it's hard to resist the beauty of an edition of Kawabata in Japanese, for example. Many years ago now a friend gave me a copy in German of *The Clown*, Heinrich Böll's beautiful novel, which I carefully filed on a shelf where it has slept since then, although sometimes I look at the spine just to give myself the satisfaction of recognising the only words I understand in German: *Ansichten eines Clowns*.

But I was going to talk about those first days in Mexico, days when I lived, again, with very few books. I got up early, headed out to one of the city's great bookshops, carefully chose a novel and went back to my room, anxious to read it right away, in one sitting. Sooner rather than later, though, the distraction returned. For years now I've had the habit of combining readings, of submerging myself more or less simultaneously in

167

several books, usually of different natures, as if maliciously making them compete with each other, or as if reading were a mysterious and complex concoction that was prepared, for example, with one hundred morning pages of *The Book of Disquiet*, three stories by Clarice Lispector in the afternoon, and some poems by César Vallejo before drifting off.

Now, as I am writing, I look uneasily at the books on the shelf: there are four or five that I haven't read, two I abandoned halfway through, and one immaculate tome that I acquired in a moment of weakness and haven't even opened. The rest I've read, and I like to think that someday I'll read them again. I won't commit the offence of confessing the number of books I've collected on this trip. Suffice to say that there are a lot, and I sincerely wonder how I'm going to get them home. Sometimes I catch myself looking for some criteria that would allow me to leave some of them in Mexico. But I don't want to. I'm sure that I will bring the whole inventory. I don't want to give any of them up, I think, with warm-hearted greed. Because maybe now I need them all.

Should I put them all on the computer, modernize these habits, turn cunning and portable? It does not escape me that this is the article of an old person, shamelessly bourgeois. And I *am* impressed that readers can move about with files now instead of books. But it shouldn't impress me. I grew up reading photocopies, and although my eyes hurt when I read on a screen, the truth is that my eyes always hurt. Really, it seems miraculous that readers can search online for .zip or .rar files that contain rare books, expensive books, books they otherwise wouldn't be able to read. And I'm still astonished that all those books can travel discretely in a laptop or on those devices that are so light and perfect.

But what can I do: I travel with books.

III.

Without a doubt, for those of us who travel with books, the return is the worst. In the end there is no more space for trousers or shirts: the bag has become a small, vacuum-sealed library.

A few days ago a friend told me that he used to get rid of a few kilos of clothes to be sure he didn't have any crises at the airport, and this confession really surprised me because I do exactly the same thing.

I like this solution, since the presence of books, for me, has always been associated with the absence of clothes. Since my adolescence I got used to buying books with the money I was given once a year to update my closet; I bought a couple of shirts second-hand as an alibi, and then I threw myself happily into rummaging around in the bookshops, so that I always walked around terribly dressed but contentedly draped in the very best literature.

December 2010

II

ROBERTO BOLAÑO'S POETRY

'Might it be that writing, in the book,
 is to become legible for each,
and, for oneself, indecipherable?'
— Maurice Blanchot

Benno von Archimboldi thought that all poetry was or could be contained in a novel. Roberto Bolaño thought that the best poetry of the twentieth century had been written in the form of a novel: 'James Joyce's *Ulysses* contains Eliot's *The Waste Land*, and *Ulysses* is better than Eliot's *The Waste Land*,' he said in an interview. In 2002 he published *Amberes* (later published as *Antwerp* in English), a book of poetry, or something like a script for a book of poetry, or a script written after reading a book of poetry. In any case he took the liberty of presenting it as a novel, or as he put it: 'the only novel I'm not ashamed of,' 'maybe because it's still unintelligible'. Novels, then, make poetry intelligible. Novels are more understandable, and they sell more copies because they're more understandable.

¶ It's the same idea that obtains in a paragraph of 'The Myths of Cthulhu,' one of the essays included in *The Insufferable Gaucho*: 'Why does Pérez-Reverte or Vázquez-Figueroa or any other bestselling author, for example Muñoz Molina or that other young man who goes by the resonant name of De Prada, sell so much? Is it just because their books are enjoyable and easy to follow? Is it just because they tell stories that keep the reader in suspense? ... The answer is no. It's not just that. They sell and are popular because their stories can be *understood*.'

¶ A good novel is, then, a novel that is understood less than a bad novel. *2666* is a great novel because almost nothing is understood, although during its thousand-plus pages there persists an illusion of knowledge, an imminence.

¶ 'Imminence is a revelation that never comes,' says Borges of art. That's what emerges from *2666*: the imminence of a revelation that never comes.

¶ Bolaño's poems are the poems Bolaño's characters wrote: the unintelligible novelist brings the unintelligible poet to the fore. The fiction writer makes the poet understandable: slightly, barely understandable. The novelist is a strategist and the poet a hero, a kamikaze. In 'Déjenlo todo, nuevamente' ['Leave It All, Again'], the first manifesto of infrarealism, written in 1976, Bolaño defines the poet as a hero: 'The poem as a voyage and the poet as a hero, revealer of heroes;' 'I repeat: The poet as hero, revealer of heroes, like the red fallen tree that announces the beginning of the forest.'

¶ And what kind of hero is the poet? Or rather: why is he a hero who reveals other heroes, and who are those other heroes who must be discovered? Discover: Bolaño is speaking of buried heroes, of the dead. The vanguard of infrarealism is really a return to the vanguards ('Leave it all, again'), a movement of loss that begins when the revolution has failed, when Latin America is a vast cemetery, a stadium strewn with cadavers and overflowing with dictators. Bolaño constructs a melancholic vanguard, one of bitter and subversive laughter: 'We're preceded by the THOUSAND VANGUARDS CARVED UP IN THE SEVENTIES / The 99 flowers

173

open like an open head / the massacres, the new concentration camps / The white rivers underground, the violet winds.'

¶ Kurt Schwitters was an Expressionist and later a Dadaist and ended up a Merzist or Schwitterist, dedicated to gathering pieces of dead letters, to chipping away at words until they became dust. Roberto Bolaño, who descends from Schwitters and from Kafka – and from Borges and his precursors – wrote poems that are clippings and novels that are albums of clippings. The only thing to do is collect the pieces and see that the images don't fit together, that they don't match up or stick together: 'Rotten poetry, rotten poetry, my love: typical dream / of a survivor. Red children no longer have nightmares, / they wish for forgiveness, to be cynical one day, to read Bataille / in French and Marx in German.'

¶ 'From infrareality we came; where are we going?' writes this 1976 incarnation of Rubén Darío, who also has something of Breton about him – a less pontifical, more solitary Breton – and Huidobro, a less solitary Huidobro, a Huidobro with more humour and less money: 'Burn all your junk and start to love until you reach untold poems.' The message continues, peremptory: 'Search – not only in museums is there shit.'

The first poems signed Bolaño, Roberto – 'poet and sculptor', according to a biographical note from the time – are disarrayed in the manner of Rimbaud, savage railings in favour of disorder. Also from 1976 comes this fragment from *Reinventar el amor* [Reinventing Love]:

At the edge of a brass bed

a blonde girl paints her nails blue while the

lights of dawn warm

the dirty panes of her only window.

The water runs in the bathroom

and her night table is a still life by some New York

primitivist.

While the radio plays a funeral march she

sits down before the mirror.

The president's body rests in a cement yard.

His birds sing along the boulevards, they raze the

gardens.

The telegraph gives the world capitals a portrait with

split lips

black blood on the lapels of its open overcoat.

And in the salons, the ladies let themselves be

squeezed a little tighter

by sweaty gentlemen.

¶ 'In the room the women come and go / Talking of Michelangelo,' wrote Eliot in 'The Love Song of J. Alfred Prufrock'. Bolaño's version is nightmarish. There are two or three cuts: scene one, the woman who listens to a funeral march in the radio; scene two, whose soundtrack is a funeral march: in the centre there is a cadaver, probably that of Salvador Allende; and scene three, that of the women who cede, who dance, perhaps, to a cynical music, maybe a funeral march or perhaps a waltz, 'a waltz in a pile of rubble', as Nicanor Parra would say.

¶ Yes: Bolaño's poems are the poems of Bolaño's characters.

175

¶ In 1983, Roberto Bolaño and Bruno Montané, now in Spain, began to publish *Berthe Trépat*, under the label – or motto – Rimbaud, Vuelve a Casa, Press [Rimbaud, Come Home, Press]. Contributors to *Berthe Trépat* included Soledad Bianchi, Guillermo Núñez, Antoni García Porta (author of two texts 'constructed using cut-ups and the successive extraction and reconstruction of various pages of the first Catalan edition of *Ulysses*'), and, among many others, Enrique Lihn.

¶ *Hopscotch*, chapter 23: Berthe Trépat believes or wants to believe that there are two hundred people in the auditorium, but there are only twenty audience members listening or tolerating her musical ramblings. Horacio Oliveira is one of them, and is ultimately the only one who endures to the end of the concert; he's the only one who doesn't walk out. Trépat is an expert in anti-structural constructions, in producing 'autonomous cells of sound, the result of pure inspiration, held together by the general intent of the work but completely free of classical moulds, dodecaphonic or atonal'. Bolaño and Montané felt solidarity with poor Berthe Trépat, like Oliveira did, and maybe that's why they paid homage to that pianist and creator of 'prophetic syncretism'; another reason, perhaps more realistic, is that Bolaño and Montané were, also, artists who were expert in anti-structural constructions, prophetic syncretists: 'After all, poor Berthe Trépat had been trying to present works in premiere, which in itself was a great thing to do in this world of the Polonaise, the Clair de lune, and the ritual fire dance.'

¶ In 'El Aire' ['Air'], one of the poems Bolaño published in *Berthe Trépat*, we can discern the elegiac undercurrent that would be present in his books from then on:

> We are the cold hands the halted act
> Of one who opened the refrigerator
> At the moment death was returning
>
> We are here to discover wonders
> Let's dream that he who couldn't relate his story speaks
> At the moment death was returning.

¶ Bolaño is an elegiac poet. His poems constitute a challenge to death, they were written against death, like those of Breton, that black humourist. It is humour that makes poetry intelligible, that in some way makes possible the scrutiny of cadavers. Death allows for jokes, cadavers do not. A cadaver is death minus the joke. To talk about that cadaver we need the joke, and language, for Breton and company, 'has been given to man so that he may make a surrealist use of it'. Bolaño's vanguard is Breton's vanguard, but it is also the vanguard of Walter Benjamin, the vanguard of those who resign themselves to the gluing together of fragments, sheltered by a diminished humour, a bitter and wavering humour, at times almost serious, at times decidedly stentorian. A guffaw of melancholy: the grin allows one to feel again that the body is body. A poem is a shot in the arm. A hit.

¶ In 1993, Bolaño won the XVIII Rafael Morales Poetry Prize for *Fragmentos de la Universidad Desconocida* [Fragments of the Unknown University]. The series includes some poems that the author had already published in his previous books (the jury never knew that, apparently), and others that he would later publish almost unchanged in *Los Perros Románticos* [The Romantic Dogs] and *Tres* [Three].

Fragments of the Unknown University is a book of clippings in which the evocation of a past full of violence and fraternity predominates, and the present is defined as a solitary and residual moment.

¶ 'Death is an automobile with two or three distant friends. Faces / that I can't forget: cerulean, cold, one step only from sundown,' writes Bolaño in the text that opens the book, and the image reappears again and again, with slight variations: 'In lost cars, with two or three distant friends, we saw /death up close'; 'Sunsets that bore witness to Mario Santiago, / up and down, frozen stiff, in the back seat / of a smuggler's car. Sunsets /of infinite white and infinite black.' Death, distant friends, sunsets, the car – which is no longer, of course, the emblem of modernity. Nor is the journey precisely Jack Kerouac's. These are other highways.

¶ In 'Self-portrait at Twenty Years,' a crucial image appears:

> And then,
> despite the fear, I set off, I put my cheek
> against Death's cheek.
> And it was impossible to close my eyes and
> miss seeing
> that strange spectacle, slow and strange,
> though fixed in such a swift reality:
> thousands of guys like me, baby-faced
> or bearded, but Latin American, all of us,
> brushing cheeks with death.

178

'*Y no hallé cosa en que poner los ojos/ que no fuese recuerdo de la muerte*,' writes Francisco de Quevedo in one of the most important poems in the Spanish Language. 'And my eyes found nothing to rest upon / that was not a reminder of death.' In sum, Bolaño's oeuvre is contained in this epiphany that will reappear, later, in the final passage of his novel *Amulet*.

¶ 'Prose from Autumn in Girona,' published in *The Unknown University* and also in *Three*, is an intermittent story, polyphonic and intimate like *Antwerp*, and perhaps also a hinge between poetry and prose. As it progresses we attend the scene of a lovers' argument, guided by a voice that scarcely gives us hints as to what caused it. This voice comes from a subject who is trying out multiple forms of distancing, who refuses and affirms the fictional nature of the stories he constructs: 'It's no wonder that the author paces naked in the centre of his room. The faded posters open like the words he puts together in his head.'

'Prose from Autumn in Gerona' constitutes a slide from poetry toward fiction. The rhythm of the prose allows the knot to be smoothed without too much force: an image being developed and a photographer who waits for it, trying to guess what it will be.

¶ *Tres* also contains two other long poems: 'The Neo-Chileans' and 'A Stroll through Literature'.

'A Stroll through Literature' is, in reality, a notebook in which Bolaño gives free reign to literary promiscuity: almost all the fragments correspond to dreams (there are as many dreams here as in 'The Part about the Critics' in *2666*) of a certain Bolaño, in which he visits Alonso de Ercilla, meets Gabriela Mistral in an African village ('she'd lost a little weight, and picked up the habit of sleeping on the floor, sitting with her head between her knees'), gets involved with Anaïs Nin and Carson McCullers and even works for Mark Twain.

'The Neo-Chileans', meanwhile, is a long poem with a beatnik tinge about a group of young musicians who travel through Chile from Santiago to the north. 'How can so much evil exist / in a country so new / so miniscule?' wonders Pancho Relámpago, vocalist of the band, who is the one who relates for the younger members the story of Caraculo and Jetachancho, two musicians from Valparaíso lost in Barcelona's Chinatown ('And what lesson can we / neo-Chileans learn / from the criminal lives / of those two South American / pilgrims?/ None, except that limits / are tenuous, limits / are relative: reeded edges / of a reality forged / in the void / Pascal's horror / Precisely').

¶ 'What this poet has of the ghostly is not so much the fact of his *not* living here – a condition that he shares with nearly the entire population of the planet,' notes Enrique Lihn, around 1981, in reference to the poems that Bolaño sent him: 'He has spent half his life abroad, in Mexico and Spain, but his poetry does not have the accent of those places. He makes one think of an imaginary country named Chile, one that rather than stripping away nationality, produces negatives of Chileans, absences of Chileans.'

'Meeting with Enrique Lihn,' included in the English collection *The Return*, is the best 'document' of the epistolary relationship between these two poet-prose writers. 'The Neo-Chileans' is dated 1993, but Lihn's judgement in a way coincides with the idea of country that guides the band of 'new patriots', the negatives of Chileans.

¶ Perhaps Bolaño's characters would not have written the novels that Bolaño wrote: they would have needed a lot of glue, and above all, resignation. The poets who go looking for Cesárea Tinajero are not the critics who chase Benno von Archimboldi, not exactly. Archimboldi is a hero, but he is not a poet: he thinks that all poetry can fit into a novel, that only a novel can communicate what poetry is. Bolaño's work tells the story of a poet resigned to being a novelist. A poet who descends to prose in order to write poetry.

¶ 'Like someone moving embers / and sucking in / the criminal air of childhood:' *The Romantic Dogs*, published first in Mexico, and later, with numerous modifications, in Spain, projects the final image of Bolaño's poetry: 'Poetry slips into dreams / like a dead diver / into the eye of God.)

Bolaño's poetry is not understandable.

¶ 'The true poet is one who is always leaving himself. Never too long in the same place, like guerrilleros, like UFOs, like the rolled-back eyes of prisoners with life sentences,' said Bolaño in 1976.

The poet is a fighter and a UFO and a condemned man. Bolaño's novels tell of revolutions and sightings and imprisonments. That is the conclusion.

June 2005

NICANOR PARRA AT THE WHEEL

I.

It isn't easy to write just now. Talking would be better, more natural. That's what one does at wakes: talk about the deceased in a low voice, with friends, in a corner. But I'm not in Santiago, and so I'm writing. I'm writing the things that I would say right now, in a low voice, with my friends, if I were at the Cathedral holding vigil over Nicanor Parra.

II.

'He's going to die any minute now,' said a college class-mate of mine in 1994, when Nicanor Parra had just turned eighty years old and we were eighteen. I asked if the poet was sick or something. 'When people are eighty years old,' he replied condescendingly, 'it's highly likely that they'll die any minute.' We were in a large group on campus, doing nothing, pretty high. Someone said there was an event at Cine Arte Alameda to celebrate Parra, and the usual four or five enthusiasts headed over straightaway – uninvited, of course, but we managed to sneak in. I don't remember much, almost nothing, about the event. I remember the place was packed. Many a rock band would love to have half the fans that Parra did.

Jumping ahead to 2003, when I first started going to his house in Las Cruces, pretty much uninvited then, too. Yes, when people are almost ninety years old it's highly likely they'll die at any moment, but Nicanor was still going strong. From that first time on, talking with him was always a true adventure. At first there was al-ways a study, a kind of recognition, like the exchange of pennants at a football game, and it would all be qualified by a few loose, exploratory phrases that were really his most recent poems, his thoughts from the week. During lunch he'd talk about what people always talk about while they eat: the joys of wine, the unbeatable pork roll from Las Cruces, the interesting colour of the tomatoes. The best part always started around the time dessert came, because then the script would take off in unexpected directions, and he didn't seem to be trying to teach anything, but one always learned a great deal.

Although the press and the academy demonstrated a persistent, sometimes insistent interest in digging around in his private life, the truth is that except for the usual enumeration of children and romances, we know very little about Nicanor Parra. His relationship with interviews was, of course, a complicated one. In general he was reluctant to grant them, saying that the questions sounded to him like interrogations. 'Every question is an impertinence, an aggression,' he declared, with paradoxical warmth. Sometimes he refused outright; other times, indecisive, he would open up long preambles that led to nothing. But even if he refused the dynamic of questions and answers, a skilled observer would leave Nicanor's house with enough material for a good article. Interviewing Parra, in fact, became a kind of elective but important course for cultural journalists in Chile.

I was a more or less involuntary witness to some of his interviews. I remember, especially, his tug of war with the journalist Matías del Río. Nicanor had agreed to talk to him on the condition that there be no questions or recordings, but Del Río took two minutes to break those rules. 'You, sir, are a pontificator, and pontiffs belong in Rome,' said Nicanor suddenly, and he stood up and walked out without another word. Del Rio didn't know whether to go or stay or what, but the story ended happily: after a while our host returned, apologized, and invited him to stay for lunch. While we ate he answered the journalist's questions *in extenso*. At one point Parra looked at me, winked, and pointed with his right index finger at the journalist's sleeve: he knew perfectly well that his interlocutor was hiding a recorder.

III.

Thanks to a series of coincidences, most of them incited by the editor Matías Rivas, not long after I met Nicanor I was put in charge of editing *Lear Rey & Mendigo* [Lear, King & Beggar], his translation of King Lear, which at the time was a semi-abandoned project. Nicanor had translated *King Lear* in 1990 for a successful staging at the Teatro Universidad Católica, but he was reluctant to publish the translation because he didn't consider it finished.

'Para traducir a Shakespeare / y comer pescado / mucho cuidado:/ poco se gana con saber inglés,' wrote Parra: 'In translating Shakespeare / and eating fish / take care: / little is gained by knowing English.' He wanted his translation of *King Lear* to be a transcription, in the musical sense of the term: the work had been written for one instrument, the English language, and it had to be transcribed for another one, the Spanish language, Chilean Spanish.

Parra sought equivalences, tried out unexpected metric combinations, broke the rhythm; he wanted, just like Shakespeare, to reconcile the high and the low, the solemn and the vulgar. Elizabethan blank verse had to come together with the metric of his own poetry, and they had to make each other more powerful: Shakespeare had to sound like Shakespeare but also like Parra; Parra had to sound like Shakespeare but also – above all – like Parra.

The translation was essentially ready, the route

decided: all that remained was to determine whether to walk in the sun, so to speak, or stick to the shade. There was a handwritten version covered in edits, and another typewritten copy that was also riddled with corrections. I consolidated them into a single manuscript and printed two copies of the result. Nicanor marked his up and I tried to record, on mine, every one of his painstaking decisions.

To see that someone I admired so much was capable of spending a full hour arguing over an adjective, or testing aloud the naturalness of a line, was a luxury for me, an undeserved lesson. I was tasked with extricating the book from him, taking it out of his hands, making him see that it was ready. But it was hard for me to rush him, because that process was, for me, pure gold. And we laughed, we got distracted too. He was always extraordinarily generous with me. We had a good time, we progressed, and nevertheless, when night fell, Nicanor was overcome by uncertainty. He considered not publishing the book, he seemed truly worried, as if in that translation of *King Lear*, his literary destiny hung in the balance.

One afternoon, my method failed: Nicanor made so many changes it was impossible to keep up with his corrections. I had to leave on the last bus back to Santiago, and I wanted to take his copy with me and get his changes down once I was home. He looked at me with intimidating seriousness and flatly refused.

And so, I had to go back the next day. I wanted to take the chance to transcribe his changes, but he wanted us to keep going. After lunch he insisted on driving me to Cartagena in his old grey Beetle so we could make photocopies. I wasn't afraid of Nicanor driving, I had already been his co-pilot a couple of times when we'd gone to eat fried fish. At the copy shop they helped us quickly, but on the way back we got stuck behind a red truck that was inexplicably going ten miles an hour. Nicanor tried to pass it, but halfway through the manoeuvre the idiot truck driver also sped up, and suddenly we were facing down an enormous bus.

For a moment I was sure we were going to die right there, on the half-empty highway at four in the afternoon, but Nicanor floored it and the other two braked and we survived by the skin of our teeth. As soon as he caught his breath he raised an eyebrow and smiled, like it was nothing. 'We almost died,' I said. He looked at me as if to say: *exaggerate much?*

We didn't die, of course, and a couple of months later Nicanor gave the go-ahead on that brilliant translation. Over the following years, now without the excuse of work, I went back to see him many times. I remember one in particular, at the end of 2010, when he was the one who visited me. I was preparing to start a class talking about a concept in the work of Nicanor Parra, when the poet himself knocked at the door, with the sheepish bearing of a tardy student. It was a beautiful gesture. I had told him over the phone that we were starting to read one of his books, and he found out the day and time of my class and arranged everything to travel to Santiago to surprise us.

It doesn't happen every day that an author walks in, just like that, on forty-something readers discussing his work, especially if the author is ninety-five years old and a living legend of poetry. That morning my students reacted timidly at first, but gradually they ventured to ask some questions, which Nicanor answered generously and at length.

Later, in the cafeteria, one of my students told me that

he'd been startled to see Parra, because he'd thought the poet was dead. 'He *is* dead, and so am I,' I replied, but my student didn't get it, I had to explain that I was joking. Some months later, in a speech to celebrate National Book Day, President Piñera made the same mistake, including Parra among the Chilean authors who 'have left us'. I don't know what the poet might have thought of that lapse. Most likely, he laughed heartily.

Day before yesterday, when he found out that, eight years later, Nicanor Parra had indeed died, Piñera tried to fix things with this pretty ridiculous sentence: 'All that remained for him to achieve immortality was to leave this earthly world.'

IV.

If I were at the Cathedral of Santiago now, with my friends, we would speak in low voices about the last time we'd seen the deceased. That's what you talk about at wakes.

It was 5 December 2014. I was thirty-nine, he was one hundred. A hundred years and two months old. I went with Joana Barossi, a Brazilian friend who translated his poems for fun, and who dreamed of meeting him. When I introduced them, he barely greeted her. For the first ten or twenty minutes, Nicanor spoke exclusively to me.

Then he put on a couple of piano *cuecas*. We commented on them, he got up to do a little dance. Only then did he speak to Joana, and with a certain solemnity; she was enchanted. He asked her to read us one of her translations, and she agreed. She started – I think – with the Portuguese version of 'Advertencia al Lector', or 'Warning to the Reader'. Nicanor looked at her as if he had the girl from Ipanema herself there in front of him.

We ate lunch, and then I thought we should get going;

it was time for his siesta. On the coffee table there was a copy of *Parra a la Vista* [Parra in Sight], a book compiled from a bunch of Nicanor's photographs that his grandson Cristóbal Ugarte had found in a suitcase. The poet started an unexpected and loquacious account in which he explained or contextualized, in detail, every one of the photos. I went out to smoke and when I came back he was still telling Joana about the photos; I went with his daughter Colombina to buy some ice cream, and when we came back he was still going; I went to the front yard, talked for maybe two more hours with Colombina and Rosita, his caretaker, and then we had to leave, but Nicanor still had material for a thousand and one nights.

It was dark when we finally left. As we were saying goodbye, with the assuredness granted her by those nearly eight hours of coexistence, Joana handed him a copy of his *Complete Works* and asked him to sign it. Nicanor hesitated a second before replying: 'Noooooo, better do it next time, Joana, next time.' Resigned but still happy, she kissed his right hand. 'This is the most important day of my life,' she told me later, in the car. I looked at her as if saying, with Parranian skepticism: *exaggerate much?*

When people are over one hundred years old, it's highly probable that they'll die at any moment, but as several friends have said, we were used to Nicanor's presumed immortality. He still lived three more full years, I could have visited him so many times. I didn't, and I'm not even there with him now, at his wake, at his funeral. All I can do is say goodbye to him like this, writing, speaking in a low voice, to no one.

Mexico City, 25 January 2018

RIBEYRO IN HIS WEB

'Every writer's face is his work,' thought Julio Ramón Ribeyro, but it's not easy to get a fix on Ribeyro's own face, since his appearance changed a lot from one photo to another: his hair long or short or half grown-out, with or without a cigarette, with or without a moustache, wearing a serious expression or a slight smile or in the middle of a surprising peal of laughter. It's as if he were choosing to put curious people off with rudimentary disguises.

Ribeyro's face is that of a law student who had contempt for the legal profession, or a Lima native who wanted to live in Madrid, who in Madrid dreamed of Paris, in Paris longed for Madrid, and so on, chasing grants and lovers, and especially in search of time to waste writing, in the solitude of Munich, or Berlin, or Paris, again, for a long stay.

Ribeyro's face is that of a solitary man who piled up dirty glasses and flicked ashes off the balcony. Ribeyro's face is the face of an eternal convalescent who was born in 1929 and died in 1994, two years after starting to publish *La tentación del fracaso* [The Temptation of Failure], the astonishing diary he kept for over four decades.

'He was, perhaps, the shyest person I've ever met,' said Mario Vargas Llosa, who is surely Peru's least shy writer. Enrique Vila-Matas, on the other hand, went mute when he met Ribeyro, and not from admiration, but simply 'because of the panic provoked by my shyness and his.' Ribeyro was a shy man who thought Peruvians were shy: 'We have an unhealthy fear of ridicule; our taste for perfection drives us to inaction, forces us to take refuge in solitude and satire,' he writes in his diary.

¶ 'My life is not original, much less exemplary. It's just one of many lives of middle-class writers born in a Latin American country in the twentieth century,' he says in his 'Autobiography'.

Even in the most confessional pages of his diary, an impersonal mood persists that keeps him safe from exhibitionism or anecdotalism. Ribeyro writes to live, not to demonstrate that he has lived. A fragment from 1977 is, in this sense, revealing: 'A true work must start from the oblivion or destruction (transformation) of the writer's very self. The great writer is not one who truthfully, in detail and intensely, describes his existence, but one who becomes the filter, the weave, through which reality passes and is transfigured.'

¶ Was Ribeyro a great writer?
Although a large part of his diary remained unpublished (Seix Barral's last publication goes through 1978), *The Temptation of Failure* reveals Ribeyro as one of the greatest diarists of Latin American literature. His stories, meanwhile, quickly earned him the title of 'best short story writer in Peru' (although there was always the joker who would define him as 'the best Peruvian writer of the nineteenth century'). In an entry from 1976, he evaluates his literary destiny with disenchantment: 'discreet writer, timid, hardworking, honest, exemplary, marginal, private, meticulous, lucid: here are some of the adjectives applied to me by critics. No one has ever called me a great writer. Because I am surely not a great writer.'

He liked to present himself as a third-string player who had scored one magnificent goal. But it must be said that during the final years of his life he played to a full stadium, responding courteously to his pestering fans.

¶ Ribeyro's stories lend themselves to piecemeal reading, inviting us to leaf through them to the rhythm of metro rides and secretive work-day parentheses. It's difficult to go back to work after receiving the brushstrokes Ribeyro prepared patiently, searching for that 'sober emotion' Bryce Echeñique talked about.

In the seventies and eighties, Ribeyro's stories made the rounds under the title *La palabra del mudo* [The Mute's Word], an allusion to the marginalized people represented therein. That is, Ribeyran characters *par excellence*: weak people, cornered by the present, victims of modernity. As Bryce Echenique, again, has observed, Ribeyro appears in his stories to be a compassionate Vallejo, stuck at ground-level.

The drive to depict that sad and unequal Lima coexists from the start with a veiled autobiographical projection, which takes on greater clarity not only in his stories, but throughout his work. Ribeyro wrote novels, plays, and 'proverbials', as he called his historical digressions, in addition to valuable essays of literary criticism, and two strange, intense books, *Prosas apátridas* [Stateless Prose], and *Dichos de Luder* [Luder's sayings] in which he lay the groundwork for *The Temptation of Failure*.

¶ While his colleagues were writing the great novels about Latin America, Ribeyro, second-class citizen of the boom, gave life to dozens of simply magisterial stories, which, however, did not live up to the expectations of European readers. And he knew it well: 'The Peru I present is not the Peru that they imagine or depict: there are no Indians, or very few, miraculous or unusual things don't happen, local colour is absent, the baroque or the verbal delirium is missing,' he says, with calculated irony.

191

¶ In *Luder's Sayings*, Ribeyro slides in an elegant reply to the question of why he no longer writes novels: 'Because I am a short-distance runner. If I run a marathon I risk reaching the stadium after the audience has already left.'

¶ Alonso Cueto said in a recent article that Ribeyro's novels tend to lose tension and interest. He was surely thinking of the forced lightness of *Los geniecillos dominicales* [The Little Sunday Geniuses], or of the slightly watered-down skepticism of *Cambio de guardia* [Changing of the Guard]. *Crónica de San Gabriel* [Chronicle of Saint Gabriel], on the other hand – his first novel – is, with utter certainty, a great work.

Of that novel Ribeyro says, 'above all it is the story of an imaginary adolescence, of a strange family, of a land both generous and hostile; it is the chronicle of a lost kingdom.' Ribeyro chooses the mask of Lucho, a Lima teenager who, in the course of a year of slow-moving life, is the target of his cousin Leticia's whims, and witness to the injustices of a world in laboured decomposition. The novel feels its way forward, searching for a precise and closed language: 'When I looked at her from up close I found, astonished, that her pupils were of such singular opacity that the light from the windows lit them without penetrating.' The lost kingdom of San Gabriel, he says in his diary when he finishes the novel, 'is the writer's time, the countless days of beauty that I sacrificed to imagine these stories.'

¶ The 1964 diary features this admirable definition of the novel, though it could also work to describe the creative process behind a story or poem: 'A novel is not like a flower that grows, but rather like a cypress that is carved. It does not acquire its form by starting from a nucleus, a seed, and growing through addition or flowering, but rather by starting with an herbaceous mass, and cutting and subtracting.'

The writer who prunes runs the risk of ending up without a garden – a necessary risk, in any case. 'Silvio in the Rose Garden' or 'At the Foot of the Bluff', perhaps Ribeyro's best stories, evoke a novelistic effect, so to speak, the same way that Ribeyro's sentences tend to brush up against the intensity of good poetry.

¶ Though I know it's too late, let me apologize now for the number of Ribeyro quotes that this essay contains. I've tried to quote as little as possible. I've failed. And in what remains of this text, I will continue to fail.

¶ A fragment from *The Temptation of Failure*: 'When I was twelve years old, I said to myself: one day I'll be big, I'll smoke, and I'll spend my nights at a desk, writing. Now I am a man, I'm smoking, sitting at my desk, writing, and I say to myself: When I was twelve years old I was a perfect idiot.'

Another: 'I have a great distrust for men who do not smoke or touch alcohol. They must be terribly depraved.'

¶ 'At a certain point my story becomes mixed up with the story of my cigarettes,' says Ribeyro, in 'For Smokers Only', his indispensable 'self-portrait as a smoker'.

He looks back on his first Derbys, his Chesterfields as a university student ('whose sweetish odour I still hold in my memory', the 'black, national' Incas, the perfect pack of Lucky Strikes ('I force my way in through that red circle when I recall those lofty nights of study, when I greeted the dawn with friends on the morning of an exam'), and the Gauloises and Gitanes that decorated his

Parisian adventures. Then Ribeyro evokes the saddest moment of his life as a smoker, when he realized that in order to smoke he will have to give up some of his books: so he exchanges Balzac for several packs of Luckys, and the surrealist poets for a pack of Players, and Flaubert for a few dozen Gauloises, and he even gives up ten copies of *Los gallinazos sin plumas* [Featherless Turkey Vultures], his first book of short stories, which he ended up selling by the pound to turn them into a miserable pack of Gitanes.

The story abounds in passages that a non-smoker will judge unrealistic but that smokers know are utterly accurate. For example, the night when Ribeyro throws himself from a height of eight metres in order to retrieve a pack of Camels, or, years later, when he solves the strict injunction against smoking by hiding some packs of Dunhills in the sand that he runs to dig up every morning.

Ribeyro deserves a primary place in the liberating library for smokers that consists of, among other necessary books, *Zeno's Conscience* by Italo Svevo, *Cigarettes are Sublime* by Richard Klein, *Puro humo* [Pure Smoke] by Guillermo Cabrera Infante, and *Cuando fumar era un placer* [When Smoking was a Pleasure], the self-help essay by Cristina Peri Rossi that includes this heartfelt poem (which non-smokers – once again – will think is exaggerated, but for us is a declaration of the utmost amorous intensity): 'It has been just as hard / just as painful / to quit smoking/ as to quit loving you.'

I repeat: these images possess an inarguable beauty for those of us who believe, as Rocco Alesina thought, that 'smoke doesn't kill, it keeps you company until you die'. It's certainly inconvenient to read that story of Ribeyro's if one is in treatment with varenicline, the drug capable of taking smokers and turning them into depressed citizens of the global world. (It is worth remembering, in this regard, the testimonials of people who, after successful treatment with Champix, confessed an enormous existential anxiety. 'Now that I don't smoke, everything is infinitely lamer,' said my friend Andrés Braithwaite, who was famous for decades for his enthusiastic puffing.)

¶ Instead of the semi-wakefulness Breton and company advised, Ribeyro preferred to write in a state of semi-drunkenness. Again, my apologies, but I can't resist citing in its entirety a section of *Stateless Prose* that could well be understood as an alcoholized version of 'Borges and I': 'The only way I can communicate with the writer inside me is through solitary libation. After a few drinks, he emerges. And I listen to his voice, a voice that is a bit monotone, but that continues, at times imperious. I record it and try to retain it, until it grows blurrier and blurrier, more jumbled, and it ends up disappearing when I myself drown in a sea of nausea, tobacco, and fog. Poor double of mine, to what terrible pit have I relegated you, that I can glimpse you only so sporadically, and at such cost! Sunk within me like a dead seed, perhaps he remembers the happy times when we coexisted, or even more, when we were the same and there was no distance to overcome or wine to drink in order for him to be constantly present.'

¶ 'Kafka is my brother, I've always felt it, but he is my Eskimo brother; we communicate through signs and gestures, but we understand each other,' writes Ribeyro.

Beyond the perceptible nearness in some of his stories of the fantastic, the similarity – the family tie – between

Ribeyro and Kafka appears, fully, in moments of veiled humour like this one: 'I am a relatively precious and fragile thing; I mean, an object that has been hard and costly to make – studies, travel, readings, jobs, illnesses – and so I regret that this object has no possibility of yielding its full potential. To acquire something and throw it away is senseless.'

Or the following fragment, which recalls the Kafka of 'Eleven Sons': 'I'm afraid that my son has inherited nearly all of my defects, along with those of my wife, which is just too much. Mine alone would have been enough to make an intelligent wretch of him.'

Please just one more, this homage to slowness: 'Why walk so fast, if on the corner where we least expect it we encounter a red light, thanks to which all those people we passed catch up to us?'

¶ In concert with the author's scepticism, Ribeyro's characters have a problematic relationship with history. It's difficult to decide if his political acquiescence corresponded to a moral imperative or if he just assembled, along the way, a suit that was tailored to fit him. The seed of Ribeyro's political – if not social – lack of commitment is in this entry from 1961, written after composing a manifesto on the role that writers should play in Peru: 'More important than a thousand intellectuals signing a virulent manifesto is a worker with a gun. Ours is a sad part to play. Moreover, what sense does it have, what decency can there be in drafting this declaration in Paris, listening to Armstrong and drinking a glass of Saint-Emilion?'

In 1970, after leaving the position he occupied for a decade at the Agence France-Presse, Ribeyro took a post at the embassy and then at Unesco, waiting out, through 1990, the rotating democracies and dictatorships. Guillermo Niño de Guzmán, his editor and friend, has this pertinent memory: 'His eagerness to maintain his diplomatic position can be understood because it was his modus vivendi (his literary income was insufficient), but it entailed an excessive cost: the loss of his political independence.'

¶ Ribeyro makes room in his diaries for some guilty reflections on loyalty. But unbelief prevails, or maybe it's the conviction that great historical gestures are mere lapses, after which mediocrity and misery are exacerbated. The news that reaches him from Latin America affects him, but he is much more affected – and he is the first to recognize it – by his long hospital stays and his hand-to-hand battles with the blank page.

At the news of the coup in Chile, Ribeyro, naturally, signs the usual manifestos, but he insists on distancing himself, on separating the waters: 'During these times Tyrians and Trojans unite, forget their quarrels, and row in the same direction, although, it must be said, not with the same goals.' The imperative to act is at odds with his pessimistic view of history: 'The two French sweepers at the metro station, wearing their blue overalls, speaking in argot, grumbling about their work – how has the French Revolution helped them?'

¶ So, who was Ribeyro? Ribeyro was, as Tabucchi says of Pessoa, a trunk full of people: 'It's as if there existed in me not one but several writers who were fighting to show themselves, who all want to appear at the same time, but in the end can't manage to manifest anything more than an arm, a leg, a nose or an ear, oscillating, messy, jumbled and a little grotesque.'

¶ A wayward entry among the diary's pages: 'From now on you no longer have any right of property over your body. I have acquired it. Your breasts are mine. Your thighs are mine. Your sex is mine. Your skin is mine. I am the owner not only of your body, but of what it supposes: owner of your pleasure and your suffering.'

¶ The crisis of the novel is, for Ribeyro, the result of artifice: 'For some time now, French novels have been written by professors for professors. The French novelist today is a gentleman who has nothing to say about the world, but very much to say about the novel,' he writes.

He goes on, then, pointing to 'modern' literature (an adjective that in Ribeyro tends to be contemptuous): 'Each new writer cross-checks his work with that of the writers who came before, not with the world. In this way we reach a rarification in the novel's material, which could be confused with esotericism.' New writers, he concludes, 'try to make of their work not the personal reflection of reality, but rather the personal reflection of other reflections.'

¶ Of Salinger's novel *Franny and Zooey* he says: 'The characters move like graduates of the Actors Studio.'

¶ This judgement about Carpentier is decisive, written after reading the first seventy pages of *El recurso del método* [Reasons of State]: 'The novel is a bazaar of proper names and erudite references. This defect is accentuated because of another character trait that I believe I see in Carpentier: the fear that for being Latin American and a Communist he will be reproached for ignorance of western culture. And so he flaunts it, but with a tropical exuberance.' Ribeyro knows how to be pitiless: 'It's as if a newly rich man shows up to the party wearing his most elegant suit and all his jewels. His style, more than beautiful, is a bejewelled style. His 'illustrious tyrant', moreover, is never made flesh, he remains words and nothing more than words. So far I don't believe in him: he is a laboured and unrealistic literary figure.'

¶ 'Need to construct my life again, my spider web,' writes Ribeyro in the mid-fifties, with full awareness that to live is to continually remake a tabula rasa. He is not that hero of Borges' who only at the last second – just before feeling 'the intimate knife on his throat' – understands his destiny. Ribeyro is not a hero but rather a man who every morning, now far away from his Lima neighbourhood, looks at himself in the shards of the familiar mirror. More than a life ordered in stages and partial defeats, Ribeyro invokes a dubious destiny every day. From there arises the predilection of readers like Bryce or Julio Ortega for 'Silvio in the Rose Garden', a beautiful story about the slippery art of reading the world.

¶ 'His lack of confidence in the future obliged him to limit his aspirations almost to the everyday sphere,' says the author in 'Self-portrait in the Style of the 17th Century'. Anyone who has made it this far with me will be able to imagine how much fun Ribeyro had writing these lines: 'without being gluttonous, he enjoyed complicated meals more than simple ones, good wine and spirituous liquors, but he was also capable of major privations, and he bore weeks of bread and butter and tap water without much suffering. He suffered, on the other hand, from lack of tobacco, and he was an aficionado of love, more of its variety than its repetition, though its absence, however, did not knock him off balance.'

The end is beautiful and perhaps true: 'He could remain alone and in fact had a certain inclination toward
solitude, and he only accepted the company of people
who did not threaten his tranquillity or bully him with
their quackery.'

August 2006

SEARCHING FOR PAVESE

I.

'I could go to the town where Cesare Pavese was born,' I
had told the editor, somewhat at random, vaguely imagining the Piedmont and not even coming up with some
commemorative event that would give the trip some
justification. Then I realized the event couldn't be any
more pitch-perfect: Pavese was born one hundred years
ago, no more and no less, in Santo Stefano Belbo, a town
of 4,000 inhabitants in the province of Cuneo, which is
reached from Genoa, Turin, or Milan. I decided to travel by way of Milan, thinking I would have time later to
go to Turin, Pavese's true city, the city where he lived for
most of his life and where, in 1950, he decided to die. In
the end I didn't go to Turin and I almost didn't make it to
Santo Stefano, since I came close to missing every one
of my many connections. I followed the trip nervously
on an oversized map I'd bought of the region, so that
my fear of missing trains had to contend with my dread
of elbowing fellow travellers every time I opened that
damned map.

II.

No sooner do I arrive than I meet Anka and Alina, two
Romanian sisters who wait tables at the restaurant close
to the station. Alina has lived here for three years with
her boyfriend, a native of the town. She doesn't speak
English, so I communicate with Anka, who comes to
Santo Stefano every summer to see her sister and to
work. Anka hasn't been to any other cities in Italy. I ask
her if she gets bored and she tells me yes, because almost no one here speaks English, much less Romanian
(and many of them still speak Piedmontese). 'There's a

Chilean in the village,' she tells me. 'You should meet him.' I answer that I'm not here to look for Chileans, I came to see the house where Cesare Pavese was born. 'But the Chilean might like to meet you,' she says. I say, to be polite, that I would like to meet him as well.

Anka recommends Il Borgo Vecchio, a reasonable bed and breakfast on via Marconi, very close to the town centre. They take me there in their car; I ride in the back seat, where I keep three teddy bears company. I ask Anka if Alina and her boyfriend have children. Anka tells me they don't, but that Alina's boyfriend is just like a child. Then she translates the conversation for her sister and they don't stop laughing for the rest of the ride.

III.

This is not a trip someone from the country of Neruda should take. We grew up in the cult of the happy poet, we grew up with the idea that a poet is someone who lets metaphors fly at the least provocation, who accumulates houses and women and devotes his life to decorating them (the houses and the women). We grew up thinking that poets collect – in addition to houses and women – figureheads of ships and five-litre bottles of Chivas. To us, literary tourism was for gringos or the Japanese, people who pay money to be wowed with marvellous stories.

Fortunately, there's none of that in Santo Stefano Belbo, a town that makes its living from vineyards and enjoys a stability that looks very much like boredom. In Santo Stefano the children learn from a very young age that a great writer was born in this town, and that he was never happy. The children of this town learn the word *suicide* at a very early age. The children know ahead of time that, in this town, as Pavese said, *lavorare stanca:* labour is hard.

The bed and breakfast is comfortable. The room costs forty euros, nothing compared to Milan. The family lives downstairs, Monica and Gabriel and their children: a nine year-old girl and a four-year-old boy who don't say hello to me, but who smile as though holding back their hellos. Gabriel has a wine shop that operates across the street from the hostel. He knows English, unlike Monica, who nevertheless talks and talks with the absolute confidence that we will understand each other in the end. The key word is *Pavese*. The only word that she says and I understand is *Pavese*.

Only now do I fully take in the landscape. A tranquil green lingers in the eyes and it seems I can take everything in with just one long look: the valley, the hill, the church, the ruins of a medieval tower. I search for the setting of *The Moon and the Bonfires*. I adjust the image to position the Belbo River and the road to Canelli, which is the novel's vanishing point, the corner where the world begins.

Then I let Monica bring me to the Centre for Cesare Pavese Studies, where I see the hundredth anniversary commemorative exhibition, which basically consists of a display of first editions. A series of discrete circles on the ground mark the route that goes from the Centre to Pavese's birth house. It's Wednesday and the house is only open on the weekends, but it's possible to visit it tomorrow if we get in touch with the person in charge. In the meantime I get in a visit to Pavese's grave, situated in the place of honour at the entrance to the cemetery.

Just as going back to Pavese's diary has been disappointing – I'd reread *This Business of Living* on the plane and I couldn't understand why I used to like it so much – visiting the village that serves as the setting of *The Moon and the Bonfires* brings on a complex emotion. Pavese interrogated that landscape with truthful questions, impelled by the vertigo of someone searching for memories within his memories. I gradually recognize the terrain I'm walking on while I think of some verses of 'South Seas', and about the poem 'Agony', which isn't Pavese's best but is the one I like the most: 'The mornings I had at twenty are now far: away. / And tomorrow, twenty-one: tomorrow I'll go out in tile streets; / I remember every stone, and the layers of the sky.' And as I walk, I recover the Pavese I prefer, precisely the one of *The Moon and the Bonfires*: 'You need a village, if only for the pleasure of leaving it,' I recite from memory. 'Your own village means that you're not alone, that you know there's something of you in the people and the plants and the soil, that even when you are not there it waits to welcome you.'

Before going to sleep, I compare landscapes like a person looking for the differences between identical pictures. For a moment I think I will stay up all night imagining that world, measuring those memories that belong to someone else, but the truth is that very soon, sleep overtakes me.

IV.

I take pictures, a lot of pictures. There is one I especially like, where Pavese's portrait is displayed in the window of a children's shoe store. There are allusions, drawings, graffiti related to him everywhere: Santo Stefano Belbo pays tribute to the poet, and there is beauty in the effort. But Pavese's hundredth birthday does not provoke shrillness. He was not such an appealing character as Neruda. Thank goodness.

To Pavese, Santo Stefano is the place of origins and dreaming, the theatre of childhood. 'Modern art is a return to infancy,' he says in his diary. 'Its perennial theme is the discovery of things, a discovery that can come about, in its purest form, only in the memory of infancy.' His thinking is close to Charles Baudelaire's: the artist as convalescent, who comes back from death to observe everything as if for the first time. Pavese takes it further: 'In art a thing can be well expressed only when it has been absorbed with an open mind. All that is left for artists to do is to go back and seek inspiration from the period when they were not yet artists, and that period is infancy.' Pavese idealized his native village, but he did so by turning it into an ambiguous territory. The character in *The Moon and the Bonfires* who comes home after living in the United States and making his fortune, returns to a place both loved and abhorred.

I'm sure that foreigners come to Santo Stefano, like me, just to see Pavese's birthplace, which turns out to be a fairly uninspiring house. 'The poet was born in this bed,' the guide tells me, and there's nothing for it but to imagine little Cesare crying like the damned. There is also a gallery crammed full of drawings that aren't at all good, hung one next to the other in order of arrival. The guide tells me these are the winning works in an annual contest held in the writer's honour. I think about how these walls crammed full of first places and honourable mentions once displayed, in their day, a welcoming bareness. But the disarray of the homage, maybe, is better.

According to Italo Calvino, the area of Langhe in the Piedmont was famous not only for its wines and truffles, but also for the desperation of the families who lived there. Calvino was thinking, surely, of the brutal dénouement in *The Moon and the Bonfires*, which I'm not going to give away here. I search, absurdly, for signs of desperation in this world of people walking slowly home from work.

I receive Anka's message: 'At eight, in the Fiorina bar, you'll meet the Chilean,' she's written on a piece of Hello Kitty stationery. Suddenly the realization hits me that it is, precisely, 18 September, Chile's national holiday. I imagine he will be glad to celebrate with a compatriot. I buy a CD and copy onto it all the Chilean music I have on my computer. But Luis, the Chilean, turns out to be a Peruvian from Arequipa. I give him the CD anyway. Luis is thirty-five years old, has lived in Italy for six years, and four years ago took up residence in Santo Stefano. He works in a water pump factory. 'I've never read Pavese,' he tells me suddenly, apropos of nothing: 'A man's got enough with his own troubles,' he adds, and he is quite right.

I talk to some of Luis's friends. Fabio, twenty-six years old, is the friendliest. We speak slowly and manage to understand each other. He doesn't like to read, he says, but like every Santo-Stefanian worth his salt he knows Pavese's work well. 'I like him because he talks about this town,' he says. 'But, deep down, I don't like him,' he corrects himself, as if thinking out loud, as if deciding on it then: 'No, I don't like Pavese.'

'I don't like the Chilean, Neruda, either,' I answer.

'I know several of Pavese's poems by heart,' says Fabio, laughing.

'I know some of Neruda's, too,' I tell him, and we laugh, and now I have a friend with whom to drink more Nebbiolo.

V.

In the poem 'The Suicide's Room', Wisława Szymborska evokes the bewilderment of friends confronting the suicide a man of who leaves behind, by way of explanation, just an empty envelope propped up against a glass.

206

Cesare Pavese, on the other hand, wrote a very long suicide note over the course of fifteen years, which ever since then we have read as a masterwork. Over the four hundred pages of *This Business of Living*, Pavese cultivates the idea of suicide as if it were a goal or a requirement or a sacrament, until finally it becomes difficult to moderate the caricature. This is not Wisława Szymborska's enigmatic friend, nor the suicidal man in a poem by Borges who says 'I bequeath nothingness to no one'. On the contrary, Pavese is aware of his legacy: he knows he leaves behind an important, accomplished body of work, he knows he has written high poetry, he knows that his novels will bear the passage of time with decorum. He had no reasons to take his own life, but he took on the task of inventing them, of making them real. *This Business of Living* is a record of theories and plans, of diatribes and digressions, but as you read there's no doubt that what prevails is the recounting of morbid thoughts, almost always extreme and at times fairly ridiculous, the thoughts of an aged youth who little by little is becoming an immature old man. Maybe you have to be like that youth or like that old man in order to appreciate Pavese's diary to the fullest extent. Maybe you have to be suicidal in order to read *This Business of Living*. But it's not necessary to be suicidal in order to enjoy books like *The Moon and the Bonfires*, *The Beach*, *Hard Labour*, or *Death Will Come and Will Wear Your Eyes*.

The greatest virtue of *This Business of Living* is that it gives clues to Pavese's work: if we took out the references to his love life, we'd be left with a slim and excellent book. It seems to me now that there are many unnecessary pages in the book: his impressions about women, for example, don't match up with the truthful or at least realistic understanding of the feminine in *The Moon and the Bonfires, Among Women Only* or in some of his poems. At times Pavese is barely witty, and rather vulgar: 'No woman marries for money; they are all clever enough, before marrying a millionaire, to fall in love with him first.' His misogyny is frequently rudimentary: 'It happens to all men in their lives that they encounter a pig. It happens to very few that they meet a loving and decent woman. Of every hundred, ninety-nine are pigs.'

Funnier and darker is the humour in a passage where he comments on the saying about one nail driving out another: for women it's all very simple, he says, since they need only find a new nail, but men are doomed to have only the one they were born with. I don't know if there is humour, on the other hand, in these phrases: 'Prostitutes work for money. But what woman gives herself unless she has calculated it first?' The following joke, in any case, strikes me as very good: 'Women are an enemy race, like the Germans.'

It's true that I'm committing an injustice by depicting Pavese as a precursor to stand-up comedy, but to disparage him is to continue the game that he himself proposed. Another brief or not-so-brief book that could come from *This Business of Living* has to do with Pavese's literary self-flagellation. At first, understandably, he doubts his own writing: he complains about his language, his world, his place in society, he disowns his poems, wants to rewrite or not to have written them at all. He wants to experience the pleasure of refusal, of starting, always, from zero: 'I simplified the world into a banal gallery depicting acts of strength and pleasure. In these pages there is the spectacle of life, not life itself. I must begin all over again.' It is not a casual observation, because it contains an ethics: the artist is forever an amateur whose successes threaten the progress of the work.

But he complains so much that listening to him at times becomes unbearable. Soon after his initial complaints, Pavese has constructed an immense body of work that gives him real satisfaction, one that allows him to be someone very much like who he always wanted to be. But now he complains all the same and a bit more: 'They tell you: 'You are forty years old and have made your name; you are the best of your generation and will go down in history; you are exceptional, authentic. ... Did you dream of anything else, at twenty?' The answer is, in a way, moving: 'I wanted to go on, take it further, absorb another generation, become everlasting, like a hill.'

VI.

Pavese was a good friend, says Natalia Ginzburg, because friendship came to him naturally, without complications: 'He had a cautious, reserved way of shaking hands: a few fingers were extended and withdrawn; a secretive, parsimonious way of taking his tobacco from its pouch and filling his pipe; and if he knew that we needed money he had a sudden, abrupt way of giving it to us; so sudden and abrupt he'd leave us open-mouthed.' In a passage of *Family Lexicon*, and in a brief and beautiful essay in that brief and beautiful book called *The Little Virtues*, Natalia Ginzburg recalls the years when she and her first husband worked with Pavese at Einaudi – difficult times that the poet had trouble settling into: 'At times he was very unhappy, but for a long time we thought that he would be cured of this unhappiness when he decided to become an adult; his sadness seemed like that of a boy – the voluptuous, heedless melancholy of a boy who has not yet got his feet on the ground and who lives in the sterile, solitary world of dreams.'

Natalia Ginzburg's opinions are well-rounded and

precise: 'The mistakes Pavese made were more serious than ours. Ours were the products of impulse, imprudence, stupidity and honesty. His, on the other hand, were born of foresight, cleverness, calculation and intelligence.' And then she notes that Pavese's main virtue as a friend was his irony, but that when the time came to write or to love he came down with a sudden attack of seriousness. The observation is crucial and, to tell the truth, it has hovered persistently over my rereading of Pavese: 'Sometimes, when I think of him now, it's his irony that I most remember and I cry, because it doesn't exist anymore: there is no trace of it in his books, and one can only find it in the lightning flash of that wicked smile of his.' To say of a friend that there is no irony in his books is saying a lot. For long passages of *This Business of Living*, in effect, the humour is limited to injections of sarcasm or mere wallops of naïveté.

'My growing antipathy for Natalia Ginzburg,' notes Pavese in 1946, 'is due to the fact that she takes for *granted*, with a spontaneity also granted, too many things in nature and life. Her heart is always in her hand – childbirth, monster, little old ladies. Ever since Benedetto Rognetta discovered that Natalia is sincere and primitive, there's just no way to live.' Friendship allows for these nuances, and Ginzburg responds in her cutting, delicate way: 'We saw all too clearly the absurd convolutions of the thoughts in which he imprisoned his simple nature; we wanted to teach him something too – how to live in a more elementary, less suffocating way. But we were never able to teach him anything, because as soon as we tried to set out our arguments he would lift his hand and say that he was already well aware of all that.'

I should state here that I stand with the sincere and the primitive, not with the know-it-all. Because without a doubt, Pavese was a know-it-all. For that very reason, his soliloquy becomes maddening. What he knew most of all, in any case, was that he suffered immensely: 'Perhaps this is my real special quality, not genius, not goodness, not anything else. To be so obsessed by this feeling that not a single cell in my whole body is unaffected.' Maybe he secretly agreed with his friend Natalia. I think of this fragment from his diary, which perhaps gives the key to Pavese's suffering: 'The man who cannot live charitably, sharing other men's pain, is punished by feeling his own with intolerable anguish. Pain is rendered acceptable only by raising it to the level of our common destiny and sympathizing with other sufferers.'

VII.

Something's gone awry with this essay. My intention was to remember, in his birthplace, a writer I admire, and it's clear that my admiration has waned. I talk it over by phone with a friend who has never liked Pavese. 'Maybe the first time you read *This Business of Living*,' she says, 'you wanted to commit suicide. All literature students want to commit suicide,' she says, and I laugh, but right away I answer, with Pavesian seriousness, that no, I never wanted to commit suicide. Maybe back then, at twenty, I was impressed with his way of expressing turmoil, his precise description of a suffering that seemed enormous and that, even so, couldn't compete with the possibility of depicting it. It's odd, I think now: Pavese struggles with language, he constructs an Italian of his own, or a new one; he validates the words of the tribe and the problems of his time. He doesn't stick to formulas, he doesn't trust in proclamations or false atavisms. He is, in that way, the perfect writer. But in another sense he is a poor guy longing to put his small wounds on display. I wonder if it was necessary to know so much about Pavese. I wonder if it truly mattered to anyone to know about his impotence, his premature ejaculations and his masturbations. I don't think so.

Pavese used to reread and rewrite his diary, to bury some hurried observation he'd made, or, more often, to ratchet up an intensity that was already quite high. In *This Business of Living*, the many self-references and the use of the second person constitute his rhetorical strategies. The second person reprimands, humiliates, but sometimes urges fortitude: 'Courage, Pavese. Take courage.' The effect never struck me as essential: any one of those fragments would work better in the first person. More than complexity of self, the second person conveys the difficulty of the division, and it always comes off as sensationalist: 'You also have the gift of fertility. You are master of yourself, of your fate. You are as famous as any man can be who does not seek to be so. Yet all of that will come to an end.' Some parts, though, are remarkable: 'You remember people's voices better than their faces. There is something indicative, spontaneous, about a voice. Given the face, you do not think of the voice; given the voice – by no means negligible – you try to envisage the person and look forward to seeing the face.'

VIII.
I reread some pages and I quickly come to appreciate him again: once again, I like Pavese.

IX.
'We only admire those landscapes that we have already admired,' he says in his diary. I wonder if Santo Stefano

Belbo has changed much over these decades. I'm sure it has. But I like to think Pavese would discern a subtle permanence.

As I wait for the train that will take me back to Milan, I reread some passages of *The Moon and the Bonfires*. The town has moved past the violence that Pavese depicts, the senselessness of a life tied to the earth. I imagine the bonfires on the hill, I remember Nuto and the lame child in the novel; I try to calibrate the distance Pavese avails himself of in order to construct that slight, dark book.

Did I like Santo Stefano Belbo? I think so, I think I liked it, or I've liked knowing that Pavese liked it. For him, the attraction carried with it, always, an implicit zone of repudiation, and this is also what has happened to me: I've hated Pavese's diary – hated the diary he loved – and I've loved his other books. I don't reach a conclusion, or I do, but it looks too much like where I started: in *The Moon and the Bonfires*, Pavese said everything he had to say. The rest, his life, is one long marginal note, nothing more than the long note to accompany a delayed suicide.

I'm still at the station. I got here too early. I decide not to look at the landscape any more, to concentrate on the book. I read: 'It was Nuto who told me that you can get anywhere by train, and that when the tracks end, the ports begin, that ships have schedules, that everything in the world is a web of routes and ports, a schedule of people who travel, who make and unmake, and everywhere you go there are capable people and there are foolish people.'

'The world is full of people who travel, who make and unmake,' I repeat out loud, as a kind of strange joke, just before I get on the train.

November 2008

213

THE TIME OF NATALIA GINZBURG

The discovery of a great writer somehow changes everything we knew or thought we knew: her books were always right there waiting for us, and we feel a little dumb for being so late to meet them. 'Occasionally I come across a book which I feel has been written especially for me and for me only,' says W. H. Auden, who immediately confesses to a comical reluctance to share: 'Like a jealous lover I don't want anybody else to hear of it.'

That is what happened to me ten years ago, when I discovered Natalia Ginzburg: I debated between writing about her immediately or keeping quiet. I let it slip very soon, of course: I wrote a short column, joyfully contaminated by admiration, in which I made the exaggerated claim that the only thing I had done in recent months was read Natalia Ginzburg. I could say something similar now: the only thing I have done over these ten years has been reading Natalia Ginzburg.

It's a beautiful lie, and a big one, because so far the only Natalia Ginzburg books I have read are the dozen that have been translated into Spanish. Specifically, into the Spanish of Spain, a language that Latin American readers understand more or less well, but whose distance – whose foreignness – is almost impossible for us to ignore. On top of my wish to have read Natalia Ginzburg sooner, I also want to know Italian. Not to learn it, but to know it now, all of a sudden. It's not so easy.

Family Lexicon is the story of a Jewish and anti-fascist family that lives through horror and only partly survives it. But Natalia Ginzburg doesn't emphasize the larger story, and hers is not the testimony of an era: she writes with precision and fluidity, with genuine love for people and words. That's why she is able to depict her time: because she brings us close to her father's grousing, her mother's witticisms, the lost language of her community. She doesn't idealize; on the contrary, she plays down the drama: she respects the ruptures, the fissures, she seeks out nuances through memory and not literature, but at the same time she understands literature to be the only form of expression.

'I have written only what I remember,' the author notes as a kind of apology for the possible gaps in *Family Lexicon*, which can be read as a memoir or as a novel written by someone who chose not to change names or events: 'Every time that I have found myself inventing something in accordance with my old habits as a novelist, I have felt impelled at once to destroy it,' she says. But she also expresses the desire for her book to be received as a novel, 'without asking either more or less of it than what a novel can give.'

This last phrase is key, since it marks the friendly but secretly categorical rejection of paternalistic or condescending gazes. There are innumerable novels and movies that seek to gain legitimacy through the formula 'based on a true story,' but Natalia Ginzburg prefers, from the reader, a valuation that transcends the merely referential. 'Only the actus purus of remembrance itself, not the author or the plot, constitutes the unity of the text,' says Walter Benjamin about *In Search of Lost Time*, and the same could be said of a singularly Proustian work like *Family Lexicon*. Ginzburg also appeals to what Benjamin beautifully calls the 'legality of memory,' which of course is internal, intransferrable, impossible to verify: only the one who remembers can access that 'legality.'

Towards the beginning of *Family Lexicon*, Ginzburg

contrasts her father's way of telling stories ('my father told them badly and made a mess of them by breaking in with snorts of laughter') with her mother's narrative habits: 'Turning to one of us at the table she would begin a story. Whether it was about my father's family or her own, she became radiant with pleasure, and it always seemed as if she were telling that story for the first time to ears that had never heard it.'

If someone – usually the father – complained that they had already heard that story many times, the mother turned to another person and went on with the story in a low voice. I like that detail a lot. When someone repeats a story we presume they don't remember that they've already told it, but often we repeat stories consciously, because we are unable to repress the desire, the joy of telling them again.

That is at the centre of *Family Lexicon*: the joy of telling. The official story tends to dismiss, naturally, what seems beside the point or superfluous. Natalia Ginzburg is not afraid of seeming naive or unserious and even frivolous; she is especially not afraid, not even a little, of humour. 'We used to have heated discussions at home about whether people were handsome or ugly,' says the writer, and right away she illustrates the point in this banal way, totally recognizable and irresponsible: 'We would argue about whether a certain Signora Gilda, governess to some friends of ours, was pretty or not. My brothers maintained that she was ugly and had a kind of dog-like snout, but my mother said she was extraordinarily beautiful.'

The great originality of *Family Lexicon* lies in its tremendous simplicity. Anyone could start with the exercise of remembering the repeated phrases of their own family and end up writing a book like this one. Imitating it (or 'applying it' to one's own life) is, in fact, a perfect writing device: put phrases together, contextualize them minimally, and then go on telling those stories. Almost anyone who follows that procedure with any constancy would end up writing a book. A very different one from *Family Lexicon*, of course, but in another sense very similar.

Natalia Ginzburg's originality lies, as well, in her refusal to look for the new in places far removed from the very nature of experience. She knew, more than anyone else, that it was impossible not to be original. That any family, any person looked at from up close reveals their singular condition. Or doesn't reveal it, but also doesn't deny it: they show their opacity, their impossible recesses, the evidence of their secret. One of those phrases or words 'would make us recognize each other, in the darkness of a cave or among a million people,' says the narrator in explanation of her project. She does it, of course, with utter clarity, beautifully: 'These phrases are our Latin, the vocabulary of our days gone by, our Egyptian hieroglyphics or Babylonian symbols. They are the evidence of a vital nucleus which has ceased to exist, but which survives in its texts salvaged from the fury of the waters and the corrosion of time.'

Natalia Ginzburg did not want to write the novel she'd been fated to write by the bloody history of the twentieth century: a survivor, a victim as she seemed to be, condemned to the literal denunciation of horror, to detailed testimonial that was emphatic and merely documentarian. She should have spoken from resentment and pain, which of course exist, persist throughout this novel, but they never come to block the course of the narration, the channelling of memory.

The result is that, for most of the story's telling, the

narrator is absent: she is the one who remembers, the one who looks, and of course the one who tells the story, but her active role is rather scarce or tacit, especially if one compares this book with the autobiographical norm. 'I had not yet decided whether to spend my life studying beetles, chemistry, and botany, or whether I would paint pictures or write novels,' she says suddenly in reference the two possible worlds she is facing, and her intrusion almost surprises us, so discreet had she been up to then.

Natalia Ginzburg's childhood dream was to win the Fracchia Prize, after she'd heard it was an award for writers. But she didn't find her style in the virtuosic imitation of the poems in fashion, but rather, as she relates in one of the best essays of *The Little Virtues*, in her family's after-dinner conversation: her sentences had to always be direct and short, because her older brothers lost patience and shushed her. Natalia Ginzburg wrote in order to participate in those conversations, not to close them. *Family Lexicon* is, in fact – it's worth repeating – a family autobiography: a self-portrait in the corner of the painting, with the small crowd of parents and siblings and friends and neighbours in the fore. The self that appears is never alone and always, rather than describing herself, wants to talk about others.

Every time she speaks of pain, the author seems to be telling us that others suffered much more than she did. This does not mean, of course, that she sweetens the facts or denies her own suffering; with lucidity and an ironclad bravery, Natalia Ginzburg shows us her characters when they were neither heroes nor villains, when they were fallible, when it was possible to love them less. And that's why we love them more.

There are books that provoke in their readers the desire to write, and others that block that desire instead.

Family Lexicon belongs, without a doubt, to the former group. It is impossible to read it without imagining that other book of our own that does not yet exist but that we must, out of pure gratitude, write.

November 2017

'In the mansion called literature, I would have the eaves deep and the walls dark, I would push back into the shadows the things that come forward too clearly, I would strip away the useless decoration,' writes Junichiro Tanizaki at the end of *In Praise of Shadows*, a beautiful essay published in Spanish by Editions Siruela some years ago. The same house has now published *The Reed Cutter* and *Captain Shigemoto's Mother*, among other Tanizaki novels, and they have announced – on a joyful sticker on the covers – that they will be gradually translating his complete works. That is good news, but there is also some bad, or at least not as good: in these first offerings, the publisher has opted to translate from the English, which is nothing new, but, by now, is just bad form. The only reason for this decision is monetary, but Siruela's books are expensive enough that the reader can also support the costs involved in a first-hand translation.

Perhaps what happens with Tanizaki is what has occurred, for example, with Kawabata, whom we also read in translations of translations, which are sometimes then handed off to writers who do the best they can to recreate the style, or what they think was the original style. These translations, at times, are astonishing exercises, as it can't be easy to imitate a prose that one has never really read. So in a way we are imitating, now, the imitators: we imagine the novels of the Japanese in the same way that the Japanese, in the past, admired the Western custom of writing novels. While there are those who affirm that the origin of the modern novel lies in *The Story of Genji* or that *The Pillow Book* can be read as a novel, those judgments call for an argument that would bore us all (especially Sei Shōnagon, the restless and delicious author of *The Pillow Book*). No argument, certainly, could paper over the enthusiasm of Japanese fiction writers for the nineteenth-century European novel, which for them was a desirable foreign language; a language they immediately learned to speak and to which they soon added their own shades.

Japanese writers perhaps erased the unnecessary in the Western novel as a genre: perhaps that's why, on reviewing their books, critics inevitably speak of 'precision' or 'fineness' and even 'limpidity', as Borges says of Akutagawa. I don't know if it's worthwhile to put Akutagawa alongside Mishima, Tanizaki with Kobo Abe, or Kenzaburo Oé with his famous enemy Haruki Murakami, since our pilgrim gaze would just find easy similarities or evident differences. They are joined, of course, by the label of 'untranslatable'; we read them – the traditional writers and the westernized ones – from an irredeemable and prolonged Orientalism, but now without guilt, perhaps even proud of the Japanesery.

There is, of course, precision, delicacy, and 'limpidity' in these two novels by Tanizaki. The narrator of *Capitan Shigemoto's Mother* draws on several sources from Japanese tradition in order to reconstruct the story of a woman whose name is unknown: we only know that she was born around the year 884 and that she was the granddaughter of the poet Ariwara Narihira, wife of old man Kunitsune and later of the minister of the Left, as well as the lover of Heiju.

The crucial moment comes when, after an abundant session of sake, Kunitsune takes the famous Japanese courtesy a bit too far: he gives the minister as a gift his own wife, his most prized possession. He is a little drunk, but he is also motivated by the sad evidence that he can no longer satisfy her. The woman goes to live with the minister and abandons little Shigemoto, whom she sees very little and in secret during the following years.

Little by little the tale develops its centre, like a photograph taking its time to dry: at first it seems to be a novel about seduction, and later one about power, guilt, impotence, or abandonment. None of these themes would suffice, however, to fully summarize the novel. The cascade of refined feelings leads up to the striking final scenes, when Shigemoto reunites with his mother.

The Reed Cutter, meanwhile, shows similar concerns: patiently, tidily, the narrator constructs the frame, then cedes the voice to a pilgrim who, in the distracted tone of one remembering childhood anecdotes, recounts a twisted love triangle. The narrator dignifies the story until we are convinced that perversity and selfishness are, ultimately, incomprehensible forms of nobility. The classical context serves Tanizaki to emphasize that need for impurity, for shadows, that he defended. The narrator comments on distant texts and does not need to shout to bring them closer, to contrast them with the present.

In Tanizaki's books, the body of the other is always a difficult mystery that at times summons condemnation, but never salvation. I'm thinking of the lovers in *The Key*, who carry out strange, profound investigations that are at times brutal, and also the protagonist couple who, in *Some Prefer Nettles*, draw out the decision to separate to the point of implausibility. Those two novels – Tanizaki's most well-known, until now, in Spanish – speak of a culture that is contaminated – infected – by the West, which Tanizaki observes with frank disenchantment. *Capitan Shigemoto's Mother* and *The Reed Cutter* are, on the other hand, more 'Japanese' novels, so to speak, in that the author insists, with a lyrical force that is nearly always dazzling, on recreating that lost world of remote rooms, half-lit.

'It's not necessary to have read Tanizaki,' says Yukio Mishima in a letter, 'to know that for him, Japan has always been a flatland at the foot of the Asian continent surrounded by the immensity of night.' I like that quote, since it reveals to what point we are foreign to the subjects and problems of a literature that, in any case, we feel at times to be disturbingly near.

February 2009

LITERATURE OF THE CHILDREN

I.

The daughter is named Pilar and the father José Donoso. The father was a great writer and maybe the daughter once thought about writing a book as well, but with the passing of the years that thought gradually became a kind of condemnation. What does one do with a father's books? Simply read them, accept them? The mere existence of those novels is a call to write one's own story; the father has lived numerously, he has multiplied himself in narrators and in characters; he has shared the experiences that others keep under lock and key, put too few coats of paint over the private life. It is necessary to read those books, and it's also necessary to stop reading them. To forget them or fill them with notes in the margins. Edit them, above all: correct them with love and distance.

In addition to his novels, José Donoso wrote a diary where he recorded, in great detail, the last thirty years of his life. The sixty-something notebooks of the diary were stored at a university and subjected to a period that seemed prudent: it would be possible to consult them fifteen years after the author's death. The liberation of those archives has awakened one or another skirmish due to fragments where the author speaks badly of some of his colleagues. But that matters very little if we imagine the scene of the daughter reading that long story that is someone else's, but also her own. To use a phrase from a melodrama: there are too many memories.

Pilar Donoso has finally published *Correr el tupido telo* [Draw a Thick Curtain], the book that sooner or later she had to write, and that in large part constitutes a response to the uncomfortable notebooks in which her father depicted her, for example, like this: 'The problem of little Pilar continues and intensifies. She has us total- ly crucified with her hatred, hatred for herself, hatred of the world, her husband and her daughters. At times I fear a murder, she is so violent and perverse.' Donoso portrays his daughter as if describing a difficult char- acter. Sometimes he says she is big-nosed, ugly, and is 'mentally limited,' and he attributes these defects to the fact that she was adopted. Other times he confesses that she is 'the being I have most loved in life'. He knew his daughter would read the notebooks, but guilt did not stop him in his decision to turn them over for fu- ture study. 'He protected himself in that future that was distant enough for him, but not for me and mine,' Pilar Donoso says now, determined to confront those memo- ries, prepared to write the literature of the children.

For a writer like José Donoso it must have been useful to forget fiction for a while and write down his thoughts without thinking much about readers. The writing of in- timate diaries tends to be associated with getting things off one's chest and it's unfair, because of that, to ask for truth or accountability in these notebooks. That he wanted to make them public is another matter. It's said that he sold them because he needed money, and maybe that's partly true, but in the fragments we've read there is evidence enough that he even fantasized about the transcendence of his notebooks: 'This page – it's won- derful and terrible to think about it – will outlive me in the climate-controlled, atom bomb-proof basements, right next to the original Lewis Carroll.'

Should Donoso have kept those pages to himself, burned them, published them? I don't know. I don't re- ally know what I think about this story. For the moment, Pilar Donoso's book interests me much more that her father's novels. I say it without irony: those of us who were born at the start of the dictatorship grew up searching for and telling the stories of our parents, and it took us too long to understand that we also had our own stories. Perhaps that's why I find the image so beautiful: a woman reading her father's notebooks and writing in the margins, finally, the notes for a story of her own.

II.

I've read the book *My Mother in Memory*, by Richard Ford, several times, and I'm always struck by the simplicity, the clarity of the gesture: without getting too caught up in conjectures, the writer puts his memories in chronological order, trusting in his memory and also, in a way, in his forgetting, since there is much that he doesn't remember or never knew about his mother's life.

Richard Ford was the only, late-coming son of a well-to-do couple. His father worked as a salesman and was only at home on weekends, and he died when Ford was sixteen years old ('and up to that moment it had never occurred to me to ask him anything'). So his mother, Edna Akin, was the permanent presence in the writer's life. The relationship is always free-flowing, although neither Edna nor her son are very given to expressing their emotions.

The tone Albert Cohen strikes in *Book of my Mother* is quite different: the biographical tale produces a turbulent reflection on the ways of expressing pain. Cohen is looking at himself on the page, trying to write well, managing to move the reader, perhaps fascinated by the will to narrate, and his guilt takes him to uncertain zones, recriminations, unforeseen tensions: suddenly the language seems to speak on its own, and the words explode on the page. It's a very beautiful book, although

I prefer Ford's, maybe because – to put it absurdly – I like Ford's mother more than Cohen's.

I also very much like *Violeta se fue a los cielos* [Violeta Went to Heaven] the book that Ángel Parra published a couple of years ago to pay tribute to the complicated genius who was his mother. With the ease of a long conversation, the son reconstructs the world that he learned about hand-in-hand with Violeta Parra, and also on his own, on valuable and daring first adventures. Every once in a while the author apologizes for the jumps and the holes in his story, since he moves forward capriciously, as though speaking aloud, as though discovering along the way what he wants to say. Those hesitations lend the narration an enormous warmth.

We meet, then, the mother who kept close watch over the freedom she gave her children, whom she turned into her accomplices, witnesses and protagonists of a scene built through force of will. We see her punishing the 'incursions' into her purse, rejecting cups of tea because 'the water didn't boil and the tea gets a white foam that I can't stand' and happily greeting the sunny mornings: 'Good morning, day; good morning, sun.' We see her confronting pain, frustration, and poverty, searching and researching until she finds a music, a world that was there but that no one had seen.

It must be hard to write about one's mother without making literature, since sometimes the memories are really inventions blessed by the passing of the years. In *Violeta Went to Heaven*, however, Ángel Parra resists 'novelizing' his mother's life, and at the end of the book she is still the complicated, passionate, fun, and wise woman that the myths depict; the warrior woman who suddenly, inexplicably, stopped fighting; the woman who sang her sorrows until she could no longer write a lyric that would let her express what she felt.

'Our parents intimately link us,' says Richard Ford, 'to a thing we're not, forging a joined separateness and a useful mystery, so that even together with them we are also alone.' The thing that unites these books is the painful acceptance of that distance, and the joy of recovering the time when one's own life seemed to coincide fully with the mother's.

III.

'My father died four years ago, one October midday, in his two-room apartment where I live now,' says Mauro Libertella at the beginning of *Mi libro enterrado* [My Buried Book], and the image hovers over us as we read: every once in a while we remember that the son is writing in the same room where his father died, where his father once worked. For Argentine literature up to now, Libertella is Héctor and not Mauro, but I say this from outside, because I'm not Argentine and I only read Libertella recently. The truth is, I don't know if I read him before or after his death: Argentines don't use the perfect tense, and they always write 'published' instead of 'has published' in author bios, so I always think Argentine writers are dead. And since I know that I always think that, right away I think the opposite: that they're alive.

To a certain extent writing always fulfils a therapeutic purpose, but in this kind of case, naturally, that dimension is more visible. 'At times I still feel like my last name doesn't belong to me,' says the author, further on: 'Sometimes I see myself as a foreigner, a usurper of these ten latin letters.' I remember that poem in which Wislawa Szymborska speaks humorously about – or against – families of writers: 'My sister doesn't write poems. / And it's unlikely that she'll suddenly start writing poems. / She takes after her mother, who didn't write poems, / and also her father, who likewise didn't write poems.' As the son of Héctor Libertella and a brilliant poet like Tamara Kamenszain, Mauro was exposed from day one to the possibility of writing. Those of us who grew up in houses without books tend to idealize literary families. But how difficult it must be to follow one's parents like that—even if you contradict them, you accept them.

Héctor made a pile of discarded draft pages and Mauro would throw himself into them, to play while his father wrote: 'The detritus of your literature, the discarded and still-warm materials you threw to the floor and that gradually formed a pyramid of rewriting – they were my private playground,' he notes, with serene and fragile emotion. It is clear that Mauro isn't interested in exhibiting his pain. He shows it without putting it on display. This is a sober and very beautiful book, which can be interpreted neither as a settling of scores nor a paean. The father comes across as a rather erratic person, one who bears the definite problem of alcoholism (he would say 'melalcoholism'), but is always conspiratorial and generous. Readers of Libertella senior will realize that *My Buried Book* is in conversation, sometimes directly, with *La arquitectura del fantasma* (Architecture of the Ghost), the autobiography published days after his death. But those unfamiliar with the father's work can also fully enjoy this book, which invites us to reread Héctor and to await future books from Mauro.

'Etymologically, Libertella means "book for the earth,"' the father used to say; 'That is the book I water every day.' It seems Mauro wanted to call his book 'a book for the earth,' but the final title is also good, full of meaning. It's the kind of title that isn't convincing at first but that grows more beautiful as the reading progresses. It would be unfair to finish this review without mentioning honesty, even though no one knows anymore what that word means. And when it comes to describing this book other words also shine, in necessary, full, inevitable disarray: nobility and love.

IV.
A. M. Homes' characters are always on the verge of becoming caricatures, except that she observes them with severity and affection, sure as she is that the world cannot be divided between good and bad people. Perhaps that's why such an impression is left by *The Mistress's Daughter*, the book in which she tells of her late-in-coming encounter with her biological parents: Homes takes pains to get to know these characters who are so painfully real; she gives them numerous opportunities even while she resists, in a way, the obligatory limelight that telling this story supposes.

At the end of 1992, when she was 31, A. M. Homes learned that the woman who had given her up for adoption was looking for her. She had known since she was a child that she was adopted, and from time to time she'd made her parents uncomfortable with her questions, but the appearance of her biological mother condemns her to recapitulate. For Homes, in any case, the conclusion is clear from the start: 'I am an amalgam. I will always be something glued together, something slightly broken. It's not something I might recover from but something I must accept, to live with – with compassion.'

The parallel life, the life of fiction, has always been with her; it takes shape now in the figure of Ellen, a lonely and regretful woman who always wanted to meet her daughter. Later we meet Norman, the very involuntary father who vacillates between accepting his daughter and erasing her completely. The relationship between Homes and Ellen is agonized: the woman wants to get her daughter back, but deep down she wants to be the daughter herself. She asks for love at the top of her lungs, a love that the daughter can't and perhaps shouldn't give her.

Norman's attitude is the opposite. At first he seems open to building ties, but he doesn't want to cross his wife by making room for his lover's daughter. Towards the end, Homes dedicates an entire chapter to interrogating her father in the style of the best lawyers: imaginary questions posed with a new resentment toward that man who had made her build up hope. Now she is merciless: only now, in the book, do the words emerge that she couldn't say at the right moment, though maybe there never really was a right moment.

In 1998 Ellen dies, and her daughter packs up her belongings in boxes that later on she can't bring herself to open. For seven years, A. M. Homes lives with those boxes and with the idea of opening them ('giddy like a child playing the game of going through her mother's purse'), and once she does it, the dictatorship of signs catches her unawares. This daughter of two fathers and two mothers suddenly accepts that strange abundance: now she also wants to learn about the multiple grandparents and great-grandparents and so she throws herself into exhaustive genealogical research. But she doesn't enjoy it much: 'I want to learn about my history, but it is daunting to become aware of so many people's lives, and to understand that most of my relatives, if not all, are ignorant of my story and even of my existence.'

It's strange to think that while this book was happening

the author was writing those other excellent, dark, and funny books that we know her for. I am sure that more than once, A. M. Homes thought about putting off that violent tumble into the mirror. The story well lent itself, so to speak, to one of those tales that give way to a long share-out of hugs; bookshops are overflowing with that affirmational and instantaneous literature, written in order to shelve suffering once and for all. But A. M. Homes knows full well that the pain doesn't end on the last page. She wrote this book not as an ending, but in order to go on, and in that lies her enormous bravery.

V.

It can't be easy to translate Jamaica Kincaid's long tirades into Spanish, her unerring phrases that advance like a vibrating improvisation, though the author by no means improvises. Quite the contrary: every word seems to obey an imperious expressive necessity; each word accuses a long re-examined absence, one evoked many times before finding the way to articulate it.

We never know if her protagonists' feelings – the hatred, in particular, that they feel or claim to feel for almost all of the people around them – are deserved or not, because the narrator is not interested in justifying her affections or her actions. She simply expresses what she feels with precision. She hates bad people, of course; she hates those who abused her, who doomed her. But she also feels contempt, in a way, towards good people. At times she becomes unexpectedly compassionate or understanding, but more frequently she rebels against any established form of good judgement. She understands the world; she understands the violence she has been the target of, but she doesn't want to please anyone. She isn't writing in order to forgive, that much is clear.

My Brother and *Lucy* can be understood as autobiographies, although distinguishing between autobiography and fiction can be, in this case, arduous and misguided (and ultimately unnecessary). In *Lucy*, the protagonist has just left her country – the Caribbean island of Antigua, a British colony until 1967 – to work as an au pair. The experience is not a bad one: the bosses treat her well, while they also, in not very subtle and nearly always funny ways, try to civilize her. The protagonist knows she is condemned to alienation, but she does not withdraw from the pleasures of her new life or her new status, and much less does she want to go back home, among other reasons because she hates her mother: 'my whole upbringing had been devoted to preventing me from becoming a slut,' she says, and soon thereafter she complains that her mother was a saint but that she didn't want a saint – she wanted a mother. (this isn't a direct quote, but I should mention I can't find anything using the word 'saint' in the book)

Lucy is a beautiful and harsh book in which Jamaica Kincaid relates, in a way, the same story as in her other books: that of a woman who saves herself thanks to literature, although saving herself means sinking a little, or at least accepting that she cannot save others. That is the main theme of *My Brother*: from her first experiences as an immigrant, we jump to the moment when the writer is living in the United States, now become a significant figure in African American literature, in harmony with a culture that includes her, with a husband and some children who love her unconditionally.

This moment of calm and legitimization ends when she learns of her brother Devon's illness. Devon is an irresponsible Rastafari who contracts AIDS and has to confront the precarious health system in Antigua, the island he never left, unlike his sister, the writer who dodged her possible fate ('having ten children by ten different men'), to become a foreigner who has trouble understanding the English her mother and siblings speak. The writer travels, then, to help Devon, and she gets him the medicines that the local doctors don't even bother to prescribe, since their only expectation is that he will die soon.

The idea of that imminent death gives way to a sustained reflection on familial bonds. The protagonist recognizes, bravely, that generosity has its limits, that she cannot renounce her place. Her brother will die and she, sooner or later, will tell the story: 'I became a writer out of desperation,' she says, 'so when I first heard he was dying I was familiar with the act of saving myself: I would write about him.'

I noted earlier that Jamaica Kincaid writes fiction or non-fiction without getting too stuck on one or the other mould, or − better said − destabilizing that difference, adding shades to it. *The Autobiography of my Mother*, in fact, is a novel and not an autobiography, a conjectural and stunning tale in which Xuela, the protagonist, imagines the life of her mother, who died giving birth to her. To her, writing a book with that title is impossible: it possesses nothing more than vague signs, dreams, and an absence that she can only fill or try to fill with words.

At the beginning of the book, her father leaves Xuela in the care of his laundress, so that the little girl only sees him when he goes to drop off or pick up his clothes. This devastating excerpt, then, is as much a complaint as it is a strictly factual description: 'That I was a burden to him, I know; that his soiled clothes were a burden to him, I know; that he did not know how to take care of me by himself, or how to clean his own clothes himself,

I know.'

The displacements continue as the father assembles a new family that is utterly foreign to Xuela. She hates her stepmother and the feeling is mutual, and she refers to her sister as 'my father's daughter whom he had had with his wife who was not my mother.' And it is not only those bonds that are unsatisfactory; further on she alludes to her own husband as 'the man I worked for but did not hate and who at the same time was a man I slept with but did not love and whom I would eventually marry but still not love.'

Jamaica Kincaid describes the violence, the senselessness, the authoritarianism and the alienation from within, without even insinuating the vanishing point in a suffocating landscape. Her books are raw, excessive, and above all beautiful, because they obey the ancient and essential desire to grind away until one obtains a little beauty among the ruins.

VI.

It starts in Córdoba, Argentina, in 1964, and it ends several times:

After a long history of fights and reconciliations, Raúl and Clotilde decide to divorce, and they meet with their lawyers and with Jorge, one of their children. Everything seems to be going well, but suddenly the father goes for a whisky and comes back with a glass of acid that he throws into his wife's face. 'On burning her, he had not eliminated the flesh he had loved; he had sublimated her by destroying her, as happens with romantic ruins,' Jorge would write decades later. At the time, at a little over twenty years old, he feels a kind of painful relief on learning that his father has shot himself, and he takes on his mother's care: he goes with her during

235

the first months to periodic operations, and then travels with her to Milan, to attend to her in the process of her facial reconstruction.

The first ending to this story is only ostensible: the mother and her son return to Argentina to recover what they can of their lives. The doctor has done a magnificent job that, nevertheless, will require regular retouching. Clotilde gives the impression she is rehabilitated, she is being reborn. But soon thereafter, in 1978, she jumps out the window. This is the second ending.

The third ending is that of *El desierto y su semilla* [The Desert and its Seed], the book that Jorge Baron Biza published in 1998. Immediately before the phrase 'The End' we read the following sentence: 'It is reconciliation I am speaking of.' Then there is a note in which the author clarifies that his original name was Jorge Baron Biza, but that, each time his parents separated, his mother demanded his birth certificate be amended: 'My current name is Jorge Baron Sabattini. I don't know if Baron Biza should be considered my other last name, my patronym, my pseudonym, my professional name, or a challenge.'

Jorge Baron Biza accepts the challenge of 'continuing' Raúl Baron Biza, an excentric Cordoban, a contradictory figure in Argentine politics, and a writer, by the bye, of pornographic novels (in his last, the one he wrote before killing himself, he writes, Jorge reads: 'Why not deny the son begotten more out of curiosity than desire? What obligation to love the newborn? Let them bear their shame, and not I their forgiveness.') Everything in *The Desert and its Seed* is true except for the names (how long did the author spend on inventing, searching for his parents' names? Minutes? Months?): Raúl Baron Biza is named Arón Gageac, while Clotilde is, in the story, Eligia. For himself, Jorge chooses a less heroic or less tragic name: Mario. The novel was received in Argentina as a major work. Three years later, however, in September 2001, Jorge Baron Biza committed suicide.

The Desert and its Seed is a great novel, although to say it like that, in canonical mode, is a little absurd. Jorge Baron Biza wrote the book he was condemned to write – a novel and not an autobiography: we are witness not to the bare facts, but rather to the desire to tell a story that resists the telling. The narrator writes to understand, although he knows there will be no revelations, that at most he will be able to shine a little light on the past. The initial image persistently accompanies the reading: a destroyed face, a lipless smile, a gaze without eyelids, suspended in semi-vigilance. To write is to record, with naturalistic precision, the light falling on that face. But this is not the story of the face: it is the story of the eye that looks at the face.

Much of *The Desert and its Seed* recreates the time in Milan, which Mario spends observing the surgeons' delicate work, distracting his mother with light readings (boom novels and magazines he orders from Argentina), avoiding or accepting the possibly beautiful women who pass through the clinic – full of illusions, their noses bandaged. Above all, he spends his time drinking like mad in a neighboring bar where he meets Dina, a whore with whom he finds not love, but a sort of silent and bitter companionship.

The Desert and its Seed is also a skeptical tale about the struggles of the seventies, which according to the narrator were led by people who promised 'punishments or paradise,' and who left power 'with extinguished eyes that only lit up when they fantasized about their past times of glory.' The heroes of those days remind him, naturally, of his father and mother, who throughout the book are compared, tacitly and constantly, with Perón and Evita.

The Milan conversations are written in *'cocoliche'*, a mixture of Italian and Spanish spoken by immigrants in Argentina that Baron Biza now 'returns,' by way of vacillations or stutterings, to Italian. The narrator's gaze is always parodic and compassionate: it is difficult to describe that voice that knows itself to be strange and that keeps watch at all times over the story's precision, at the risk of deforming it. The novel fills up with impurities and tricks that are not surprising, that don't want to surprise: *this is literature*, the narrator seems to be saying between the lines, and there is a great deal of bitterness in that warning.

April 2008 – June 2013

III

WRAPPED TREES

The story of *Bonsai* is the long story of a short book. Nine years ago, one morning in 1998, I was reading a newspaper and came across the photograph of a tree wrapped in a sheer fabric. The image belonged to the series *Wrapped Trees*, by Christo & Jeanne-Claude, those artists who've spent decades travelling the world wrapping landscapes and national monuments. I remember that I wrote, in those days, a poem that wasn't very good that talked about wrapped, restricted trees. And then I came across bonsais, so similar in a way to Christo & Jeanne-Claude's trees, although stunted, by force, through the whims of pruning.

Writing is like taking care of a bonsai, I thought then, I think now: to write is to prune the branches until you make visible a form that was already there, lying in wait; to write is to illuminate language so the words say, for once, what we want to say; to write is to read an unwritten text.

I wanted to write – I wanted to read – a book that was called *Bonsai*, but I didn't know how: I only had the title and a handful of poems that grew and shrank with the passage of the months. The controversial beauty of bonsais led me to a scene or a story that I didn't want to tell, but rather only to evoke: the story of a man who, instead of writing – of living – chose to stay home watching a tree grow. That man wasn't me, of course, but rather a blurry character that I gazed at from a certain distance. In the spring of 2001, however, that distance shrank a bit, because two friends gave me a little elm tree ('so you'll write your book,' they told me), and I found myself suddenly converted into the character of a story I hadn't written yet. I cared for the bonsai as best I could:

242

I got manuals, consulted experts, and even, in a fit of paternal responsibility, subscribed to the Spanish magazine *Bonsai Today*. Soon after that I left to spend a year in Madrid. When I came back, the elm was completely dried out.

I don't remember the precise moment when *Bonsai* started to be (or seem like) a novel. I distrusted fiction; I especially distrusted my ability to tell a story, or that I even had, a story to tell. I didn't want to write a novel, but rather the summary of a novel. A bonsai of a novel. Borges' advice was to write as if composing the summary of a book that was already written. That's what I did, or what I tried to do: summarize the secondary scenes of a non-existent book. Instead of adding, I subtracted: I wrote ten lines and erased eight; I wrote ten pages and erased nine. Operating by subtraction, adding little or nothing, I arrived at the form of *Bonsai*.

I wrote the novel, finally, during the first months of the year 2005. Before I published it, I read it and liked it, although it was no longer the book I had wanted to read. Soon after that I started *The Private Lives of Trees*, a novel that in more ways than one is the inverse of *Bonsai*. But that's another story, I think. Walter Benjamin said that the art of telling stories is the art of knowing how to go on telling them. I don't know if I really understand the phrase, and now I feel I'm misquoting it, but it seems an opportune one to end on. Again: the art of telling stories is the art of knowing how to go on telling them.

Walter Benjamin said that storytelling is always the art of repeating stories. I don't know if I really understand the phrase, but it seems an opportune one to end on. Again: Storytelling is always the art of repeating stories.

August 2007

THE NOVEL I LOST

I never thought of *Bonsai* as 'movie material'. I never thought of the book that way, so when a director asked me for permission to adapt it I was really surprised and I didn't know what to say so I just turned him down. Later Cristián Jiménez asked me and again I refused, but this time I asked him to let me see his work. And it so happened that *Ilusiones ópticas* [Optical Illusions], his first film, moved me in a way nothing had in a long time. I was captivated by his way of seeing things, which I felt to be very different from my own. But it also felt, on another level, very close, familiar. Then I gave up playing the stubborn writer and I felt proud that someone like him appreciated my book.

I trusted instinctively and almost immediately in Cristián, and I decided that, whatever happened, in no case would I be the typical writer who resents his novel's adaptation. And so I decided that if I didn't like the film, I would just keep quiet. But I had a good feeling about it. I thought, above all, about the final scene of *Ilusiones ópticas*, the marvellous Paola Lattus and Iván Álvarez de Araya forehead to forehead. I won't give it away here, but to me that was one of the most risky and beautiful endings I've ever seen in a film (and on top of that, incredibly, it is a happy ending).

¶ For Cristián, writing the script wasn't easy. There were several times he felt himself foundering. Every once in a while we would get together to have lunch and talk about the novel, and my position was strange but fairly comfortable – I didn't feel artistically implicated, so to speak, in the film: it wasn't my movie, I had no obligation, and moreover I was writing *Ways of Going Home*, which completely absorbed me. Cristián asked me questions no one else had asked, because he read *Bonsai* over and over again, savagely, affectionately. I remember most of all how one morning I opened the door for him and he said to me, by way of a greeting, like a policeman: 'We need to talk about Emilia's death.' And I really did feel a little guilty for having killed her.

¶ My first contact with Jiménez took place mid-2008, a year after *The Private Lives of Trees*, my second novel, was published. And the afternoon we met up for the first time, in the big Olán restaurant on Seminario, I had just written a couple of pages I'd spent months searching for, and I was happy because I was starting to get close to what would end up being *Ways of Going Home*. I mention this because there is an important relationship between this novel and the film, which ended up appearing almost at the same time.

There are some traces of this process in *Ways of Going Home*; for example, the mention of *Good Morning*, the film by Ozu, who was one of the filmmakers Jiménez and I talked about – because sometimes we also met up to watch movies. By then we were a couple of friends who talked about anything, while he drank tea (like the characters of his movie) and I drank coffee (like the characters of my book). We never completely forgot, though, what it was that brought us together. From our conversations I culled small supplementary convictions about literary creation. As I watched the way Cristián tackled the material, I thought again about the specificity of literature, that classic question of structuralism: what is the literary, strictly speaking, in a novel or a poem – what is it that can't be done by other means, in another language?

¶ When Cristián sent me the first version of the script, I started out reading it in a basically sporting state of mind, but the experience affected me in a way that was unexpected and radical. It's difficult for me to express this idea: I had known that the novel would become something else, another very different, foreign work, and I really did want that. But as I read the script for the first time, even though I thought it was good and I recognized some marvellous solutions in it, I felt like my novel had been violated or erased, like the book was not going to exist anymore.

That afternoon, almost without realizing it, I went out for a walk, and I headed toward the house where I was living when I wrote *Bonsai*, and I smoked several cigarettes while I looked at the façade. In *Ways of Going Home*, the protagonist does something very similar, but now I'm unsure of the timing and I don't know if I wrote that scene before or after the afternoon when, to put it conventionally, I was in mourning.

I like to think that when we publish books, they are like children leaving home: we wish them well, but there is little or nothing we can do for them. And we are much more interested in the book we're writing now, the one we are raising now. That afternoon, sitting on the curb, I thought that from then on my novel would live very far away, and that maybe it was on its way to becoming one of those ungrateful children who never call home.

¶ What came next was simply time. Between the novel and the film there are all kinds of differences, and some of them are divisive. I'm glad for that. Of course, if I had made the movie, it would be very different: it would be set entirely in Santiago, it would have different music, a different rhythm, a different mood: everything would be different. But I don't make movies. And, in another sense, I feel very close to what Cristián saw in my book. It's a privilege, no doubt about it, for someone to read your book in such depth, and to crystallize their own, autonomous reading of it.

Later I found out that Trinidad González, an actress I like a lot, would be in the movie, and that the main character would be played by Diego Noguera, which made me happy because I had just seen him in *Turistas* [Tourists], by Alicia Scherson. And then I spent four months in Mexico City, and that time coincided with the filming; I was very sorry about that, since I would have loved to crash the film shoots and filter a little more into that world.

¶ When *Bonsai* was published, in February 2006, some writers reacted irately towards the novel, arguing that it was not a novel but just a long short story Defining the novel as a genre is impossible, but in any case the idea persists that it is a long story, two hundred pages or more (and the longer the better, the more a novel it will be). I hadn't wanted, strictly speaking, to write a novel, but rather a kind of simulacrum or summary of a novel: the same way that a bonsai is and isn't a tree, I wanted a book that was and wasn't a novel. Aside from that, if *Bonsai* had been published along with another story, people would have called it a long story, and no one would have accepted it as a novel. But I didn't want to publish *Bonsai* accompanied by some other story. For me it was, a book, a single unit. That was the project. I even thought at one point of adding a subtitle: *A Toy Novel*. Cristián Jiménez's *Bonsai*, on the other hand, is a movie, and not a short film.

¶ I remember an essay in which Susan Sontag says that a film that is an hour and a half long is equivalent to a short story and not a novel, and that this is the great mistake of adaptations, since filmmakers find themselves obliged to over-simplify. This was also my biggest fear, which is why I hadn't accepted the previous offers: I didn't want them to simplify the book in any way. I didn't want, especially, for the movie to shout what is whispered in the novel. Cristián felt the same way. In an initial meeting I asked him if he thought the novel seemed 'filmable', and he replied that no, it didn't at all. That was precisely why he was interested in adapting it.

It's very strange for the novel to be shorter than the movie. You can read *Bonsai* in less than an hour, and the movie lasts ninety minutes. And although in this novel the characters pretend to have read a book, I like to think that, cramming for an impending test, in this case some school kid will choose to read the novel.

¶ I still can't decipher what I felt when I first saw the movie. The screen was in some way a mirror, because many of the phrases those characters said were ones I had written or lived. And even so it wasn't mine, it belonged to Cristián and to the actors and the almost unbelievable number of people it takes to make a movie. I felt a long mixture of happiness and serenity. And the certainty that I had lost that story: that if it belongs to me now, it is in a new and profoundly collective way. And that is overwhelming and weird and beautiful.

April 2012

NOVELS – FORGET IT

'I'll say up front what I have to say and without literature,' writes Clarice Lispector in 'Report of the Thing', a beautiful and very strange story that investigates the 'infernal tranquil soul' of an alarm clock. I don't know a better definition of the act of writing, or at least a more precise one, since it emphasizes a fact that is, for me, essential: that to make literature it is necessary to not make literature.

Books say no to literature. Some. Others, the majority, say yes. They obey the market or the holy spirit of governments. Or the placid idea of a generation. Or the even more placid idea of a tradition. I prefer books that say no. Sometimes, even, I prefer the books that don't know what they are saying.

I would have a hard time looking for real affinities with a style or movement, especially because I would prefer not to have a style and not to adhere to any movement. I wouldn't know how to be consistent. I wouldn't know how to order myself under a common precept or cause. And it would be unnecessary, surely. I like to read. It might seem strange to say that, but I'm really not so sure anymore that writers like to read. I don't know if it was Sting or Bono who said that when he heard a very good song he felt jealous that he hadn't written it. I don't know if it was Roberto Juarroz or Marcelo Pellegrini who wrote this poem that demonstrates to what point Sting's or Bono's envy is absurd: 'To read what I want to read / I'd have to write it / But I don't know how to write it / No one knows how to write it.'

We write in order to read what we want to read. We write when we don't want to read others. But most of the time we want to read others; that's why I don't understand

Sting's (or Bono's) envy: often, almost always, we want to read what others write; we write only when others haven't written the book that we want to read. That's why we write one of our own, one that never turns out to be what we wanted it to be. We say no to literature so that literature, for its part, will say no to us. So the book will be, always, a space that we weren't expecting; a way out, but not the way we were expecting.

'Not knowing how to write could perhaps be exactly what saves me from literature,' says Clarice Lispector, again. In the non-fiction chronicles of *A Descoberta do Mundo* [Discovery of the World], Lispector insists on the desire that her stories not be stories, that her novels not be novels, and not out of any attachment to a forced experimentalism or to the kind of commonplaces that literary workshops, return to again and again, with admirable patience: Lispector does not seek to surprise or captivate the reader. It's more that she herself wants to be captive of a story that she could just abandon, but that she goes on writing to find out what it's like, how much is left, when it began. 'Very strange poems are permitted. Novels, then, forget it...' she says suddenly, out of the blue, and that story of hers about the 'infernal tranquil soul' of an alarm clock ends in this beautiful, abrupt way: 'And now I am going to end this report on the mystery. It so happens that I am very tired.' I don't think there is a more legitimate reason to end a story than that its writer is tired. While Clarice Lispector rests, I'll open a parenthesis.

My generation is the last whose literary education was, fundamentally, national. We grew up reading Chileans – dead Chileans, to be precise, since the living ones were finishing up their exiles or perpetual house arrest of those years. In my house, as in the majority of middle-class houses, the library consisted only of a collection of cheap books that came free with the magazine *Ercilla*. The Ercilla Library included several dozen titles coloured red for the Spanish series, brown for Chilean literature, and beige for world literature. There was no collection of Latin American books. There was, for us, no Latin American literature. *Doña Bárbara*, *Martín Fierro*, and Borges' *Fictions* figured among the books of world literature, and if I remember correctly the most recent title of the Spanish books was *Niebla* [Mist], by Unamuno. My generation grew up believing that Chilean literature was brown, and that there was no such thing as Latin American literature. When, at the beginning of the nineties, we started seeing literature of exile and Latin American books and books by gringos and Europeans and Japanese, we read our own writers as if they were foreign and the foreigners as if they were our own. Yukio Mishima was our Severo Sarduy. César Vallejo was our Paul Celan. Macedonio Fernández was our Laurence Sterne. Raymond Carver was our Raymond Chandler. Álvaro Mutis was our grandpa. Robert Creeley was our mute friend. Emily Dickinson was our first love. And Borges was our Borges.

From that complete disorder, from that late meeting comes the current landscape. Some of us changed countries and came back more Chilean than ever. Others stayed in Chile and turned British or American or Swedish. It's no joke: a lot of Chilean writers thought it was a tragedy that Bolaño was Chilean. Maybe it bothered them that he didn't renounce his nationality. I'm not exaggerating if I say that most Chileans don't want to read Chileans, much less Latin Americans. They want, in the best case scenario, to read Sándor Márai. I don't know if that's a bad thing. Maybe it's good, it's better to read Sándor Márai. I haven't read him. I am, probably, the only Chilean writer who hasn't read Sándor Márai.

I close parentheses to return to Clarice Lispector, though only to recall the moment when, in the middle of a chronicle, she stops and breathes and says: 'I am writing with a great deal of ease and fluidity. One must distrust that.' That's how we are in Chile: we distrust fluidity, the ease of words; that's why we stammer so much. It's not a criticism, just a description. We distrust writing, as well. We stammer, as well, in our writing. A clear divorce persists between spoken language and written language: there are many words and phrases that are said aloud to each other but never written. Gabriela Mistral fought against that divorce, as did Nicanor Parra, Enrique Lihn, or Gonzalo Millán; they dared, each in his or her own way, to write in search of a Chilean language. Violeta Parra ventured to discover it, to create it, and, as if that weren't enough, to sing it.

The great and secret theme of Chilean literature is that abyss between what is said and what is written. What Neruda invented, really, was an elegant stutter, a literary phrasing that favours circumvention and endless digression. Anti-poetry saved us from that short-lived rhetoric. The direction that started with Parra continued with Lihn and with Juan Luis Martínez, but these are only some names on an interminable list. With Juan Luis Martínez, in fact, Chilean poetry abandoned verse. Today, very few Chilean poets write in verse. I don't know if they write in prose, but I'm sure they don't write in verse. Chilean poets forgot Neruda long ago. But fiction writers didn't. Fiction writers write – we write – inwardly, as if the novel were, really, the long echo of a repressed poem. Maybe we need to find that poem, unwritten but present in Chilean novels. We would have

252

to write the poem and something else, something that refuses it.

'Novels are the poetry of stupid people,' said the poet Eduardo Molina, who never wrote poems, but plagiarized whatever French writer he felt like. At the start of the nineties, however, Chilean fiction writers steeled themselves courageously, or at least that's what they, back then, used to say. They trusted entirely in their ease with words. They trusted blindly in the idea of being *representative*. They held very strange meetings during which they discussed whether Chilean literature was this thing or the other. It seemed that, finally, fiction writers were overcoming their inferiority complex from not being poets. They even christened the city, the people: there were discourses in which Santiago de Chile figured as a great city, a great city happy to suffer the same problems of which big cities complain. They talked of kids with their Walkmans, differentiating them from other kids – the ones without Walkmans – that those writers had only heard tell of. And there were even those who embraced the death rattles of their youth creating a parallel world called McOndo.

In short, to each his own. I prefer to write in a nameless city or one that constantly changes its name, a city that is always Santiago or nowhere. I prefer to write without sociologists or cool-hunters sharpening their gaze. Nothing further away, for me, than the experience of the *boom*. One of the best novels I've ever read is *No One Writes to the Colonel* (and one of the worst, now that we're on the subject, is *Memories of my Melancholy Whores*). But in Chile we read the boom late, we read almost everything late, fortunately. Arguing over the boom would be, for me, as stimulating as debating the ins and outs of Góngora vs. Quevedo.

253

But I was talking about the moment when Clarice stops and takes a breath and says: 'I'm writing with a great deal of ease and fluidity. One must distrust that.' I was talking about my generation, the generation of a group of friends whose works have little to no similarity. A generation without manifestos and without any more history than the books we have written. A generation that distrusts its possible youth and at times stops and breathes and says: 'I'm writing with too much ease. I must distrust that.' A generation that prefers very strange poems to novels.

Novels, then – forget it. I, at least, would rather talk about books. 'A novel, these days, is anything placed between front and back covers,' says the Uruguayan writer Mario Levrero in *The Luminous Novel*, his greatest work, which he wrote by forcing himself to write it, knowing beforehand that what he wanted to write was impossible. That's why, instead of the novel, he narrates the distractions that sidetrack him from the novel: his arguments with spellcheck – which, when Levrero writes 'Joyce', suggests changing it to 'José' – or his adventures in Visual Basic, dreaming up a programme that lets him know when it's time to take his antidepressant. It's not so surprising that the happiest moment in *The Luminous Novel* is when Mario Levrero manages, finally, to fix Word 2000. Surely, Word 2000 is easier than writing that unfathomable novel that Levrero writes but doesn't write. But to write the luminous novel it is necessary to pass through the dark novel; to make true literature it is crucial to turn to, as he says, fraudulent literature. Novel without a novel; literature without literature.

Sometimes it works. Sometimes we depict nothing more than the forgettable scene of a writer observing the exhaustive failure of his plans. In my case, the books

I've written were imagined differently. But I don't have much imagination: I have, perhaps, a good memory or a good will to remember or a good involuntary memory. When I wrote *Bonsai* or *The Private Lives of Trees* I didn't know very well what I wanted to depict. Maybe nothing. Anything I can say about those books is posterior to their writing, and it corresponds, rather, to what I thought the first and only time I read them after they were finished. In both books I obeyed the sole wish to deploy images that seemed valid to me. Now I think that on writing those books I wanted to name lives that were mediocre and not at all novelesque, the lives of those of us who grew up reading books that were red, beige, and brown. Now I think that I wanted, maybe, to talk about characters who didn't want to be or couldn't be characters, perhaps because they are *Chilean*. Maybe I wanted to talk about our poor vegetal past, about imposture, fragile new families – in sum, about the life that, as John Ashbery says, is 'a book that has been put down,' and about death, about other people's dead and my own. But maybe I'm making this up. Maybe I didn't set out to do anything but find, for myself, a passable prose. Maybe I talked about what I did because I didn't want to or couldn't speak any other way. All literature is, in the end, a failure. All literature is personal and national. All literature struggles against itself, against the personal and against the national, because, as Henry Miller writes at the beginning of *Black Spring*, 'What is not in the open street is false, derived, that is to say, literature.'

We write, we pass like obedient hunger artists through a cage that is new and nevertheless familiar; we recover, every time, an absurd transparent disguise. What is the conclusion? None or all of the above. I like that poem by Jean Tardieu whose final verse says: 'I don't know,

I don't know, I don't know.' And that poem of Mark Strand's that at the end says 'Et cetera, et cetera'. And that beautiful song that says 'quizás, quizás, quizás'. But better to end, for now, without literature.

September 2007

NOTEBOOK, FILE, BOOK[2]

I'm going to talk about notebooks, files, and books, about pens, typewriters, and computers, but also, in a way, about being back here at the University of Chile after so much time. Those of us who decided to study Literature in this department twenty years ago didn't have a very clear idea of what we wanted. Our greatest passions were reading and writing, and the idea that pleasure could dovetail with obligation seemed marvellous to us. But it also must be said that for many of us, studying literature was also a way for us to not study law, to not study journalism: it was a way to not do what our parents wanted us to do.

Almost all of us wrote poems or stories or something unnecessary that we wouldn't even consider labelling. Around the second or third week of classes, we organized a reading that took place in this very auditorium: we hung up flyers all over campus, several students from upper classes and from other departments attended – maybe a teacher or two showed up as well. The place was full, but we still weren't happy after the event was over, because the audience had been cold and pretty ungenerous. Back then we didn't know that at poetry readings and literary conferences the audience is always like that: serious, dry, led by brow furrowers, that kind of urban tribe dedicated to chipping away at the confidence of public speakers.

Nor did we know, though we soon found out – as the rumour spread about how bad we first-years wrote

2 Speech read on 18 March 2013 in the College of Philosophy and Humanities at the University of Chile, as part of the inauguration of the academic year organized by the Department of Literature.

– that the fact that we read in public made us suspicious. Wanting to write was a sign of naiveté: everything had been said already, literary history's last rites had been administered; we had to be very credulous to think we could add anything, to think that what we were trying to say could be important. 'Distrust everything / Distrust everyone / Distrust them // Live in a state of suspicion,' says a poem Roberto Contreras wrote about those years written by. I met Contreras in March of 1994 on the first day of classes: I remember we gravitated towards each other because we both had long hair and were terrified about possible hazings – back then it was common for incoming first-years to have their hair cut off by older students.

Even if people accepted that it was legitimate to write, to *want* to write, our generation was still suspicious: what could we have to write about, we who had grown up like those trees people tie to broomsticks: asleep, anesthetized, repressed. We all had different lives, but that was something we had in common: our childhood under dictatorship, and now this sudden, supposed democracy. It was a complicated time, so grey, with Pinochet still in charge of the armed forces and en route to becoming senator-for-life. I'm talking about suspicions, and it's worth mentioning that in that time, arrest for suspicion was still legal.

Maybe it was true that we were asleep, but it was like when we realize we're dreaming and try to wake up, but can't; we know that with a little effort, like someone kicking off the bottom in order to reach the water's surface, we could wake up, but we just can't to do it. Being young, as I've said, was no advantage in this case, or at least we didn't feel it to be one. Because there was also that other suspicion – a perfectly reasonable one, it must be said – that always hounds literature students, young readers: the suspicion that we hadn't read enough.

Things being what they were, we had to play the game, accept the challenge, and some of us did. In the years that followed there were many memorable classes in which we tried to prove that we read widely and well, that we could come at the teachers with opportune and confounding questions. I am sure that I have never again discussed books with the passion and latent joy of those years. And though we really did read a lot, we pretended we'd read it all, that we navigated a copious bibliography with unrealistic ease. Because we didn't want to put up with that disparagement anymore, that suspicion, again, every time we spoke or tried to speak about literature.

Years later I wrote a book about two literature students, Julio and Emilia, who pretended they'd read Proust, and I imagined them here, in this university. Intuitively, I mean: I wasn't driven by the urge to depict something concrete, or to communicate some message; it was more that I wanted, while I wrote, to delve into certain images, to play, to constitute or insinuate a presence. Also to pay homage to some authors who had shaken my foundations, writers as different from each other as Juan Emar and José Santos González Vera, Yasunari Kawabata and Macedonio Fernández, María Luisa Bombal and Felisberto Hernández. I also wanted, I suppose now, to inhabit or construct a distance, to cover the melancholy with a light, almost imperceptible patina of humour and irony.

Midway through the book appears the character of Gazmuri, a novelist returned from exile who has written a saga about Chile's recent history. The man needs someone to transcribe his latest novel, handwritten in Colón notebooks, because his wife, who usually does the job, doesn't want to. Julio is a candidate for the job; he has read Gazmuri's novels closely, and he admires him. During the interview they talk about the novel and also about writing. The old man asks Julio if he is a writer, whether he writes by hand, and he ends up denigrating or looking down on him because he doesn't. Young people don't understand the drive of writing by hand, he says. He tells Julio about a noise, a strange equilibrium between elbow, hand, and pencil.

Gazmuri stood for tradition, experience, legitimacy: he had lived, he had written. And it fell to Julio to be the secretary, the typist, in the best case scenario, a consultant. On one side was the old writer who, complying with some kind of unwritten protocol, was ending his career like the majority of his colleagues, successful or not: that is, pontificating against the present, and intimating that they were the last. That is, that they would take literature to the grave, so to speak, so that no one else would write after them. On the other side was the challenge faced by young writers, apprentices like Julio, like us: to find oneself with the weight of words, to reconquer their necessity, search incessantly, even when they – the words – have become even more transitory, more perishable, more erasable than ever.

The suspicions persist; only the sign or the emphasis varies. The current generations, for example, grew up reading and writing on a screen, and it would be so easy to invoke that fact to disqualify them: it's said they don't possess the experience of the book, which makes them second- or third-degree readers. They have a different idea of reading, because for them, *literature* is a synonym more of *text* than *book*. I am more interested in positions like that of Roger Chartier, who puts these changes in historical context and warns against dismissing new forms of writing and reading brought on by the digital revolution.

I share the fear provoked by the presumed disappearance of books, but I also subscribe to the fervour around the democratizing effect of electronic books. It could be no other way, because, like almost all of my generation, I grew up reading photocopies: the first incarnation of my library held a few books, but its greatest treasures were the spiral-bound photocopies of works by Clarice Lispector, Emmanuel Bove, Roland Barthes or Mauricio Wacquez. And my generation felt that photocopies of *La Nueva Novela* [The New Novel], by Juan Luis Martínez, of *Proyecto de Obras Completas* [Complete Works Project], by Rodrigo Lira, or any book by Enrique Lihn, was more valuable than any first-edition Neruda.

Another thing that happened in those days, in the first half of the nineties, was the massification of personal computers. To a certain extent we resisted it: we were not, as they say now, digital natives; we were a transition generation in that sense, too, as well as the transition to democracy. Most of us still turned in our papers typewritten, and in some cases handwritten. It was hard for us to imagine that poems and stories could be written directly on the computer. Maybe for us those long texts, full of crossed-out words and smudges and scrawled in the notebook or sketchbook, *were* the poem – that those wine or ash stains were also part of the poem. To move it to the computer, make a clean draft, was to subject it to a significant loss, a thinning: it meant accepting that the poem was finished, that it had died.

We grew up sitting through interminable handwriting sessions, patiently covering the five or six pages they gave us as homework: we were the last or maybe the penultimate class who really exercised our hands, because

261

for us, writing came to be fully, only, handwriting. Educated, ultimately, in the old way, there was a point in our childhood when we believed that being a good student meant having good handwriting and a good memory: many of our classes consisted only of teachers dictating material that they might not have even understood themselves. I'm not saying this no longer happens. I'm afraid that in spite of educational reforms and counter-reforms, in many Chilean schools even today the teacher dictates, the students write, and no one understands anything: the words pass from one to the other and no one enjoys them, no one lives them. And if a student interrupts it's only to ask, shaking out a cramped hand, 'Wait, please, slow down.'

What *has* definitely changed is handwriting, as is clear when I have to correct tests: they're filled with some real hieroglyphics, shaky signs that are intricate and unintelligible. I'm not complaining, in any case; quite the contrary: I identify with those scrawls, since I never achieved the sophisticated, fluid, and well-crafted handwriting that abounds in my generation and even more in those of our parents and grandparents. Although I never stopped writing by hand, my handwriting didn't improve. I think every letter I ever wrote ended with the line: sorry for my handwriting.

In his novels *El Discurso Vacío* [The Empty Speech] and *La Novela Luminosa* [The Luminous Novel], Uruguayan writer Mario Levrero takes on these subjects in a lucid and unusual way. *The Empty Speech* testifies to the moment when, for lack of practice, we no longer recognize our own page. The anecdote from *The Empty Speech* is minimal: since he hasn't been able to change his life, Levrero tries – modestly – to change his handwriting, filling notebooks in an attempt to 'reform' his hand-written prose. This 'graphologic self-help' does not seem to obey any literary challenge: he has no intention of writing the 'book about nothing' that Flaubert wanted, or of vindicating the surrealist method. Rather, he wants to delve into the relationship between handwriting and personality: 'I have to allow myself to grow larger through the magical influence of graphology,' he says, and then gives this funny clarification of his reasoning: 'large letters, large me. Small letters, small me. Pretty letters, pretty me.' The calligraphic efforts that the book includes are serious, funny, and abundant: 'B B B B B B B B B B B B *Bien*, once again I'd forgotten how to write B. The problem is that I forget where to start drawing it, and if it doesn't come spontaneously, I can't manage it by thinking about it. There's a trick somewhere, and I just can't find it.' The author writes 'Usted' just because he needs to practice the upper case U, and he fearlessly goes deep into the surface, aware that he is perhaps inaugurating, so to speak, 'a new era of boredom as literary current'.

In spite of the bullying, we kept on writing. I'm exaggerating, of course, because there were some spaces, extremely valuable ones like the polyphonic poetry workshop Códices, directed by Andrés Morales, where I made friends I still have today. Back then the only way to disseminate our work was in print, and naturally we dreamed of publishing books. Very soon we did, in editions that we financed by asking friends for money, in small print runs that circulated hand to hand.

In those days, in section C of the newspaper *El Mercurio*, there was a segment called 'Books Received' that simply stated that certain works existed, nothing more: author, title, publisher, number of pages. In most cases, that was the highest point in the history of those

263

books' distribution. I say this because the generation after ours had blogs and photologs and web pages where they put their poems, manifestos and counter-manifestos, the strategic reviews, the lists of philias and phobias, the fights and warm reconciliations that animate the life of every literary generation.

We arrived late to all that, and we didn't understand it well: our fights were ferocious, we were as alcoholic or more so than the average Chilean poet, but we didn't show off. Compared to the younger writers we were shyer, we stuttered more, and maybe we were also more proud. Because we were irritated by the idea of promoting ourselves, of showing ourselves, of discursively calling upon youth, or bothering the rock stars of Chilean poetry to ask for the inevitable prologue, the inexorable letter of recommendation.

And we still believed in paper, and sought in it a possible, elusive legitimacy. To put it another way, we still read the newspaper; it took us a while to realize that the press no longer had the tremendous importance it had had until then. And we still wrote by hand, in notebooks, epigonally, silently. And we hated computers.

No, we didn't hate them, me least of all:

I'm the son of a computer technician and a programmer, so that I can say without doubt that I owe my life to computers. If I resisted them it was because they represented something established, given, obligatory: the opposite of writing. And nevertheless, in another sense, I also tried to understand the programmes, and whether I liked it or not I was always the one called upon for design or transcription. For that 1994 reading, I was in charge of designing the flyers in a rudimentary Page Maker, and some days later I formatted the first novel of another classmate and friend, Jaime Pinos, for La

Calabaza del Diablo, the press my classmate Marcelo Montecinos was starting.

The times that I went to my father's work and he showed me the immense computers in the systems area, expecting me to react in amazement, I made sure to fake interest. But as soon as I could I went to reception to play with the typewriters there, an electric one that I found magical, and a conventional Olivetti that I also liked and that I knew well, because my mother had one just like it at our house. I could say, then, with only a little trickery, that my father was a computer and my mother, a typewriter.

The typewriter was an auratic object, complex but understandable, decipherable, lovable. The obvious artifice of the carbon paper, the white-out, the meticulous gesture of applying corrector fluid: I liked to look for the mistakes, search the surface of a page that passed itself off as good, but contained those vacillations that in the end gave it – the paper – a certain humanity.

'Our writing tools are also working on our thoughts,' said Nietzsche, who, as Friedrich Kittler affirms, with the adoption of the typewriter in the final stretch of his lifetime 'changed from arguments to aphorisms, from thoughts to puns, from rhetoric to telegram style'. Starting with Tom Sawyer – the first novel written on a typewriter in the history of literature – and moving through the works of poets like e.e. cummings and bp Nichol (among so many others), and the consecrated last vintages, typewriters profoundly modified literary production in ways that were at times contradictory, personal, or circumstantial. Speed, for example: at the end of the fifties, José Donoso was still a very slow typist, but precisely for that reason, when he thought a text called for a different speed, he would write directly on the typewriter. Jack Kerouac was much faster, according to Truman Capote's famous phrase: 'That's not writing, that's typing.' For the poet W. H. Auden both typewriting and handwriting were useful 'critical' tools: 'Most people enjoy the sight of their own handwriting as they enjoy the smell of their own farts. Much as I loathe the typewriter, I must admit that it is a help in self-criticism. Typescript is so impersonal and hideous to look at that, if I type out a poem, I immediately see defects which I missed when I looked through the manuscript.'

There are still, of course, writers who refuse to move to the computer, like Cormac McCarthy, Don DeLillo, or Javier Marías. In *The Story of my Typewriter*, Paul Auster declares both his love for an old portable Olympia, and war against not even computers, but electric typewriters, due to the 'motor's constant buzz, the discordant drone of the pieces, the alternate current vibrating and changing frequency in the fingers.' In part five of *2666*, the writer Benno von Archimboldi rents a typewriter to transcribe his first novels, but when he runs out of money he decides to ask for an advance from Sr. Bubis, his editor. Astonished that the author doesn't have a typewriter, Bubis sends him one as a gift, and Archimboldi uses it over the course of books and travels: 'Sometimes he went to the shops that sold computers and asked the salespeople how they worked,' says the narrator. 'But at the last minute he always balked, like a peasant reluctant to part with his savings.' When laptop computers appeared, however, Archimboldi does buy one, and the fate of that mythical Olivetti on which he'd written his first books is more or less the same as that of all typewriters: 'He flung it off a cliff onto the rocks!'

There's a different story in *Moo Pak*, by Gabriel Josipovici, in which Jack Toledano speaks against computers. When his friends tell him that with word processors he can play with sentences, he replied that he doesn't want to play with words, that that's why he stopped writing by hand: 'In the days when I wrote by hand... I would spend a day playing with one sentence or perhaps one paragraph, turning it this way and that and when I finally got it to sound as I wanted it to it would late in the day and I would be worn out.' With a typewriter, on the other hand, 'you have to go forward, you have to keep typing, and that was the saving of me.'

As Josipovici's character says, writing on the computer is quite similar to writing by hand, in more than one sense. Writing on a typewriter is considered, nevertheless – maybe because of the myth, the romantic image promoted in the movies – more genuine, more authentic than using the computer.

Published in 2005, one year after Mario Levrero's death, *The Luminous Novel* is a strange work from the get-go. The author started to write it in 1984, at 44 years old, on the eve of a bladder operation. Because of his fear of going under the knife, he rushes his writing and gets through the seventh chapter. The operation is a success, but once back home the author realizes the novel is a failure: Levrero burns two of the seven chapters and the novel is left incomplete, an impossible project.

Sixteen years later, however, the Guggenheim Foundation approves the project and the author has a grant that enables him to dedicate himself entirely to writing. It is, now, August 2000, and Levrero progresses as best he can, which is little to not at all. And it's just that he can't go back, he can't legitimize the old idea: 'The inspiration that I need for this novel isn't just any inspiration,' he says, 'but a particular one, tied to events that lie in my memory and that I must revive, by force, so that this novel's continuation is a true continuation and not a simulacrum. I don't want to use my profession. I don't want to imitate myself. I don't want to take up the novel again where I left it sixteen years ago and continue as though nothing had happened. I have changed.' The fragment I just cited appears in 'Diario de la beca' ['Diary of the Grant)'], a text that the author started as a kind of stimulus to writing, but that very soon takes on a necessary flight of its own. Almost the entire novel will consist of a record of the impossibility of its writing.

In 'Diary of the Grant', Levrero lists his distractions, of which there are many, all very worthy: reading or re-reading old mystery novels, going on timid outings in the company of a woman who has stopped loving him, or buying a truly comfortable armchair. Without a doubt it is easier to buy an armchair than to write the novel, but Levrero has a terribly hard time deciding between a grayish-blue model (ideal for sleeping) and an attractive *bergère* (ideal for reading), and he ends up buying both. Then, faced with the unbearable Montevideo heat, Levrero realizes it will be difficult to sleep or read or write without air conditioning.

In the same way that *The Empty Speech* gestures toward the difficult fullness of the handwritten page, *The Luminous Novel* assumes the bastard nature of the typed text, as the computer becomes one of the book's main characters. Levrero transcribes the arguments he has with spell check – which allows the palabra *coño* (cunt) but not the word *pene* (penis), and suggests changing 'Joyce' to 'José' – is a consummate solitaire player, and knows enough Visual Basic to stay up until nine in the morning coming up with a programme that will let him know when it's time to take his antidepressant. Sometimes he writes by hand simply to punish himself for abusing the computer; other times he accepts his addiction and enjoys it.

The Uruguayan edition of *The Luminous Novel* is some five hundred-odd pages: the four hundred of 'Diary of the Grant' (incorporated as a gargantuan prologue), plus the negligible pages written in 1984, and a remarkable chapter-story titled 'First Communion', the only 'real' result of the blessed Guggenheim grant. There is also a brief epilogue in which Levrero vents his doubts about the nature of the book: 'I would have liked for it to be possible to read the grant diary as a novel; I had the vague hope that all the open plot lines would have some kind of climax. Of course, it was not to be, and this book, altogether, is an exhibition or museum of incomplete stories.' But right away – contradicting his own words – the author demonstrates the evolution of some of those plot lines. There are some seemingly scattered actions or incidents whose reappearance gives the project a certain unity. While the incompleteness Levrero refers to may be the book's prevalent characteristic, the plot lines *are* resolved.

This is what Ignacio Echevarría points to in an essay centred on the mystical dimension of *The Luminous Novel*. He gives as an example how Levrero dedicates several fragments to describing the cadaver of a pigeon on the neighbouring patio. The recurrence of this image – the narrator's meticulous observation as he relays the minimum changes the scene undergoes – gradually takes on, with the passage of the days and the pages, an indisputable allegorical value. The diary of the grant closes with a mention of the cadaver's current state; its permanence is, for Echevarría, the permanence of the Spirit, 'of its mark, even there where it seems to have been wiped out.' To observe that cadaver is to linger on

269

the inert and to bring it to life, just as writing is waiting for an illumination that is delayed and never arrives.

The character longs for a unity that is no longer possible to access through traditional routes (was it ever?). The tapestry is torn and it is absurd to force or improvise junctures. Walter Benjamin said that assemblage implies a renunciation, a loss: introduce a short novel, for example, with hundreds of pages that testify to its impossibility. This is not the ludic exaltation of the *Museum of Eterna's Novel*. Levrero's humour is different, strange, as the job of the jokes is to accompany and to a certain extent legitimize the tragic.

Levrero – author or character – never stops digging into the (new) materiality of writing: he never gets used to the computer, but nor does he reject it, the same way that he never managed, in *The Empty Speech*, to reform his handwritten prose. In an interview with Álvaro Matus, Levrero says that his novel *La Ciudad* [The City] is a plagiarism of Kafka. 'I read Kafka at night and I wrote by day, trying to seem like him. I thought that was the way to write. It came out badly, but my intention isn't all that obvious. I wanted to do something like translating Kafka to Spanish.' Even in *The Luminous Novel*, observations that recall Kafka abound, but it's a Kafka who writes in Word 2000 (and fixes it).

In the middle of 1999 I bought (or more like I obtained, because I paid over many, many instalments) one of those immense computers that ran Windows 95. I don't know if that winter was really as terrible as I remember it, or if I just couldn't hack it, but the fact is I got into the habit of warming my hands on the CPU, and one day I even put it in my bed and slept several nights with my arms around it. I like that image: an object that at the time seemed so sophisticated ended up serving such a basic purpose as keeping me warm. Years later I included that anecdote in 'Memories of a Personal Computer', a story that I wrote with the idea of showing computers as relics of the past, as technological advances that we've moved beyond. It was an elliptical way, as well, to talk about literary generations, because back then some writers still insisted on the computer as an emblem of the new: I thought it would be funny to demonstrate or at least depict the obsolescence of those machines (and those discourses).

I don't think it's one of the functions of literature to imagine what the iPhone 18 will be like, but it would be absurd to behave as if the periodical changes in technology experienced over the past thirty years had not altered our experience of the world, our everyday life, and our way of writing.

Did novels change when we began to write them on the computer? Of course they did, but who really knows how. People say that it used to be more difficult to write a book, but that implies an understanding of writing as a physical activity, as if the novel were better the more calories the author burned on its writing... It's like when critics don't dare write a negative review of a book because it has a lot of pages, and it must have taken a great effort to write it. It's also said that these days it is easier or more frequent to start out by writing the ending or any intermediary sentence, but obviously no novelist was ever obligated to start with the book's first paragraph.

Would Flaubert's writing have taken less time if he'd been able to cut and paste like mad, dazzled by those commands that allow you to search and replace, detect cacophonies and all kinds of repetitions, in search of perfection? Who knows? It is undeniable, though, that word processors have systemized the logic of assembly. Some writers think that the way to be or seem modern (or post-modern or post-post-modern) is to adopt, in their writing, structures similar to blogs, or chats. But even in the most conservative texts we can see the assemblage: even if all fragmentariness is denied, even if one imitates the classic paradigm like Jonathan Franzen does, the text owes more to the aesthetic of the historical vanguard than to the nineteenth-century model or realism. Today more than ever, the writer is someone who builds meaning by putting pieces together. Cutting, pasting, and erasing.

For my part, I think there is a central fact: because of computers, text is ever less definitive. A phrase is today more than ever a thing that can be erased. And the proliferation of words is such that we must like ours a lot in order to keep them. When I write, I employ several procedures, and although the text projects – I hope – a certain singleness, the multiplicity of its origin is decisive: each phrase has had to pass through several tests to verify its right to exist, to demonstrate that it is worth adding something to the incessant rush of words. Often I write by hand and then move to the computer, but sometimes I handwrite what I've written on the screen. I enlarge and shrink the text, change the font, the line spacing, and even the spacing between characters, like someone trying to recognize a single face in various disguises. And I read out loud, all the time: I record and listen to the texts, because it seems to me a sentence should also pass that test.

I'm very slow, I take an enormously long time in approving a phrase, and I'm almost incapable of considering a text finished. And it's hard for me to imagine another way of writing, a pure form, so to speak. And when I receive the printed book, when it arrives in the mail, the happiness competes with a kind of mourning: with the book in my hand, I have the silly, melancholic thought that I'll never be able to write it again.

THE BOY WHO WENT MAD FROM LOVE[3]

'I'm sad, and I'd like to be sadder,' says the narrator o
El Niño que enloqueció de amor [The Boy Who Went Ma
from Love]. I like that phrase for its simple severity; it i
recognizable, and it can, for that reason, feel troubling
It is said that this novel by Eduardo Barrios, publishe
almost exactly one hundred years ago, has aged badly
But it's odd to put it like that, as if it were books and no
readers who aged. It's not my intention, in any case, t
defend this novel. It's a Chilean classic, or more precise
ly a school classic, and as such has had to stand up t
the questions of thousands or maybe millions of readers
When it was published it was considered controversial,
brave and disturbing book, and maybe the first questio
to ask would be: how much of that power has been lo
along the way?

But I don't know if I'm writing this in order to respon
to that question. I read *The Boy Who Went Mad From Lov*
when I was nine years old. Of course, I would like t
know exactly who the boy was who, in 1984, read th
story of that other boy who went mad with love. Muc
has been written about the fluctuations of taste, almos
always with a feeling or conviction of superiority asso
ciated with the present. Now we read better: that's wha
we believe. How to annul or even confront – to not sa
combat – that conviction of superiority? Even if we lon
for innocence or childhood, there emerges the shrillnes
of speaking, here and now, recapitulating and imposin

3 This lecture was given on 10 December 2014 in the Nicanor
   Parra Library at Diego Portales University, as part of the Secon
   International conference '?Qué leer? ?Cómo leer? Lecturas de
   juventud' ['What to Read? How to Read? Readings of Youth']
   organized by the Chilean Ministry of Education.

processes, hastening the end and rushing to conclusions, disguising gerunds, as if we really were solid, as if we were already made, formed. As if the rereading I did not long ago of *The Boy Who Went Mad With Love* were in essence more genuine than my reading at nine. We write, now, as if we were not going to disavow what we think, what we are. It's better for that to be the impulse, because otherwise we wouldn't write, we would stay stuck in silence. But it's worth remembering that when we talk about childhood or adolescence we display, first and foremost, our implacable capacity for forgetting.

I'm talking about students and teachers, of course. And I can't resist telling this story. I was 23 years old and I taught class at a school in Curicó. I travelled for three hours there twice a week to face down those sophomore, junior, and senior students who were utterly indifferent to anything I had to say, and who demonstrated that indifference by throwing paper in my face. That's another story, anyway. What I want to tell here is what happened one morning with the only student who paid attention in class. I took care of her, yes. Since I put up with such intense and constant humiliation, the fact that there was a student in the first row who listened closely to me seemed, all things considered, like a kind of indulgence of fate, maybe a hopeful message. But I also understood that this student always paid attention in her classes, not only in mine: she listened to me because she always listened, not because I deserved it or she was especially interested in what I was saying.

The morning in question, I asked the students if they had started reading *The Metamorphosis*. Of course I knew the answer: noooooooo. I knew it and expected it, I wanted that answer, because I was dreaming up the most difficult test in the world, the test that would consummate

275

my revenge with a bloody string of Fs. After the general negative, this student, the only one who paid attention, said that she *had* read *The Metamorphosis*. I asked her if she'd liked it and she replied with an immediate, categorical no: how could she possibly like a book about a guy who wakes up one morning turned into a bug? 'It's gross,' she told me. 'And totally unrealistic.'

'It's a metaphor,' I told her. She asked why, or maybe she asked for what. 'Haven't you ever felt like a bug?' I asked her. 'Haven't you felt like your parents don't pay attention to you, that you're a nuisance to other people?' The girl started to cry. And not like in the movies. In the movies, the tears come slowly, one at a time, like the timid tributaries of a timid river. But she burst out crying the way children cry: first a confused and brief look of disconcertion, and then the explosion of snot and tears. I was impressed by her reaction, although of course the mistake had been mine, an immense mistake, as I thought later, too late. Maybe, for example, the girl had just lost her mother. I thought of the thousands of family problems that my words could have multiplied by a thousand. It wasn't that, it turned out, but I had touched a nerve. And I had transferred my own feeling that I was a bother; I was the one who felt like a bug. I was the one who, more intensely than anyone else in that room, wanted to be somewhere else. The story ends here. I'd like to say that the girl turned into a fanatical reader and that now she is working on a post-doctorate specialized in Kafka, but I don't think so. The only thing I heard about those kids was three or four years later when one of my students – a different one, one of the troublemakers – was among the finalists for Miss Chile. I still felt proud; I don't remember if she came in second or third. Miss Congeniality, she was not.

276

'Let others boast of the pages they have written; I am proud of those I have read,' said Borges, recurring to the false modesty of one who knows he has written lasting pages. Some, almost everyone, believed him. The gesture of defining oneself more as a reader than as writer is elegant, but it is also a bit demagogical and comfortable. Faced with resonant and inopportune questions, it is better to rewind the tape to the moment when we discovered, in books, some kind of foundation. It is a safe zone, perhaps, or one that is less unsafe. And the image quickly constructs a life where there was something stable – reading – and something unstable – writing. As writers we change all the time, and that's why we publish a second, a third, a twentieth book: because the first one wasn't enough. As readers, that dimension is uncertain. We recognize books that changed our lives. But we also change as readers, sometimes radically.

They say that we turn into writers when we stop identifying with the protagonist and start identifying with the author. Not the narrator, but with the author: with the person who was able to multiply into various characters, to meticulously design the novelistic edifice. I like that idea, but nevertheless it presumes a defeat: in effect, the moment comes when we stop identifying with the protagonist, because we are attending instead to the structural signs, the technical details. Though perhaps it would be better to say, simply, that we no longer seek what we sought before. None of that makes us better readers, though, even if, blessed by a university professor's credentials or a literary critic's furrowed brow – or even the tics of a writer – we might seem so, we seem so.

The Boy Who Went Mad From Love was not obligatory reading for me; on the contrary, as Wisława Szymborska says, it was one of my first non-obligatory readings, one of the first books I read in complete freedom, with no other purpose than to enjoy myself. This is the first moment in the life of every reader. When it's said that a child likes to read, what in reality is being said is that he likes certain books, because if those books were not available and there were others that he didn't like, that child wouldn't like to read. I know it sounds like a tongue twister, but I think it's important to accept that there was a moment when we read to entertain ourselves, without anyone telling us that reading was important, telling us to turn off the TV and read a book, all those things that sound so desperate in the reading promotion campaigns. No one read in my house, but all of a sudden some books arrived and I looked at the titles and I chose one called *The Boy Who Went Mad From Love*. And although it was a sad book, if someone had asked me I would have said it was good. Maybe I would have said it was funny, but not to trivialize it. I would love to know whether I cried when I read it. I think it's something I would remember. But I don't know.

I'll move a little more quickly, in a list now, though I don't know if it's a chronological list, because these lines will cross in the life of any reader:

There are the first non-assigned readings.
There are the books we read when we liked to read, when reading was already a habit.
There are the books we read because they had to be read.
There are the books we read because someone recommended them.

This is important. Someone tells us, 'read this book, you'll like it'. Maybe the phrase is: 'Read this book, you'll like it. I didn't like it, I thought it was shit, but you, you'll like it.' Or maybe: 'Class, read this book, which bored me profoundly, but since you all are children and you don't know anything, since you have no experience of life or any intellectual formation, you'll like it.' I think that's the line. What I am going to say is absolutely obvious, but it makes sense to emphasize it, because it's often forgotten: a teacher should never work with books they aren't interested in, books that they don't find, in some way, relevant. Not relevant for the history of literature. Relevant for their lives. Maybe the ideal would be: a teacher should never give his students books he understands completely. He should share with his students books that fascinate him because he doesn't entirely understand them.

This is key, I think: what matters to us in a book is associated to the feeling that there is something we don't fully understand. The happiness of reading is linked to the possibility of rereading. To knowing that the book will remain there, that we can read it again. It's like that joke where a fool says that he watched a movie two times, and the second time he didn't understand it. Why would the guy watch the movie a second time, if he thought he understood it the first? The best pedagogical situation, the ideal situation – and I'm not discovering anything by saying this – is a conversation between two people who possess different knowledge about a book, knowledge that puts an entire life into play, but that for that very reason can't be understood entirely in a hierarchical key. I always found the image of the know-it-all teacher to be obnoxious. And the insurmountable beginning of that antipathy is in the scene of the teacher who asks his students about what they've read, and when they don't respond or they reply that, deep down, no book has ever really interested them, it's all off to a bad start. In the best case, the students will accept the intellectual challenge. In the best and most infrequent case.

I can't imagine a situation more averse to reading than the wait leading up to a test. *What will they ask me? I have to pay attention to everything.* From uncertainty we move to those partial certainties, which perhaps make us feel something of pride: they will ask about this or that, the teacher always asks about secondary characters, so that reading becomes a function, and the important thing is the test, the performance. Later, it gets worse and worse. At university, we read in order to feel validated by the professors, or rather to challenge them, and later, now professors ourselves, we read so that none of our students can call us out, we take on the responsibility of knowing it all. We compete with them, constantly on the defence; maybe the only thing we teach them is to compete.

I'd guess that no one starts to read in order to become a professor or a literary critic or a writer. I don't understand why the idea that something entertains has come to mean, for many readers, that it's banal. It's more than clear that we are not all entertained by the same thing. When I say that I think a novel by Roberto Ampuero is boring, I mean exactly that: I got bored when I read it. And I'm sure that someone out there could object to my idea of entertainment.

Three years ago, for example, I stopped liking literature. I know that sounds very dramatic, but what can we do, it's what happened. I don't know how long it lasted, maybe two months. I'd been writing in the Chilean media for almost a decade, first in a newspaper, then in another and another: since this is Chile we're talking about, where there are more or less three newspapers and approximately two magazines, during those ten years I wrote in all the Chilean press. At first it was the ideal job, but over time it became less and less pleasant: after a while I couldn't stand the obligation to be more or less up to speed, in particular that feeling that everything I read, sooner or later was leading up to a text. I felt that leisure had become obligation. That I had irrevocably contaminated the space of reading and writing. Because the columns every Sunday were my reading comprehension quizzes, my achievement test, my weekly exams. I read in order to offer my opinion, to have something to say in the end. In sum: obligatory reading.

I stopped writing in the newspapers, and it was one of the best decisions I've made in my life. Of course there were many reasons I stopped, some of them very personal, even more. Maybe the most personal is, paradoxically, the most relevant here: I needed to clear the space of reading of all impulse of obligation. Starting then, I almost completely abandoned the habit of finishing books. I'm ashamed to put it like that, because it's very simple, it's the simplest mechanism imaginable: if I get bored, I stop. Of course, it's difficult to establish what it is that bores me, but the fact is that as soon as I get bored I close the book, probably forever.

What I hope for now, as a reader, is exactly what I was looking for when I was nine years old: not to get bored. I can say it in just a slightly more sophisticated way: what I look for is to forget that I am reading. Forget myself, and since I'm a writer I guess that means, as well, forgetting that I'm a writer. What I seek is to fall into the trap, and for that it's necessary that I not be able to recognize it. I guess that in more than one way, I've been ruined, corrupted by literature, but I also think I can see the trick because those books were written with trickery. Whatever the case, I'm reluctant to think that I am now, in essence, better than the boy who at nine years old read *The Boy Who Went Mad From Love*. And I suppose I should finish these lines by talking about whether or not I liked the novel. I'm sorry, I was lying. I haven't reread it yet. I'm going to do it now. And I'm going to finish it. As long as I don't get bored. I want it to make me cry.

FREE TOPIC[4]

I'm grateful for this invitation, which I accepted happily but also with surprise, because it's rather strange to be invited into one's own home. This sounds like a polite phrase, but it's strictly true, and I'm going to prove it:

Almost exactly eight years ago I was on the fifth floor of this department, sitting on a bench, smoking, with my suitcase beside me. There was nothing anomalous about this scene, because back then it was permitted, or at least it wasn't totally forbidden, to smoke inside the building. Nor was it strange for me to have that suitcase with me, because I often hauled around books for my classes. Though maybe the suitcase itself was an exaggeration, because a bag or a small carry-on would have been enough, but I was and still am in love with that black suitcase with its swivel wheels, whose existence seemed to me miraculous. I'm no expert in these matters, but it still seems inexplicable to me that it took so long to invent the suitcase with swivel wheels. First they invented the wheel, and I guess at some early moment in history or pre-history they invented the suitcase, but it's inexplicable that the two inventions both existed so long without combining, and that even then it would take several more decades to arrive at that inarguable masterpiece that is the suitcase on swivel wheels [5].

As I was saying, I could often be found on the fifth

4 Speech given on 30 May 2016 at the Department of Communication and Literature at Diego Portales University, as part of the lecture series (Cátedra Abierta) in hommage to Roberto Bolaño.
5 In *This Must Be the Place*, by Paolo Sorrentino, there is a character who claims to be none other than the inventor of the suitcase with swivel wheels. It must be said that *This Must Be the Place* is a damn good movie.

283

floor waiting for my students alongside that suitcase that for me was so beloved, and probably every time it happened, one of them gave me the classic joke about getting kicked out of my house. That afternoon almost exactly eight years ago, it was not one, not two, but three students who in a span of maybe five minutes, always in the light tone of a joke in passing, tried out variations on the same formula: 'Hey, teach, you moved out?' 'Uh-oh, someone's in the doghouse,' 'You living in your office now?' I responded casually, shaking my head and smiling, and of course I didn't tell them that yes, I had moved out of my house that very day, and that for a few hours at least I was, in effect, living at the office.

I hope you'll understand, then, to what point it's true that in this department I feel like I'm in my own house. A house I was never thrown out of, one that I never left. Now I feel like I've invited myself over for dinner, and part of me is waiting patiently at the set table while the other part buys bread and looks for ripe avocados – I feel like in addition to speaking I'm out there in the audience, and as such I distrust what the speaker is saying, which in any case is good, because as I write this I'm impelled by the same criteria I follow when writing a story, a novel, or anything else: to not get bored, to avoid the autopilot of a borrowed style and also the routine tics that appear, almost imperceptibly, in one's own writing. I want to write a speech capable of keeping even a person like me awake; that is, someone with an apparently irreversible case of ADD.

On a less solitary note, the invitation to one's own house entails a reproach, a not-so-subtle irony, a 'we have to talk'. That's why after I accepted the invitation I asked right away, in alarm, what we would have to talk about, what would I have to talk about, what is the subject of this conference. But it was a false question, because I already knew the answer – I already told you I've been here a long time, over twelve years, and of course I remember the morning I was sitting – or rather standing – listening to the first of these lectures, given by Ricardo Piglia in early 2007, and from then on I was almost always in the audience, and I was also oftentimes tasked with presenting writers whose works I admire. So it was a false question – of course I knew that the people invited to this lecture series are asked for a talk on a free topic: We have to talk, but we can choose what we have to talk about.

Now that I think about it, it's a little strange for a lecturer's topic to be left open. In general we writers are asked to talk about the boom, or about the current or future state of or the latest trends in or the rebirth or the death of Latin American or Chilean or Santiagoan literature, or about the crisis in or the existence of literary criticism, and although the risk of repeating ourselves becomes ever greater and more evident, we almost always accept, because we are a community, and because one way or another we have a good time, or at least we keep each other company, which is another way of saying we're a bunch of nerds, because we really are interested, for example, in the future of literature. Although maybe we also agree to give or attend these conferences for less splendid reasons: when it comes down to it, after the second glass, even the worst boxed red seems worthy of being complimentary.

I want to talk about that mundane morning when the teacher, tired of being creative and probably of being a teacher, hesitates a few seconds before giving the assignment. Because he's already asked his students to write about summer holidays and winter holidays and even about the long weekend, about the National Festival and about Christmas, about the Naval Battle of Iquique and about the most recent earthquake and the one before that. And so he has no other recourse than to command them to write about what they want, and then the slippery notion of 'free topic' floods the room and it's like an unexpected overdose of autonomy. It's a prize and also a problem, because in any case they're obliged to write, it's an obligatory free topic. The teacher walks unhurriedly around the room, in theory concentrated on imposing silence, although maybe he is also thinking about how to make it to the end of the month, or about the cute, inaccessible maths teacher, and during those forty-five minutes the students write something, anything, doesn't matter, no problem: free topic.

Obligated to the free topic we discovered, first of all and with just a little anxiety, that we had no topic, but maybe also, after that, we saw how one phrase summoned another and the story, mysteriously, took off. We discovered that we didn't need a topic, that writing could be a beautiful and noisy way of keeping quiet; that writing was also a way to put off the immediate obligation to contribute to the conversation, to say something opportune or intelligent; that to write was to suspend the present in a moment of utter intensity, with the promise of a conversation making our eyes and ears sting; we discovered that, in writing, we could be crude, capricious, dumb, boring, unfair, confessional; we discovered, as Violeta Parra said, 'that writing soothes / the torments of the soul'.

Later, much later, the desire arises, almost always ambiguous, reckless, and anxious, to show what we've written to a friend or to someone who is said to *know something about literature.* Only then, when we're driven by the urgency to publish what we write, whether it's on the bulletin board or in a book, whether we post it on some wall or – in that frankly desperate act that is the postmodern version of the bottle in the ocean – send it by mail to absolutely all of our contacts, only when for the first time we behave like readers of what we have written—only then do the topics appear. And perhaps on speaking retrospectively about our texts, we massage them, we condescend to a conversation that is different from the one we were going for: we translate, we betray our writing. Creation itself, on the other hand, feeds on that lack of a topic. We can spend entire months or years opening the file without ever being entirely clear what it is we're saying. Devastated by the uncertainty of the topic, we are also blessed by the certainty that, though we may not know the subject, when we write we are doing *something*, there is definitely something there, something presumably valuable, or maybe something whose true value we doubt over and over, but that by now we couldn't renounce, because we wouldn't know how to.

Nothing guarantees us that the text we work on for days, months, years, will at some point seem publishable to us. One doesn't write in order to publish, even if we've already been published and we know that someone could be interested in our soliloquy. The part of me that is sitting with you in the audience distrusts this kind of affirmation, because someone who publishes books obtains a kind of legitimacy, and maybe loses the vocation of defeat that is implied by spending hours talking to no one. And the only way I see to confront that distrust is to read you, right now, a text I worked on for months and then decided not to publish, but whose existence I find in some way as undeniable as it is problematic. The same way that, when we're asked what our novel is about and the only reasonable answer would be to reply 'read it,' the only way I can talk about these failed texts is to show them and make that failure explicit.

And why not read a failed text, a text I didn't want to publish, since I feel at home here, and on top of that they gave me a free topic? Maybe only here, in the frame of this conference, a text that I don't like but that I feel affection for (and that I want to feel affection for) can and deserves to exist. Maybe now I can read it as if I liked it, and in that way the text and I can be at peace. It's called 'El Amor Después del Amor' ['Love after Love']; I think that title is lame, too, but it will go on being called that. All the same, now, as I read it, I'm finally killing it, and maybe just maybe I'll forget it:

II.

The first Argentine human being who had any influence in my life was a beach volleyball player, maybe twenty years old, a six-foot-tall blond guy who, in the summer of 1991, got it on with my girlfriend. It happened at the yacht club in El Quisco, and some of my classmates happened to be there, and later they described the event in detail, on the school bulletin board. And then my torment began, but looking back I think it was a good thing. It was good, of course, to know. It's always better to know. And it was also good to be a cuckold at such an early age. I think one of the most important moments in life is when we find out that someone cheated on us. It's necessary to go through that, to have been there.

I learned a lot in those days – those weeks, months – when everyone either made fun of me or felt sorry for me; in the end it's the same thing. There were two or three loyal friends who never mentioned the subject in my presence, and if they made fun of me they did it discreetly. And oh how important is discretion and camaraderie. Hugo Puebla, for example, told me a joke to console me. It was about a guy who comes home limping with his face all bloody, and his wife asks him, 'What happened to you?' and he tells her that he'd been beaten up by a group of people because they'd confused him with an Argentine. 'And why didn't you set them straight?' she asks, and he says, 'Because I love it when those fuckers get their asses beat.' When I thought about my girlfriend and imagined that Argentine giant with his hands on her, I remembered that joke and told it again to myself; I drew it out indefinitely, and it was a delight, an antidote, a consolation.

These sad events engendered in me an immense prejudice against Argentines, against beach volleyball, and even against summer. Luckily, the following year, I went to Guanaqueros and met Natalia, a beautiful *porteña* who was underage, which in any case wasn't a problem, since I was also a minor; she was even a few months older than me. Our relationship lasted only a week in person, but we kept it going for some months by writing letters. Back then the album 'El Amor después del Amor', by Fito Páez, was a big hit. I couldn't stand Páez's voice – still can't. It seemed to me like he was making fun of his listeners, like it was a parody, and that no one who sang that way could expect to be taken seriously. But even so, I thought 'Tumbas de la gloria' was a profound song, and I also liked another three or four from the cassette, but when she asked me I of course said I liked the whole thing, I said I loved it, and then she took out an astonishing apparatus that let us both connect our headphones to her Walkman and the cassette went on and on, because the thing had auto reverse.

The song I liked the least was precisely the one that gave the album its title. I thought it was horrible – still do – but what could I do, she liked it, and we learned it by heart, we even analyzed the lyrics: 'El amor después /del amor tal vez/ se parezca a este rasho de sol': 'Love after/ love perhaps/ is like this ray of sun.' Not much there to analyse, the song was just bad, but Natalia explained to me that couples had another stage, a phase when they stopped loving each other and something else started that wasn't love, but love after love, and I imagined two little old people singing the song and trying to screw, and I doubled over with laughter.

Nati – she didn't like to be called that, her girl-friends called her Nata, which is the Spanish word for that gross film that forms over hot milk – went back to Buenos Aires, and we started exchanging letters right away. I wrote her long and dramatic missives telling her about Santiago, my family, my neighbourhood, and she answered me with perfect grammar (which was very important to me) and even some skilful drawings, and she'd add other details, perfume or locks of her blond hair, clippings of her painted fingernails, and even – but only once – five little drops of blood. I asked her to describe Buenos Aires for me, and she replied with the funny line that Buenos Aires was like every other city in the world, only a little more beautiful and a whole lot uglier. For better or worse, my sentimental education owes a lot to those letters, which very soon, quite reasonably, she stopped sending, though I went on writing her for a while, because in those years my defining characteristic was persistence.

The next summer, my parents planned a vacation in Frutillar and they invited Luciano, an old friend of theirs from across the Andes. We stayed in two cabins: in the large one slept my parents, my three sisters, and Mirtita, Luciano's daughter. Luciano and I slept in the other, although truth be told I slept very little because I was depressed, even if in those days I didn't know it, and it would take me forever to realize it – I was depressed for so many years, my entire adolescence and the first part of young adulthood, and if I'd only known it then everything would have been so different, I think, goddamit.

The day before the trip I had asked my mum, who worked downtown, to buy me a book by the poet Jorge Teillier, and she'd got mixed up and bought me a book of stories by Jaime Collyer, so I had no choice but to read it. In the other bed Luciano smoked, drank whiskey, watched the inanities of the Festival de Viña del Mar on TV, violently scratched his left cheek, and also talked to me – 'go on reading, you don't have to answer me,' he'd say, but then he'd come out with some comment that would turn into a question, and I, in effect, obediently, said nothing, but he still waited for an answer. So I'd say a few words, and that was enough for him, he was grateful for that, and finally he'd fall asleep with the glass perfectly balanced on his chest, as if every day of his life he had fallen asleep with a half-finished glass of whiskey balanced on his chest. Luciano was fat, had reddish skin and was almost completely bald, as I think all Argentine men are once they reach a certain age. And even though later on I behaved so badly with him, I have to say that at that moment he struck me as a pleasant person.

Back then my father was obsessed with fly fishing, and when he wasn't fishing he spent his time practicing casting in the grass, obsessively working on his technique.

Luciano was, in theory, his partner, his buddy, but he got bored almost immediately, so sometimes – really almost always – he went with my mum and the girls to the lake, or he played football or went hiking with me. One day we passed a sparse outdoor market in the Plaza de Armas, and one of the stalls was selling books. All the Argentines I have ever met in my life have been big readers – you'd think they spent all their time reading, although it also seems like they dedicate themselves exclusively to drinking mate or watching football or writing editorials. Luciano, on the other hand, didn't like to read: he peered at those books from afar, distrustfully, as if sensing some future boredom, and he gave a faint, prudent smile as if in muffled celebration of non-reading. I *did* like to read, but I mostly read poetry; it was unusual for me to read novels, but that summer I just felt like reading novels, and I chose three more or less at random. Luciano paid for my books, which I would like to thank him for publicly right now, and he was on the verge of buying a novel he had unenthusiastically picked out for himself, but then at the last minute he changed his mind. 'Who am I fooling, *boludo*, I'm never gonna read it,' he told me, with absolute, contagious happiness.

I went out that night, but they were dancing to some impossible music at the club so I went right back to the cabin, planning to finish the book by Collyer, which I was enjoying. I thought Luciano would still be in the other cabin playing rummy or old maid or dominos with my parents, but he was already settled in his bed hitting the whiskey and devouring a slice of the extraordinary cherry pies that the owner of the cabins baked. I ate a piece too and I tasted the whiskey – officially, because I'd already tried a few sips when I got up to take the glass off Luciano's chest. But this time he offered it to me, poured me a glass with some solemnity, and asked me how many ice cubes I wanted (four!). It was a rough J&B, pretty terrible, but I was up to it.

The next night we started properly drinking, and by the fourth or fifth night of masculine complicity, since he did nothing but talk to me about women, I told him the story of his compatriot, Natalia. At one point he asked me to describe her physically, and the truth was I'd never been in a situation where I'd had to describe her, Nati was so beautiful I'd decided not to say anything about her looks, because I'd thought there was no need to describe an Argentine girl, it was all right there in the word *Argentine*, or rather you only had to describe them if they were abnormal, that is, if the Argentine girl *wasn't* beautiful, which was unrealistic or at least infrequent. Still, I tried to describe her, and I think I was, to a certain extent, persuasive.

'And? You give her that hot beef injection?' Luciano asked me. The expression made me laugh. And ok, so I had *not* given her that hot beef injection, but I lied and said I did. What I hadn't realized was that Luciano thought I was secretly or openly talking about his daughter Mirtita, who was two years younger than me, blonde and thin and pretty, but I wasn't into her, her beauty was fairly humdrum. I had trouble believing that Luciano could really think I was talking about his daughter. I let out a nervous giggle that he read as a cynical chuckle, and then things went all to hell, because he pounced on me and I had no choice but to apply my rudimentary method of self-defence, which basically consisted of kneeing him in the nuts, and while he was writhing in pain on the floor he told me he'd always wanted to give it to my mother.

It seemed so silly, Luciano was like a kid who was trying to compete with me, and then I remembered a clever dialogue from school, when González Barría told González Martínez, 'I'm gonna go fuck your sister,' and González Martínez replied triumphantly 'I don't have a sister,' but González Barría counterattacked right away with this abominable but self-assured phrase: 'Last night me and your mum made you one.' Yes, it's horrendous, but I still couldn't get over how fast Barría's comeback had been, and it was so clever that Martínez didn't even get angry, and they even slapped each other on the back, and when I remembered all of this I had a true attack of laughter, but it was not the right moment for those memories, since the more I laughed the more my roomie yelled, and what came next is confusing, because now everyone was there, even the girls and my parents, there in the room with us and shouting, it was a real disaster, and I don't remember how the night ended up, but by the next day the group had dissolved and the Chileans slept in one cabin and the Argentines in the other, and my three sisters blamed me; only my mother came to my defence. My father told me that it was the last summer holiday I would spend with my family, which was absolutely, any way you looked at it, good news for me.

Three years later, my parents split up. It was terrible. Or for a while it seemed terrible to me. When I was growing up, every once in a while my father called me and my sisters in and told us that he and my mother had decided to separate, and that we would have to choose whether to go with him or stay with her. It was a very cruel joke, but it was practically a family tradition, one he enjoyed enormously because he always managed to convince us in the end, he was very dramatic and eloquent, and my mother would berate him for it later but he laughed a lot, maybe he was on drugs or something. That's why, all those years later when they told me the news, I thought it was a joke, and they had to explain to me many times that no, this time it was for real. I cried a little, two fingers of tears. Two fingers of tears with four ice cubes. Later, once I was calmer, once there was no option but to accept it, I thought it had come too late. I thought something ambiguous. Something like: oh, they're alive. It seemed unnecessary to separate. They had to stay together, period. But they wanted to exist. They insisted on existing.

A few months later I found out, in the worst way possible, that my mum had a boyfriend. It's difficult to be the son of a woman like that, so overflowing with talent and breasts. I curse the day I was weaned, at twenty-five months old; everything had been fine, and then all this other shit began. And one afternoon my mum, that fabulous woman whose legs are so covered with freckles invited me for dinner. Suspicious. We lived in the same house. 'Come for dinner,' she said. She called me. On the phone! She got her hands on my (Chilean) girlfriend's number, called and asked to speak with me. My old lady was nervous, I know her. She said 'I want to invite you to dinner.'

'What time, more or less?' I asked, acting coy, just to raise the tension. It was going to be at six, it was always at six. I knew the answer, but my stomach still hurt when she said: 'Six.' I arrived a little early, on purpose. And then I saw her embracing another man. And maybe there's another lesson here. Maybe we should all at some point see our mother kissing and touching and rubbing against the body of someone who isn't our father (or us).

But it was still too much to see her with that guy. With Luciano, *che*, yes indeed. Fatter, redder, and balder.

I couldn't believe it. That man had attacked me, he was an alcoholic, a cherry pie addict, a professional snorer, and on top of all that he didn't read. He didn't read! An Argentine who didn't read, how could you, Mum?! And he didn't even drink *mate*, just his little coffees all day long.

While I calmed myself I saw the whole family go out to the yard, and how confusing it was to look out through the window of my room: my sisters with their moody boyfriends, my mother with a chubby, veiny, reddened Argentine arm around her, and they all went smiling and smoking and sitting around the table next to the same arbour where as kids we'd run around chasing our dogs and cats and rabbits, now buried, all of them, in the garden. I approached. I didn't look at my sisters or their moody boyfriends. But I looked at my mother with a hushed love: she was still silent, her little face trembling. And then I looked Luciano straight in the eyes and with all my rage, with all my heart, with raw hatred, a hot, murky, Nerudian tear on my cheek, I spat out what seemed to me the ultimate obscenity, the worst, most terrible, hurtful and irrevocable insult, the worst expletive ever meted out: *Argentine*.

III.

I know very well why that story failed: because I never, throughout the entire process of writing it, stopped thinking. I let myself be carried along by the story, by the pleasure of telling, of course I did, but I never lost control, never managed that warmth or madness that makes us reach beyond our intentions and presumed skill. A person can laugh at his own jokes, but sometimes it happens, as now, that the text deep down doesn't say anything, doesn't add anything, isn't worthwhile. I could never consider it finished; every time I open the file I'm unsure whether I should keep giving it mouth-to-mouth or if I should just perform last rites on it. I've just presented this story to you as if it didn't matter to me, but of course it does; I've just read it to you and I tried to read it well, to make it sound good. I can't deny its existence or my inability to let go of it, to turn it in. I understand the piece as playing with voice, I understand it as a parody, and although without a doubt it is a pretty ridiculous story or a fairly stupid one, its comic intention obvious, I thought all that would be simply left behind, out of the blue; I wanted something to appear and it just didn't.

This explanation could be longer, but I don't want to over-intellectualize a very simple feeling: I was never convinced. Or to put it in an even more basic way: I don't fully like the narrator or the characters or anything about this story. I also hate some of the jokes but still I cannot erase them without feeling I'm being unfair. And nevertheless I can't deny, as I was saying, that it exists. I can't eliminate it, though it's a fact that I am very good at destroying texts. I suppose this happens to all writers, whether they admit it or not. Or maybe it doesn't, maybe I'm projecting my own foibles, just to feel included. I'm struck by those writers whose books seem to be the result of a fixed or infallible method. I'm unsettled by the smug flavour in the discourse of the professional writer, *à la* Vargas Llosa. I say this without irony, probably with envy; I would like to be more disciplined and less obsessive. I'd really love to fall asleep every night lulled by the feeling that the day had purpose, that I'm progressing, that it's a mere matter of settling in at the computer every morning with a litre of coffee, some cigarettes, and a few Bengay patches, to finish, in x number of working days, my novel.

Speaking of Vargas Llosa, three years ago I read a review he wrote of *Plano Americano* [American Map], Leila Guerriero's monumental and brilliant book that had just been published by the press of this very university, and that Vargas Llosa praised generously and unreservedly in the newspaper *El País*. That Vargas Llosa would celebrate *American Map* didn't surprise me, just like it wouldn't surprise me if, for example – to cite another Nobel winner – Barack Obama praised the book. But there *was* something surprising in the review, specifically in the first paragraph, which begins like this: 'Every time I return to Madrid or Lima after several months away, I'm greeted at home by a depressing sight: a pyramid of books, packages, letters, emails, telegrams, and messages that I will never be able to read in full, much less reply to...' Of course, this introduction exists to prepare us for the dazzling discovery, among that pile of unsolicited parcels, of Leila's book. I love that image, and I find it admirable/enviable as well that Vargas Llosa manages to stay away from email – probably so he can concentrate on writing – although, if I understand correctly, he only receives email when he is in one of these houses, and for some very mysterious reason, the emails that reach him in Madrid are not the same as the ones he receives in Lima. But what really disconcerts me is that at both his houses, in Madrid and Lima, Vargas Llosa still receives such a quantity of telegrams, when I'd thought they had gone extinct a long time ago. I would have loved to be in the audience a few weeks ago – when Vargas Llosa gave about twenty-three talks at this university – to ask him what those telegrams said, who sent them, and from where. I imagine things like this:

CONGRATULATIONS stop NOBEL stop

IREADALLBOOKS stop GOOD stop

COME stop CONFERENCE CHILE stop OPEN
ARMS stop

I PREFER MANUEL PUIG stop

CONVERSATION IN THE CATHEDRAL stop
TIME OF THE HERO stop MAGNIFICENT stop
LATEST NOVELS NOT stop

That last one is less likely – it would be very
expensive.

Sorry, it's possible that many of the people here today
have no idea what a telegram is. Nor am I an expert –
I've only received two telegrams in my life. Both were
sent by my maternal grandma on the occasion of my
birthday, and curiously enough, both were on the same
day. I belong, instead, to the fax generation, but I do
remember having thought at some point about the specificity of telegram messages: the overwhelming sequence
of transmissions, the un-danceable but to a certain extent contagious rhythm of Morse code, and especially
the somewhat comical effect of that linguistic economy
that meant some words had to be cut and articles and
prepositions left out, playing at the limits of intelligi-
bility, for the very reasonable purpose of saving a few
pesos. Telegrams were, to put it one way, like the haikus
of correspondence, although, far from any lyricism, a
telegram's arrival was really associated to bad news, and
in cowboy movies, to the hiring of a gunslinger.

I suppose it was just a slip-up on Vargas Llosa's part,

something like the explosion of nostalgia for a world in which telegrams exist, a nostalgia that rhymes with the death of western culture he decried in his book *La civilización del espectáculo* [The Civilization of Spectacle]. I don't want to even think of how depressed the author must have been when he wrote that essay laying into – though without interrogating them much – practically every contemporary manifestation of culture, and also the press, especially gossip magazines. And it's thanks to those very tabloids, ironically, that we now know Vargas Llosa doesn't seem so depressed anymore.

I don't miss telegrams, but of course I do miss the young man I was twenty years, maybe twenty kilos ago, when, for example, I read Vargas Llosa's novels and was dazzled. Although to tell the truth I don't really miss those days, when, maybe unconsciously, the rhetoric of the telegram clipped our sentences and made us think that every word would cost us dearly. We were completely seduced by language, we were so anxious to say something, anything, but we also felt the inhibiting weight of high culture, and we couldn't bring ourselves to take the baton. A poem published in a Xeroxed magazine, our money pooled to print a book: it would be so easy to construct, using those events, a supposed heroism, a minimal but consistent odyssey, and of course a mysticism, a collective spirit that we've never lost. But that sort of nostalgia is such a bummer.

We started out a little debauched or dazed by scepticism, but we wanted to belong to something, anything, and maybe that's why we ended up shouting along, even if we didn't really understand the lyrics, to a song that said 'I don't belong here'. We felt the need to have a song, a topic, but we were also reluctant to accept the ones that supposedly corresponded to our generation. And that never stops, I'm afraid, that normalizing pressure, the improvised assignment of labels and categories, the tiller of the topic that fixes and entombs and that almost never goes much beyond a more or less poor and literal reading, made to contain.

We write to multiply ourselves, we write, Fogwill used to say, in order to not be written, but we are written anyway. That's more or less the subject of 'The Autobiographical Novel', another failed text that I wrote about a year ago, and that I've never published and never will.

It goes like this:

IV.

Kalámido Crastnh sits beside me on the train. We'd met the night before, at a dinner with some poets who defined themselves as savage detectives, although there was little about them that was savage and the only thing they were interested in investigating was how to avoid paying the bill.

Before we said goodbye, Kalámido told me that he had read all my books and he wanted to interview me. He seemed to emphasize the word *all*, which I found a little alarming, because I have some books I'd rather no one ever read again. Nor did he tell me whether he had liked them, and of course I didn't ask. Since we had tickets for the same train, he suggested we do the interview during the trip.

I don't know if the train is moving quickly or slowly, but I'm sure that it's advancing. I open the computer and start typing very quickly so he'll think I have an urgent matter to resolve. I don't like interviews, though I do like starting them, because that means that at some point they're going to end.

Kalámido studied philology in the exclusive Oincaskc Unyiversadorc, and later did a master in Hyper-Journalism at the same university ('but in a different department,' he clarifies), before starting his PhD at the prestigious University of Ertyuing, from which he graduated with the highest honours. Even so, in spite of his intimidating curriculum, the first thing he asks me after he turns on the recorder is the following: 'Are your books autobiographical?'

I pretend not to understand the question. Kalámido rephrases it in this way, pronouncing each word painstakingly – with conviction, one might say: 'How much in your books is fiction, and how much is real?'

I try to imagine Kalámido in his native Llaslamnlcmas, a small city to the west of Nlncclael, more or less close to the beautiful Lake Aslvfvsd. I see him as a child, in the snow, waiting for an improbable rainbow, and later, as a teenager, reading with devotion and disconcertion Emilia Qwerty, Pol Uiop, or the weird Asd Fghjkl. I think that Kalámido would never have bothered Emilia Qwerty with a question like the one he has just asked me.

It's not a good comparison, because Qwerty never gave interviews, but I don't think Kálamido would have posed a question like that to skinny old Uiop or to Fghjkl, and they *did* give interviews (maybe too many). I feel offended, but I let it pass; I've suffered much worse humiliations. I hold my tongue, but not very tightly; I'm just too sociable. I decide to reply. And I decide, moreover, although I know that this is completely unnecessary, to tell the truth.

'My books are 32 per cent autobiographical,' I tell him.

I'm afraid Kalámido will think my words ironic. That

is not my intention. My answer is totally honest. I went to a terrible school where they only taught us maths, so I'm used to this unhealthy level of exactness. Luckily, my fear is unfounded: Kalámido notes the figure down in his notebook, takes two sips of a tea he got from I don't know where, and looks straight at me, as though thinking out loud—as though looking at me out loud, if that were possible.

'I knew it, 32 per cent,' he says.

'And I knew you knew it,' I lie.

'And I knew you knew I knew,' he says.

And we go on like that a while, hell yeah. There's a good vibe between us. We like each other. Kalámido could be my friend, I think. We should give it a try, hone the rhythm of the friendship little by little. I think that's how you dance to the beat of friendship: laughter, silence, laughter, silence, laughter, silence. Hell yeah.

Kalámido asks me about the future of Latin American literature and about the future of literature, period. And about the future, period. And about the future of the word *future*. And about the future of the word *word*. It all flows, it's all going marvellously, until we reach the crucial, the terrible, the world champion of difficult questions: the desert island.

What book would I bring to a desert island? Since I'm no dummy, I try to negotiate: I propose that instead of a desert island we work with the idea of a sparsely populated island. Kalámido replies that the premise of the question can't be modified, because his editor is a tyrant. I ask him, them, to let me bring more than one book. He shakes his head no. I tell him his question is depressing. I tell him that the last thing I would do on that shitty island is read.

Kalámido approves my answer with a complicit laugh

and he shares a little of his tea with me. It's all very good. The interview hasn't ended, but I'm sure that at some point it's going to. The train advances quickly or slowly or maybe it's inexplicably come to a halt, I don't know and I don't care: the only thing I want, for now, is to go on answering Kalámido's questions with total, absolute honesty.

V.

The part of me that is sitting out there in the audience hates this text, and the part that is up here talking to you does too. The guy who wrote that text is annoying and ridiculous, and the story is horrible but I also like it... The only part I really like is the end, which got away from me. If the text failed it's because I never managed to break away from the topic. I was angry, just a little, and almost without realizing it I started to whip up a kind of festive complaint that is not all that different from the presumption I criticize writers like Vargas Llosa for. I thought I knew very well what I was talking about, but I wasn't looking; I spoke as if I were outside of and not within what I am observing or parodying or criticizing. And writing is, as more than one person has said, seeing oneself in the crowd. And one of the few things I am truly clear on is that I don't want to be outside. That I belong and I want to belong.

In sum, I'm finishing up now, crying onstage:

They say that there are only three or four or five topics for literature, but maybe there's only one: belonging. Perhaps all books can be read in function of the desire to belong, or the negation of that desire. To be part of or stop being part of a family, of a community, a country, of Chilean literature, a football team, a political party, a rock band, the fan club of a rock band, or at least a group of scouts. That's what we write about when we're given a free topic, and also when we think we are writing about love, death, travel, telegrams or suitcases with swivel wheels. That's what we always talk about, seriously and in jest, in verse and in prose: belonging. And that is, or was, of course, the topic of this lecture. Stop.

Acknowledgements

The custom of including an acknowledgements section
at the end of books is, as far as I know, fundamentally of
the English-speaking world, or in any case isn't usual in
Spanish-language publications. This does not mean, of
course, that writers of Spanish are ungrateful. Ultimately,
there are so many people I have to thank that it is tempting
not to thank anyone, especially in order to avoid forgetting
someone. But here it goes:

This book was originally published in 2010 and then a
few times more, always with slight expansions in the text.
The original idea and selection were the work of Andrés
Braithwaite whom I thank in capital, bold letters, with a
glass of champagne and tears of emotion. I would also like
to thank Nurit Kasztelan and Ana S. Pareja, editors of the
Argentine and Spanish editions.

Many thanks to the editors of the first and at times
second versions of the texts collected here: Marcela
Aguilar, Marcos Avilés, Yenny Cáceres, László Erdélyi,
Diego Erlán, Emilio Fraia, Raquel Garzón, Andrés
Gómez Bravo, Winston Manrique, Ana María Navales,
David Noriega, Jaime Rodríguez, Emily Stokes, Vicente
Undurraga, Diego Zúñiga, and, especially, Cecilia García-
Huidobro, Rafael Lemus, Álvaro Matus, Andrea Palet,
Matías Rivas and Héctor Soto.

I could never sufficiently thank the dedicated, tireless,
thorough, and brilliant work of Megan McDowell in the
translation and editing of this book, which poses difficul-
ties that are different and in some ways greater than the
translation of other books of mine that Megan has done
before. I also thank Jacques Testard, the editor of this
beautiful press Fitzcarraldo Editions, for his clarity and
buena onda and his valuable comments in the editing of this
book. And thanks to all the editorial team, of course. And
I also especially thank the poet and translator Rodrigo
Olavarría and the novelist and birdwatcher John Wray,

who generously read and commented on this English version.

Finally I thank Silvestre, my almost three-month-old son, and Jazmina Barrera, his mother. Or more than thanking them I ask forgiveness, because I was typing these lines very loudly and I've just woken them up.

A.Z.
Mexico City, February 2018

Fitzcarraldo Editions
243 Knightsbridge
London, SW7 1DN
United Kingdom

ISBN 978-1-910695-63-0

Design by Ray O'Meara
Typeset in Fitzcarraldo
Printed and bound by TJ International

fitzcarraldoeditions.com

Fitzcarraldo Editions